KEEPING SCORE

MEASURING THE
BUSINESS VALUE OF LOGISTICS
IN THE SUPPLY CHAIN

ISBN 0-9658653-1-2

Council of Logistics Management
2805 Butterfield Road
Suite 200
Oak Brook, IL 60523-1170
www.clm1.org

Printed in the United States of America.

KEEPING SCORE

MEASURING THE
BUSINESS VALUE OF LOGISTICS
IN THE SUPPLY CHAIN

James S. Keebler
Karl B. Manrodt, Ph.D.
University of Tennessee

David A. Durtsche
D. Michael Ledyard
Computer Sciences Corporation

COUNCIL OF LOGISTICS MANAGEMENT

TABLE OF CONTENTS

ACKNOWLEDGEMENTS

Developing a work of this nature cannot occur without the support of many people from many different places. The authors would like to take this opportunity to thank a few of the people who have made the most significant contributions to this study.

First and foremost, we would like to thank the business and professional community who shared their experiences in hopes that the logistics profession could learn from their successes and frustrations. More than 500 executives responded to our surveys, giving us insights into their key issues and how they manage them. Nearly two dozen companies opened their doors to our team of case study researchers, bringing forward professionals from different parts of their organizations to discuss our agenda and how they use measurement to drive their business. Their experiences form the core of our message and provide the real insights into measurement's true benefits and barriers. Those companies, and the individuals most responsible for facilitating the case study interviews, are as follows:

3M – Gary Ridenhower and Dennis Fabozzi
Avery Dennison – Frank Hathaway
Caliber Logistics – Christopher Healy
Compaq – Greg Granger
Department of Defense – Roger Kallock
Graybar – Bill Nephew
H. E. Butt – Ken Allen
Ingram Micro – Deb Siek
International Paper – Don Washington
Loblaw – David Dundas
Martin-Brower – Steve Spoerl
Modus Media International – Kate Vitasek
Motorola – Frank Castronovo
Nabisco Foods – Rick Blasgen
Owens & Minor – Jim Grigg

PageNet – Don Murphy
Service Merchandise – Gary Sease
Sun Microsystems – Debra Caster
Texas Instruments – Bryan Vonfeldt
Tyson – Mike Roetzel
W. W. Grainger – Rick Adams
Welch's – Dee Biggs

We received expert guidance and direction from the Council of Logistics Management's Research Evaluation Committee. Bryan Kelln of General Cable Corporation chaired the committee and was assisted by Rick Balla of GTE Supply, Dr. Bernard La Londe of The Ohio State University, Kathleen Mazzarella of Graybar, Bill Perry of i2 Technologies, and Dr. Elaine Winter of the Council's staff. We appreciate the significant time and valuable contributions this knowledgeable group has made available to this work.

We wish to thank our friends and colleagues within our respective organizations—Computer Sciences Corporation and the University of Tennessee—for their support and contributions to the project. Within CSC, Steve Keener sponsored the effort and made it possible. Steve Biciocchi, Gerry Boltin, Chuck Poirier, Chuck Troyer, and Steve Stulck spent many hours reading, discussing, and adding their experiences to our drafts. Brad Bush, Gary Jones, and Jerry Lavely furnished valuable input during the life of the project. We could not have conducted the survey and collected the results without the efforts of Alan Weaver. At the University of Tennessee, Dr. C. John Langley, Jr., provided valuable insights during the course of the study. Gregory A. Riser and L. Michelle Bobbitt added many long hours during the entire project, but especially helped us analyze survey data. They provided the first insights into the data, and pored over all the paths of inquiry that characterize these types of studies. Dr. Amy Cathey was our resident statistics expert. Finally, many of our colleagues in the university's Department of Marketing, Logistics, and Transportation covered our classes and other research responsibilities, which gave us the opportunity to fully pursue this study. To them we owe our thanks. There were many others in both organizations who gave freely of their time and experiences to support and encourage us, and we only wish that we had the space to thank each of them.

The actual words on the page, more often than not, belong to our editors, Bernie Thiel and Bob Buday of The Bloom Group LLC. In addition to their literary skills, Bernie and Bob brought substantial subject matter knowledge to the project and provided the invaluable reality check. If they didn't understand a point we were attempting to make, odds are that the reader would struggle as well. Pat Wright, an editorial affiliate of The Bloom Group, also contributed heavily to the writing of the text. We also want to thank Georgia Cady and Eileen Brockhurst of CSC, and Kim Kerrigan for the artistic value they brought to the graphics and layout, which make this book so easy to read.

On a more personal note, we would like to thank our spouses and families, who quietly endured the long hours we spent away from them, the vacations and holidays interrupted by reading and writing, and the blank looks prompted by our preoccupation with the book during the often far-too-brief periods spent with them.

David A. Durtsche   James S. Keebler
D. Michael Ledyard   Karl B. Manrodt, Ph.D.
Computer Sciences Corporation   University of Tennessee

EXECUTIVE SUMMARY:
THE LOGISTICS MEASUREMENT IMPERATIVE

Do you know whether your logistics operations are enhancing or eroding shareholder value?

Do you have capital tied up in slow-moving inventory, funds that should be going to growth initiatives? Can you quickly identify and recover that capital without affecting service?

Do you know whether you are providing enough—or too much—service to customers, and the impact on your bottom line?

When a major customer says that your service is not meeting its standards, do you have the information to respond?

Are you sure that your logistics organization is aligned with and focused on the company's strategic goals?

The ability to answer questions like these depends on how well you "keep score" in logistics—that is, how well you measure the performance of your logistics operations. In today's business world, effective logistics measures increasingly are separating the leaders from the laggards. Certainly, measurement has become critical to the success of many business operations—manufacturing, engineering, merchandising, and others. Managers in many industries quickly have adopted tools like "balanced scorecards" to monitor the health of their activities and make necessary changes.

However, few business areas need to be measured more extensively, more frequently, and more effectively than logistics. This is in part because logistics has so many "moving parts"—products, orders, information on orders, and so on—that flow through numerous points (factories, wholesalers, retailers, and carriers) around the world. This creates many places where things can go wrong. In addition, logistics represents a significant share of overall costs, and any major cost center must be monitored. Most importantly, logistics capabilities have become a key basis of competition in industry after industry. In fact, in industries such as retail and computers, companies like Wal-Mart and Dell have set the standard for logistics as the basis of competition. Consequently, the measurement and control of logistics is critical to your firm.

High-performance logistics requires mastering the discipline of measurement. To improve the performance of any business activity, you must understand how well it performs today. In other words, you must measure it. If you need better performance, you must make changes to the activity, and then measure its performance again to ensure that the changes are going in the right direction. Given that customers' demands typically increase over time, you will have to continue to measure and make the operational changes necessary to meet the new performance standards cost-effectively.

The benefits of effective logistics measures can be substantial. First, logistics measures can help pinpoint inefficiencies and reduce costs. For example, a logistics measurement program at 3M has helped make a significant reduction in the costs of logistics during a five-year period. Second, logistics measures can be instrumental in improving service. The same measurement program has helped 3M improve their on-time delivery by 32 percent in a three-year period. Finally, good logistics measures can help managers decide what services and service levels to offer various customers by giving them insight into the costs of providing those services. Modus Media International, a $700 million manufacturer and distributor of computer software and manuals for high-tech companies, used detailed logistics measures to score its customer relationships and focus on profitable business. The result: Modus Media has improved its profitability dramatically.

Yet for most companies, two straightforward questions are far from simple to answer:

- How are we performing for customers?

- How are our suppliers performing for us?

Research on the logistics measurement programs of more than 350 companies showed that while the majority were measuring the performance of some logistics activities, few were measuring their performance where it really counted: with customers and suppliers. Most logistics managers are focusing their measurement internally— on the performance of warehousing, transportation, and other logistics activities—not externally, on those activities that *collectively* satisfy their customers. Until now, logistics measurement itself has focused on monitoring the performance of individual logistics *functions* instead of tracking the performance of end-to-end logistics *processes*. For the first time, this book examines the measures critical to high-performance logistics processes and shows you how to implement them.

Why is there such little useful measurement occurring in logistics? There are several reasons. The first is that a successful measurement program is hard work. It demands the commitment of top managers, who must persuade employees, customers, and suppliers that the return from measuring performance across the supply chain is worth the substantial effort. In many companies, effective measurement forces a cultural change, one in which people learn to evaluate by the numbers and seek improvements across functional boundaries.

Secondly, the measures used to evaluate logistics performance are often out of synch with corporate strategy. Logistics often is monitored by yesterday's strategy. Meanwhile, senior management may have shifted its direction and failed to communicate this to managers located far from headquarters in the warehouses and on shipping docks.

The third reason effective logistics measurement has failed to take hold is that there are often too many measures being collected. These measures are set independently by functional managers who lack accountability for an entire business process. A procurement manager, for example, looks for ways to reduce inventories. But a store manager who reports to a different division head is not concerned with minimizing inventories. He is rewarded on sales volumes, which means minimizing stockouts by maximizing inventory. Contradictory logistics measures like these are rampant in organizations.

A fourth reason for the lack of useful measurement is that companies are reluctant to provide information on their performance. Logistics measures appear threatening to workers—and their companies—who wonder what their boss or their customers will do with the data.

Lastly, logistics measurement is beset by problems with language. There can be substantial disagreement over the definition of basic terms, which can remain dormant until there is a problem. For example, to some manufacturers, "on-time" shipments means meeting predetermined dates when their goods leave the plant or the warehouse. To customers, "on-time" means when they take possession of the goods at a specified time and place. This disagreement on basic definitions can cause major misunderstandings.

These misguided measurement practices must end if companies are going to compete in today's ever-changing supply chains. Research conducted for this book found a strong association between measurement and operational performance. Companies reporting a major logistics advantage over their competition were more likely to measure their logistics processes than companies whose logistics performance was trailing the competition. The reasons for measuring logistics are clear:

- To drive revenue growth by providing the service that keeps current customers satisfied and attracts new ones. Logistics measures help you understand specifically how well you are meeting customer expectations. This helps you to turn adversarial relationships into true "trading partnerships."

- To identify additional revenue opportunities by differentiating the way you deliver your product or service. Logistics measures can help you uncover value-added services your customers may be willing to pay for, at additional profit to you.

- To improve profitability by reducing operating and administrative costs significantly. Logistic measures help you pinpoint the cost, time, and quality of your logistics operations. They can help you identify ways to take inventory out of your system, freeing up cash and enhancing shareholder value.

- To improve profitability by scrutinizing your activities with customers and suppliers. Measures can help you determine which customers are profitable and which are not. They also can help you decide which suppliers are most effective to deal with, and how to reduce costs and improve efficiencies for both organizations.

- To help you determine conclusively whether to make costly operational improvements. All logistics managers should seriously consider having performance data before seeking funds for operational improvement programs.

While good logistics measures are now instrumental to business success, they are not easy to develop or implement. This book explains the lessons learned from the successful logistics measurement programs of companies such as Modus Media, 3M, Caliber Logistics, Graybar, Texas Instruments, Tyson Foods, International Paper, Motorola, Welch's, and H.E. Butt. The critical lessons are many:

1. **Make sure logistics measures are in synch with strategy.** Different business strategies have very different implications for logistics. Being the low-cost provider means having efficient logistics operations, which can conflict with a strategy of providing tailored customer service. Effective logistics measures are ones that help managers execute their company's strategy.

2. **Truly understand customer needs.** Do not assume you know what customers expect or that their needs will remain static. Motorola's pager division once measured its delivery performance according to how often orders were shipped on the dates it had set. On this measure, the business unit enjoyed a very high rate of on-time shipments. However, many paging and cellular service providers were dissatisfied with Motorola's performance. The measure did not compare Motorola's delivery performance to the shipping date requested by customers. Motorola began tracking the delivery according to customers' requested date of receipt. This measure and other initiatives have helped the company reduce its lead time with PageNet, a large customer, from 120 days to 30 days.

3. **Know your costs in providing logistics services.** Deciding how much customer service to offer and at what price requires comprehensive cost measures. With this information, managers can do sophisticated cost-benefit analyses on different logistics service scenarios.

4. **Take a "process" view of logistics.** Logistics measures must be defined first at the business process, not functional, level of

an organization. This means grouping all logistics activities into three key processes: Sourcing/Procurement, Fulfillment, and Planning/Forecasting/Scheduling (Exhibit A-1).

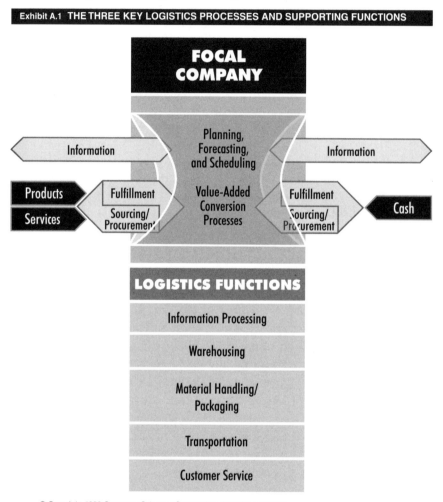

Exhibit A.1 THE THREE KEY LOGISTICS PROCESSES AND SUPPORTING FUNCTIONS

Logistics measures must let you monitor the performance of these processes. The day when companies across a supply chain use the same measures to monitor their combined performance will be the day when *order-of-magnitude* improvements in logistics performance across the supply chain will be truly possible. However, most industries are not at the point of making this a reality because there is little agreement today in any supply chain about how to measure performance. Companies can start down the road of supply chain improvement by instituting process measures with key customers and suppliers.

5. **Focus only on key measures.** While there are hundreds of ways to track logistics performance, about two dozen measures are important. These are process measures. They track the overall performance of the sourcing/procurement process and the fulfillment process in terms of time, cost, and quality. Measures of logistics functions and activities must be derived from these process measures.

6. **Stop ineffective measurement activities.** Measures are ineffective when they are subjective, when they obscure bad performance, and when they provide misleading statistics. Many measures used today are subjective. For example, rating a supplier's on-time performance on a scale of one to five without data on the percentage of deliveries that arrive as promised is a subjective measure. Logistics measures must be objective to be useful. Customer surveys that average a company's performance across several measures such as on-time delivery, cycle time, and accuracy make it difficult to pinpoint problems. And statistics can be used to distort reality.

7. **Use information technology.** Gathering, processing, and analyzing thousands, even millions, of bits of information every day on logistics performance require advanced information systems. Some organizations do not capture the right information. Other companies capture information differently in each business function or business unit. Trading partners usually gather logistics information differently, which makes it difficult to compare logistics information. Fortunately, several major technology developments spell progress for logistics measurements: supply chain management systems, enterprise resource planning software, and data warehouses. Information technology rapidly is becoming a powerful tool for logistics measurement.

So what exactly is a *good* measure? As research was conducted for this book, 10 characteristics of good logistics measures emerged. These are listed and described in Exhibit A.2. When thinking about the measures in your own company, you can use this list as a quick check to help you determine, at a high level, whether your measures

A good measure:	Description:
• Is quantitative	• The measure can be expressed as an objective value
• Is easy to understand	• The measure conveys at a glance what it is measuring, and how it is derived
• Encourages appropriate behavior	• The measure is balanced to reward productive behavior and discourage "game playing"
• Is visible	• The effects of the measure are readily apparent to all involved in the process being measured
• Is defined and mutually understood	• The measure has been defined by and/or agreed to by all key process participants (internally and externally)
• Encompasses both outputs and inputs	• The measure integrates factors from all aspects of the process measured
• Measures only what is important	• The measure focuses on a key performance indicator that is of real value to managing the process
• Is multidimensional	• The measure is properly balanced between utilization, productivity, and performance, and shows the trade-offs
• Uses economies of effort	• The benefits of the measure outweigh the costs of collection and analysis
• Facilitates trust	• The measure validates the participation among the various parties

are on target or may need some help.

With these principles in mind, you can begin instituting effective logistics measures. To do so, managers first must assess the measures already in use. Here, the emphasis should be on identifying the measures themselves, and not on the performance levels those measures are indicating. Managers then must develop process measures—i.e., measures such as on-time delivery, complete order cycle time, total delivered cost, and quality of product received. The emphasis on the process measures will depend upon the company's business strategy. After prioritizing which process measures to develop first, logistics managers then can build a "prototype" solution to test in the field. This initial model may lack data that will be required later. However, the prototype lets managers work out the bugs before they make major investments in collecting data and developing new information systems. The measures are revised, sometimes several times, before they are rolled out. Before they institute the measures, logistics managers must educate employees on how to use them. They also must revise incentive systems so that old measures and reward systems do not impede the new measures.

Measurement programs like the ones described in this book rapidly are becoming merely the table stakes for staying in the game of competition. Why? Several forces are at work here. With pressure to enhance shareholder value, senior managers are looking at ways to streamline their logistics processes and reduce costs. The commoditization of products is forcing companies to differentiate themselves, and logistics is becoming a key differentiator. Wal-Mart, The Home Depot, Costco, and other retailers are consolidating more and more purchasing power into fewer hands and are driving up the logistics performance of their suppliers. The globalization of markets and the rapid growth of electronic commerce already are revolutionizing the conduct of business. Through the power of the Internet and other technologies, once-stable supply chains for products such as PCs, music, books, and publications are being disrupted. Consumers and business buyers increasingly are shopping online. The story of online booksellers like Amazon.com soon will play out in many industries, from steel production to automobile manufacturing to food distribution. That story is this: *The best distribution system wins*. Now is not the time for logistics managers and senior executives to be complacent about the performance of their logistics operations, no matter how superior they may be.

These fundamental forces are inescapable. They will make this year's performance targets obsolete in three years, maybe sooner. They may make this year's logistics *processes* obsolete in 10 years or less. Unless the right measurement system is in place, logistics managers and senior executives will have neither the basis for determining the adequacy of their logistics operations nor the roadmap for improving them.

There is still time to get started, but the window of opportunity is getting smaller by the day. As General Electric CEO Jack Welch has said, "If the rate of change inside an organization is less than the rate of change outside, the end is near." The rate of change in nearly every industry supply chain is accelerating. Companies like Dell are using the Internet and the telephone to go direct to customers, bypassing wholesalers and retailers. Others, like Wal-Mart and The Home Depot, have amassed astonishing buying power through logistics systems that provide superior price and availability for customers.

Unless logistics managers keep up with the changing world outside, their companies soon will find themselves trailing seriously behind. Effective logistics measures are the first key step in staying in the game of supply chain improvement. Executives who can put the right measurement systems in place will give their companies a major advantage in a world where logistics truly has become the competitive difference.

1

THE SUPPLY CHAIN
REVOLUTION
IS JUST BEGINNING

Logistics is in the limelight. Once viewed by corporate executives, the business press, and Wall Street as a backroom function with about as much strategic impact as the mailroom, the delivery of raw materials and finished goods to their appointed destinations has gained new-found respect as a source of cost savings and competitive advantage. The topics of logistics and supply chain management are now center stage in the executive suites of major corporations around the world. Logistics conferences today overflow with attendees once considered far-removed from day-to-day logistics concerns in their companies—heads of marketing, customer service, finance, manufacturing, sales, R&D, and engineering.

The press trumpets the virtues of companies with leading-edge logistics, as well as the woes of organizations whose logistics lag behind. *Business Week, Fortune, Forbes,* and *IndustryWeek* shower Michael Dell with accolades for his $16 billion company's uncanny ability to incorporate the most recent technologies into PCs, while squeezing prices and inventory levels well below those of Compaq, IBM, Gateway, and Hewlett-Packard. Dell builds and delivers PCs to order in five days, with less than one week's inventory. In the retailing world, Wal-Mart is hailed for managing inventory with the precision of a Swiss watchmaker. At the same time, American auto makers are publicly derided for unwieldy distribution practices that account for as much as 30 percent of an automobile's sticker price. Auto industry executives see their distribution operations as ripe for renewal.

Even in war, the spotlight shines on logistics. Lieutenant General Gus Pagonis was widely hailed for his efforts in rapidly amassing the military might that forced Iraq out of Kuwait during the Gulf War.

After the war, in 1993, Sears, Roebuck & Co. hired Pagonis as its top logistics executive and made him a member of the retailer's powerful executive committee. Rubbermaid Inc. brought in a Desert Storm four-star general—Lee Salomon, as senior vice president of procurement—to streamline purchasing and logistics.

Perhaps the strongest indication of logistics' preeminence in many companies is that the logistics function has become a springboard to the executive suite. According to corporate-ladder expert Eugene Jennings, professor emeritus at Michigan State University who has been studying career paths in U.S. companies since 1947, the best path to the top of many companies is now through logistics.[1] Manufacturing had the inside track during the 1940s, and sales (late 1950s and early 1960s), finance (1970s), and marketing (1980s) also have had their day. Two of the most recent "role models" for logistics are DaimlerChrysler President Tom Stallkamp, who had led the company's procurement and supply operations, and H. Lee Scott, who in 1979 began his career with Wal-Mart in logistics. In early 1999, Scott was promoted to the number-two position, chief operating officer and vice chairman. Several industry experts believe Scott will be CEO by the year 2000.[2]

Logistics, indeed, has come a long way. It has emerged from the backroom and has become a force for competitive differentiation. It is clear that companies that respond quickly, with low inventory and consistently superior service, can pull ahead of the pack and may even command premium prices for products that are commodities.

The reason is that customers now evaluate their suppliers not on their products alone, but increasingly on the set of services they offer for making maximum use of the products. For example, a growing number of manufacturers offer customized delivery options, integrated planning and forecasting programs, or electronic access to order and shipment status at the customer's convenience. At Toyota's car assembly factory in Lexington, Kentucky, truck drivers delivering parts make a quality check before leaving the supplier's dock. Increasingly, the value of a product is not just the product itself but also the services and information that suppliers "wrap around" the product—the "value bundle."

In many cases, the service and information components of the bundle are influenced greatly by logistics. For some companies, they are the bundle's differentiating features—the company's competitive edge. Marketing and sales departments now tout their organizations' logistics performance as a key selling feature. Cross-functional teams that include logistics professionals are vital in making the sale. And after the sale, the supplier's logistics performance is often the determining factor in a customer's decision to stay with or switch suppliers.

THE NEED FOR EVEN BETTER LOGISTICS PERFORMANCE

Despite the heightened importance of logistics—and the improved performance of manufacturers and retailers during the past two decades—much more progress must be made. In 1997, KPMG Peat Marwick and the Massachusetts Institute of Technology studied 18 Fortune 500 consumer products manufacturers and retailers and found strong improvements in costs, cycle time, and inventory turns during the prior 12 months. Still, the companies reported wide variation in logistics performance, with many retailers not using such efficiency-minded practices as cross-docking and customer-direct shipments.[3]

Research conducted for this book uncovered a significant disparity in logistics performance and practices. Survey responses from 355 U.S. manufacturers, transportation providers, and retailers—as well as case studies of nearly two dozen companies—showed time and again companies struggling to make improvements in logistics operations and others making major strides.

Why were some companies great at logistics while others floundered? There were many factors at work, but one, in particular, drove superior logistics performance: the existence of properly structured and well-utilized measurement programs. Companies that frequently and quantitatively assessed their inventory levels, on-time performance, shipment costs, and other key operating metrics were better able to understand how their performance compared to the competition's and how well they were meeting customer demands. They also were more likely to know where there were bottlenecks in their many warehouses, routes, and other operations. And, most important, they better understood what they had to do to correct problems—often before they even happened.

The best-performing companies did not create logistics measures in a vacuum. Companies such as 3M, Motorola, Welch's, and Modus Media made sure that the measures they used on the ground floor of their warehouses, transportation operations, and other logistics infrastructure were in synch with the company's overall business strategy. For instance, companies whose strategy was to excel in customer service were not driving their logistics staff with measures emphasizing cost reduction.

In general, the research found that a well-aligned, well-executed measurement program could benefit a company in three primary ways: significant reduction in operating costs, dramatic improvement in customer service, and the pursuit of new growth opportunities. While aggressive companies with excellent measurement programs often have realized more than one of those benefits (and, in some cases, all three), a target of one is only a good starting point.

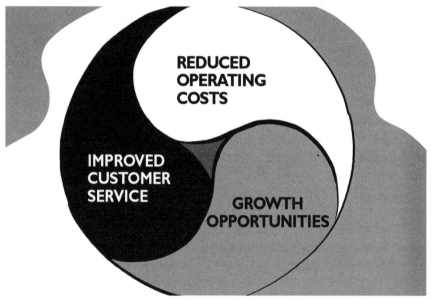

- *Reducing costs.* Measurement programs are well-suited to generating cost savings because they shine the spotlight on inefficiencies. Effective measures can help companies understand which customers are profitable and which are not; which suppliers offer truly "lowest total cost"; which services really add value and which just add cost; and which internal processes are fraught with excess hand-offs, rework, and redundant activities. For example, 3M, known for creating entire markets through such innovations as Post-it notes, realized its customers wanted easily accessible information on current orders. Now, from the time they place their orders, customers can check order status electronically. 3M has markedly improved the reliability, speed, and efficiency with which it ships its products, in part through a detailed measurement of all critical activities in order fulfillment. Because of 3M's ability to deliver its products reliably—and have customers view its real-time performance—the company has enjoyed preferred positioning in catalogs, shelf space, and other key sales outlets. Its logistics improvement initiatives also have cut 3M's costs significantly.

- *Improving service.* By replacing subjective, ratings-based customer-satisfaction surveys with objective measurement programs, companies can get more accurate pictures of how they are serving customers—and pinpoint and correct problem areas rapidly. For some companies, such programs actually serve as the heart of their ability to attract and retain customers in hyper-competitive industries, mature markets, or low-margin businesses. In the automobile industry, for example, Caliber Logistics has boosted the efficiency and effectiveness of logistics operations through measurement programs. Caliber Logistics, which provides distribution services to the automotive and other industries, has worked extensively with a replacement-parts division to ship parts to automobile dealers faster and less expensively. Caliber Logistics monitors their customer's end-to-end logistics operations, and that lets the automotive supplier take a comprehensive view of its logistics processes and better balance tradeoffs. The result: Caliber Logistics has improved customer service dramatically, thus solidifying its business relationship with one of the world's largest manufacturing companies.

- *Generating healthy growth.* Having an intimate understanding of logistics costs and performance can help companies weed out unprofitable customers and spur profitable growth. By knowing which performance capabilities place a company in customers' favor, which customers are its best (and worst), and how it stacks up against the competition, a company can focus logistics resources on the business that really pays off. At Modus Media International, a midsize company that manufactures and distributes computer software for powerhouses like Microsoft and Sun Microsystems, a program that measures the effectiveness of its overall operations has had just such an impact. The logistics measures also have helped the company far better understand the profitability of customer relationships. By focusing on customers it can serve at a fair profit and dropping others whose demands were too costly, Modus Media boosted its earnings during a two-year period. Perhaps even more important, Modus Media's logistics measurements have been adopted by other high-tech customers. By taking the lead in supply chain measurement, Modus Media has more control over the rules of the competition.

Unfortunately, however, those companies are the exception, not the rule. The gap between companies whose logistics processes are performing well and those that are doing poorly is widening. That is due, in part, to the companies' widely divergent ability to measure their performance. In some companies, measurement programs do not suffer from lack of internal skills in designing and implementing them. Rather, managers fail to recognize that measurement programs are needed in the first place. A surprising 20 percent of companies that responded to the survey conducted for this book do not compile such fundamental logistics performance measures as on-time delivery or order fill rates.

Continued failure to measure, measure the right things, or act appropriately on the data will spell disaster for companies whose success is increasingly dependent on logistics. That is due to a number of larger market forces that, for the foreseeable future, are raising the bar on logistics performance.

FORCES OF CHANGE

Amidst the daily pressure to keep a company's logistics operations running smoothly and to satisfy customers, it is easy to lose sight of the bigger picture within which logistics operates. In this case, "bigger picture" means the set of competitive, regulatory, technological, customer, and other forces that, individually and combined, require companies continually to improve their logistics processes and, occasionally, to make wholesale changes in them. The need for improvements in logistics performance will, in turn, increase the need to measure and monitor that performance. Five trends, more than any others, will require logistics managers to make continual improvements in their operations, large and small:

- *Continuing cost pressure:* Cost reduction is still high on the list of corporate initiatives. While revenue growth is the focus of most companies as the new millennium nears, cutting costs remains a top priority—and logistics is one of the biggest targets and best opportunities for improvement.

- *Product commoditization:* As markets mature and become saturated, once-innovative products and national brands become commodities, which forces companies to find new ways to differentiate their offerings.

- *Growing power of customers:* With retail chains growing larger and more demanding, manufacturers of consumer goods must emphasize customized service more strongly.

- *Globalization:* As more U.S. companies source, produce, and sell globally, the supply chain assumes greater prominence in daily business operations. Operations is one of the few areas that companies—working internally and with trading partners—still can mine for significant service improvement and cost reduction.

- *Electronic commerce:* The rise of the Internet is challenging the status quo of many industries, strongly influencing the way trading partners interact.

For logistics managers, those forces of change will be inescapable. They will create the need for massive improvements in logistics performance—well beyond the impressive gains many have made to date. The programs and systems used to measure those improvements are critical to the initiatives' success. The following discussion reviews these forces individually and examines their potential implications for performance measurement.

The Supply Chain Faces the Scalpel

In industry after industry, the first force that will drive companies to higher logistics performance is the never-ending quest to cut costs, better utilize assets, and increase revenues. CEOs cannot seem to squeeze enough dollars out of their organizations' research and development, manufacturing, marketing, sales, and distribution operations. Why? For starters, today's era of low inflation makes it virtually impossible for many companies to boost profits through price increases. The prospect of low inflation, or even deflation, and sluggish market growth has forced multibillion-dollar marriages of such companies as Exxon and Mobil, Daimler-Benz and Chrysler, and British Petroleum and Amoco—as well as a multitude of significant mergers in the consumer goods, retail, and pharmaceutical industries.

The demands of Wall Street create more pressure on senior corporate managers to reduce costs and increase revenues. The global battle for capital and the rising influence of institutional investors have forced nearly every CEO to build and vigorously promote his or her program for enhancing shareholder value. Of course, "feeding the Wall Street beast" by boosting shareholder returns requires continual cost reductions and better asset utilization on one hand and profitable revenue growth on the other. Thus, as *Fortune* 500 companies hack away at the cost of distribution, manufacturing, purchasing, finance, engineering, and product development, process improvement initiatives rage on.

In many companies today, no area is more highly scrutinized for cost-reduction potential than logistics. It is seen as one of the best ways to keep costs low, equipment and facilities utilized, and customer loyalty high. For instance, Texas Instruments Inc., the $9 billion semiconductor manufacturer, is working closely with distributors of data communications and electrical equipment like Graybar to root out costs in the procurement and acquisition of maintenance, repair, and operating supplies. Through partnership and an aggressive program, they have reduced the cost of procurement by more than 15 percent of the total cost of goods.

The $600 billion U.S. auto industry is chasing supply chain efficiencies on an even grander scale. After more than a decade of extracting costs from manufacturing and product development, General Motors, Ford, and DaimlerChrysler are aiming much of their streamlining efforts at their unwieldy distribution networks. In the U.S., distribution represents nearly one-third of the cost of building and delivering a new car.[4] The expense in getting cars from factories to dealerships represents 10 percent of distribution costs and 3 percent of total manufacturing and distribution expenses. Outbound logistics costs are not the only distribution expenditures auto makers are squeezing. There are also the inbound logistics costs associated with getting purchased components to automobile assembly plants. All told, the cost of purchased components—including inbound

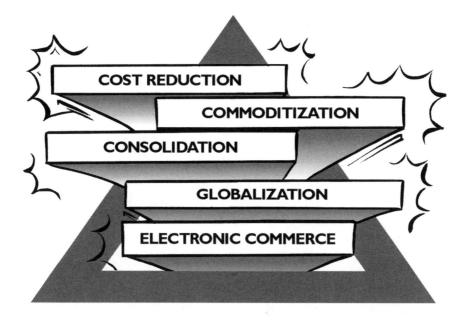

logistics—is 45 percent of total manufacturing and distribution costs for U.S. auto makers.[5]

The groundswell in the early 1990s to reduce costs in American companies through asset divestitures, process improvements, workforce reductions, and other means no doubt will continue. Those initiatives are being linked with programs targeted at earnings growth. Key performance measures for logistics process improvements are becoming the rule rather than the exception, as companies realize the need to compete—not just product to product, but also logistics process to logistics process—to achieve profitable revenue growth with maximum asset utilization and operational efficiency.

Products Are Becoming Commodities

Industries such as food, beverage, paper, and building materials find it is getting more difficult to differentiate products based on their features and quality. Increasingly, they are seeing that what customers value is moving from the product itself to the service with which it is delivered. To distinguish such commodity products, many manufacturers now are competing on service as well. As more products become commodities, companies must use logistics to differentiate themselves.

Logistics-based services help the retailer, and sometimes the end customer, get maximum value from the product. In the early 1990s, Coca-Cola's Japanese bottling operations were hailed for tailoring the company's delivery operations to the particular needs of stores and vending machine operators.[6] In Japanese supermarkets, Coke delivery personnel set up displays and make sure shelves are in order. For smaller, family-run stores, they even help process bills. Such value-adding activities are key to opening up new market segments.

Manufacturers like Baxter International have gone to great lengths to differentiate their products through logistics. The Illinois-based medical products company not only supplies hospitals with a wide array of products, it also can take responsibility for monitoring inventory and managing the logistics of the hospitals. Like Baxter, many other companies find it hard to compete on price and innovation alone. In such markets, a company's logistics operations can become the basis of competition.

The Customer Calls the Shots

The consolidation of companies in most supply chains is placing greater bargaining power in the hands of larger and more technologically sophisticated customers. In nearly every segment—manufacturing, distribution, and retailing—there are fewer competitors and, therefore, there is a greater concentration of power. From steelmakers and tire manufacturers to office products distributors and toy stores, competition that had once numbered in the dozens or hundreds has been reduced greatly—in some cases, to a handful.

No where is this more evident than in the continued consolidation of retail power and the demands of increasingly knowledgeable and demanding consumers. The rise of Wal-Mart and Target in the discount store segment, the growth of "category-killer" stores like Toys 'R' Us and Best Buy, and the ascent of warehouse and membership clubs have concentrated greater retail power in fewer hands (Exhibit 1.1). Nineteen years after opening its first store, The Home Depot generates more revenue ($30 billion) than all U.S. hardware stores combined.[7] Wal-Mart (with revenues of $139 billion), Target, and Kmart control more than two-thirds (69 percent) of all U.S. discount store revenue. In the U.S., mass retailers account for more than half (52 percent) of all toy sales, more than one-third (37 percent) of all consumer electronics sales, and one-quarter (25 percent)

America's Largest Retailers

1990 Rank		1999 Rank	
Company	**Annual Revenues**	**Company**	**Annual Revenues**
1. Sears Roebuck	$55,971,700	1. Wal-Mart	$139,208,000
2. Wal-Mart	$32,601,600	2. Sears Roebuck	$41,322,000
3. Kmart	$32,080,000	3. Kmart	$33,674,000
4. American Stores	$22,155,500	4. Dayton Hudson	$30,951,000
5. J.C. Penney	$17,410,000	5. J.C. Penney	$30,678,000
6. Safeway	$14,873,600	6. The Home Depot	$30,219,000
7. Dayton Hudson	$14,739,000	7. Kroger	$28,203,000
8. A&P	$11,164,200	8. Safeway	$24,484,000
9. May Dept. Stores	$11,027,000	9. Costco Cos.	$24,270,000

Source: *Fortune* magazine

of sporting goods purchases. Retail giants also control large shares of the sale of non-prescription drugs (23 percent) and pet supplies (19 percent).[8]

| Toys | Consumer Electronics | Sporting Goods | Non Prescription Drugs | Pet Supplies |

Even in Europe, once the bastion of the independent shopkeeper, retail power is concentrating. During the past 25 years, hypermarkets—cavernous retail outlets typically located outside city centers, featuring grocery, housewares, garden supplies, and other consumer products—have been gobbling up large shares of the food business. In France, hypermarkets account for about half of food sales, and in Spain they account for about one-quarter.[9] Consolidation in the U.S. grocery industry also is picking up speed, due in no small part to the increasing encroachment of Wal-Mart onto the grocery scene.

Retailers not only got bigger in the 1990s, they got smarter—smarter about exactly what is or is not selling well in Peoria at 5:00 p.m. on Saturday. Educated consumers are exerting pressure on retailers. Today, customer loyalty is defined simply as the lack of a better alternative.[10] A new customer loyalty equation has emerged:

Service = Loyalty

Logistics plays a critical role in delivering that service. Companies like Wal-Mart and Costco have developed the ability to have suppliers restock the right goods and weed out poor performers faster than competitors. That allows them to outperform their retail rivals both in terms of the prices they can offer customers and the margins their accountants track. By now, any retail chain that wants to survive this onslaught realizes it must become far more sophisticated in inventory management and information systems.

Manufacturers are being asked to provide customized pallet configurations so that shipments can go directly through the retailer's distribution center and on to a particular store. A growing number of retailers ask their suppliers to come in and manage their inventory in their stores and distribution centers. All this requires manufacturers to do more work, absorb more cost, take more time, and incur more risk to keep the business. To the immense purchasing power of a Wal-Mart or Target, not even the mightiest of suppliers can say no— not even Procter & Gamble. As a result, the pressure forces them to become extremely efficient. Supply chain optimization is the rallying cry, and logistics improvement is at the heart of the movement.

Immense buying power plus exhaustive knowledge of what is selling at the checkout counter make a powerful combination called "clout." The Home Depot, Wal-Mart, Toys 'R' Us, and Target have it, and they use it to demand continually better performance and better terms from their suppliers. For manufacturers, the message is, "Comply or die." In return for volume, large retail chains expect rock-bottom prices and great service from their suppliers. For the thousands of manufacturers supplying these retail outlets, this means only one thing: Life on the supply chain will only get tougher. As a result, measuring logistics performance is vital.

Global Sourcing, Production, and Selling: The World Gets Smaller

The logistics operations of many manufacturers and retailers face even greater pressure and complexities because their CEOs want to "go global." The push to sell into foreign markets is fueled by both opportunity and cost. The opportunity is to expand into markets like Southeast Asia, which has been developing rapidly for American companies. For example, as part of its decade-old globalization push, Whirlpool Corp. in the mid-1990s established five factories in

Southeast Asia. Those factories now generate $400 million in sales.[11] The company also bought the European appliance business of N.V. Philips, the Dutch electronics and consumer products giant. Whirlpool, which 10 years ago had virtually no European sales, is now the number-three appliance company in Europe with sales in excess of $2 billion. Philips, in turn, bought television manufacturer Magnavox to increase its share of the North American consumer electronics market.

Staying responsive to the needs of the increasing number of global retailers also keeps logistics managers of manufacturers and distributors awake at night. In the 1970s and 1980s, specialty retailers like Laura Ashley, Gucci, and Benetton, and general merchandisers such as Marks and Spencer and Sears, expanded outside their home countries with varying degrees of success. During the past 15 or so years, they were followed by retailers like Wal-Mart, Swedish furniture dealer IKEA, and Toys 'R' Us, as well as specialty stores such as The Gap, The Body Shop, and The Disney Store.[12] As vendors strive to keep up with the demands of such global brands, they are bound to find their logistics operations increasingly stretched—and stressed.

For their part, retail logistics professionals are under increasing pressure to devise cost-effective and timely ways to bring goods produced in far-flung locales to the shelves of their U.S. stores. A retail buyer's ability to find a bargain on goods in the Far East is negated if it costs too much or takes too long to ship the products to U.S. stores. These long supply chains have to be lean, flexible, and agile, with minimal inventory. As the entire world becomes a single mega-market, and delivery requirements grow in complexity, logistics managers will face a new set of challenges.

The Commercialization of the Internet

The last driver of supply chain improvement may turn out to be the most significant: electronic commerce. As if pressures from consumers, customers, and existing competitors to renovate the supply chain were not enough, consider the vast insecurity generated by the growing number of Internet startups looking to cut out whole links of the chain. As the rate of change accelerates and companies look to cyberspace to enhance their logistics performance, logistics managers have to keep pace.

Although still a tiny sliver of today's retail pie, Internet shopping by consumers has grown from virtually zero in the mid-1990s to nearly $8 billion in 1998, according to Forrester Research, a respected market research company.[13] For the 1998 holiday shopping period, the firm projected $3.5 billion in Internet purchases alone. A report by Boston Consulting Group found that online shopping during December 1998 jumped 230 percent from the same month in the previous year.[14] By 2003, online retail sales in the U.S. are projected to top $100 billion, representing 6 percent of domestic retail spending. And Forrester predicts that 56 percent of all U.S. households will be connected to the Internet by 2003 (Exhibit 1.3). It will be increasingly common for travel services, computers and software, books, stocks, consumer electronics, housewares, and other items to be purchased over the Internet and shipped directly to homes.

The prospect of Internet retailing already has a number of large retailers rethinking logistics. One great example is the jockeying for position in book-distribution channels among Amazon.com, its competitors, and its channel partners. The Seattle company has dramatically redefined book buyers' expectations by delivering—sometimes in days instead of weeks—obscure, long-forgotten titles missing from the shelves of even the biggest of book "superstores." By the end of 1998, Amazon's 12-month sales were running at a rate of more than $1 billion. In fact, Amazon's market capitalization was larger than either of its two biggest competitors, Barnes & Noble and Borders. That meant that in the three years since its launch, Amazon had grabbed 3 percent of the U.S. retail book market—half the share of Wal-Mart—and was rapidly gaining on Barnes & Noble and Borders (each of which have a 25 percent share).[15, 16]

Exhibit 1.3 THE DIGITAL DECADE

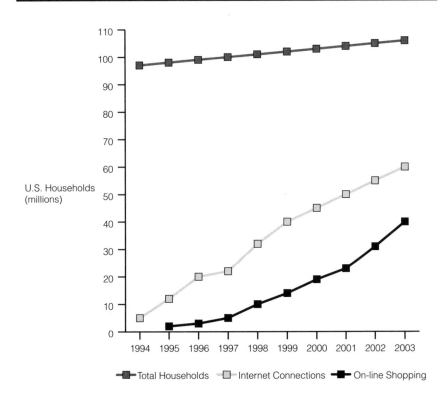

Reproduced by permission of Forrester Research Inc.

Two years after Amazon's launch in July 1995, Barnes & Noble, the largest bookstore chain in the U.S., awoke from its slumber. In 1997, it went online with its own book-selling site. Yet a year later, Barnes & Noble's online sales were only one-tenth of Amazon's. Perhaps frustrated with its progress, in November 1998, Barnes & Noble made a radical move: It announced its purchase of the book industry's largest distributor, Ingram Book Co., for $600 million. Barnes & Noble asserted that buying Ingram (which also supplies Amazon) would speed the time it takes for books to go from warehouses to homes. In fact, Ingram's 11 distribution centers will be able to deliver books overnight to 80 percent of Barnes & Noble's customers.

The point here is not to predict whether Amazon, Barnes & Noble, or some other bookseller will prevail. Rather, it is to make the following observation: Whether or not Amazon ever makes money—or even survives—the Internet startup already has shaken up the book industry. And if the book industry's experience with Amazon is a harbinger of things to come, the supply chains of other industries also figure to change significantly as a result of electronic commerce.

Another indication of the Internet's potential is the fact that some highly successful manufacturers are willing to risk their relations with traditional channel partners to get a stake in online sales. In 1998 Compaq Computer Corp., the world's largest manufacturer of PCs, launched an online PC sales business despite dealer opposition. By February 1999, Compaq was conducting $1 million of business a day through its Web site [17] and claimed it was on track to generate 20 percent of its total annual revenues from Web sales within a year.[18] In a similar move, Hewlett-Packard launched its own Web site, "Shopping Village," to sell PCs direct. In the meantime, such direct PC marketers as Dell and Gateway were attracting increasing numbers of sales through their Web sites. By late 1998, Dell's Web site was processing daily orders worth $3 million, meaning the company would do about $1 billion of business a year through the Internet. Customers who browsed Dell's Web site and then ordered by fax or phone placed another $7 million in daily orders.[19]

PC companies are not the only companies building electronic connections to customers. That arbiter of "athletic fashion," Nike Inc., announced early in 1999 that it was beginning to sell footwear and apparel directly to consumers online, eventually relaunching the site with a wider variety of products.[20] And manufacturers like Mattel Inc. see the Internet as a way to counteract the growing power of retailers. In February 1999, the company told *The Wall Street Journal* that it is counting on the Internet and other direct marketing channels to reduce its reliance on retailers like Toys 'R' Us and Wal-Mart, which make up 30 percent to 40 percent of Mattel's sales. In 1998, to the toy maker's dismay, those retailers had cut their toy inventories. "If the retailer is not going to be aggressive, we'll find another way to put our products in front of the consumer," Jill Barad, Mattel's chairman and CEO, told the newspaper.[21]

What impact does the rapid growth of electronic commerce have on logistics? While the ultimate impact is yet to be seen, early signs suggest that the distribution systems of many Web retailers are not ready to handle direct selling efficiently. Consumers, attracted to the convenience of Web shopping, expect quick delivery of the goods they order. But many were dissatisfied with the service they received in the holiday season of 1998.[22] Surveys and press reports disclosed widespread inventory shortages and delivery delays. One survey of online shoppers found that less than half (37 percent) of them planned to buy over the Internet during the next Christmas season.[23] Apparently, some companies' logistics operations were not ready to handle Web shopping in peak periods.

While home online shopping has grown at a furious pace, business-to-business electronic commerce has exploded. Like Amazon's upheaval of the U.S. book distribution system, the changes in business-to-business electronic commerce are likely to rattle many old industrial supply chains. Forrester Research predicts the amount of worldwide commerce conducted over the Internet is expected to range from $1.4 trillion to $3.2 trillion by 2003.[24] The $3.2 trillion would account for almost 5 percent of all global commerce. Already, computer and communications equipment and components companies like Cisco Systems and Intel are doing billions of dollars in online business. Cisco, a manufacturer of routers, switches, and other computer network gear, says it does nearly 60 percent of its business through the Internet—to the tune of more than $1 billion a quarter. That portion of its business is expected to reach 80 percent by 1999.[25]

In the heavy manufacturing industry, two major players are making their bids to exploit the Internet. Eaton Corp., a diversified manufacturer based in Cleveland, announced plans to use its Web site to transmit and process electronic invoices, shipping notices, and purchase orders. The move is expected to slash the per-invoice processing cost for Eaton and its trading partners from $70 to $7.[26] Steel producer LTV Corp., also in Cleveland, launched a venture with two other steel manufacturers to sell excess and damaged steel inventory over the Internet. The venture's Web site will feature both product catalogs and an auction service through which customers can purchase steel. LTV and its partners plan eventually to expand the site to let customers pay for purchases and check order and shipping status online.[27]

All that means the Internet could become the ultimate driver of supply chain efficiency. Logistics managers now must ask themselves the "What if?" questions: What if our distributors began buying our products over the Internet? What if their customers began purchasing our products through them over the Internet? What if those customers came to us to purchase our products directly? What if our competitors' products were available over the Internet? In each case, what might be the Internet's potential impact on manufacturing, inbound supply, and outbound supply chain operations?

The answers could be discomfiting. Logistics professionals now must think about their strategic role within their companies and how they and their operations can continue to add value. They must help their companies understand whether and how they can exploit electronic commerce. And they must ask themselves what new ideas and training they need to succeed in a world where electronic commerce is reshaping age-old supply chains. Considering how fast things move in the world of Internet commerce (where the term "Internet year" means a few months), now is the time to be asking those questions. Otherwise, a company might find itself like Barnes & Noble or Compaq—rushing to catch up but still far behind.

WATCHING OUT FOR "TRIGGER POINTS"

Pressures to cut costs, grow revenues, boost share price, differentiate commodity goods, be responsive to ever more-powerful customers and consumers, stay competitive with foreign rivals, streamline global operations, and deal with the Internet will increase pressures on logistics managers. Those forces, separately and together, are raising the performance bar for supply chain operations in many industries. What is acceptable today in terms of on-time delivery, cost to serve, inventory carrying costs, inbound and outbound freight costs, information integration, order status, and other performance metrics may be unacceptable a few years from now.

Do not expect those forces to disappear. They have been in place for a number of years (even the Internet dates back to the late 1960s), and they will march on for the indefinite future. Consider them sewn into the fabric of business. Yet as powerful as they are, they are not the only forces that logistics managers must worry about. Another set of challenges also must be considered. These developments are less evolutionary, occurring within fairly well-defined time periods. These events are "trigger points." These volcanic disruptions are difficult to ignore and even harder to manage. They are earthquakes that change the landscape and open up new opportunities. Well-known trigger points of the past two decades include:

- New regulations that open up new competition: Remember the deregulation of the trucking and railroad industries in the 1980s.

- Economic and political upheavals that change worldwide economics: Recall the oil embargoes of the 1970s and the Asian economic crisis of the late 1990s.

- Technological breakthroughs that make old systems obsolete: Look at the contortions through which enterprise resource planning (ERP) software puts many logistics managers.

Logistics executives must be prepared for such trigger points. Their mindsets, plans, and operations will have to be flexible for logistics processes to change quickly and without much warning. However, knowing whether and how logistics operations must change requires a clear understanding of how well those operations perform today. In turn, intimately understanding a company's performance requires measurement systems that keep track of performance, and the underlying factors that influence that performance. Only then can logistics professionals understand the alternatives, leverage change, and come out on top.

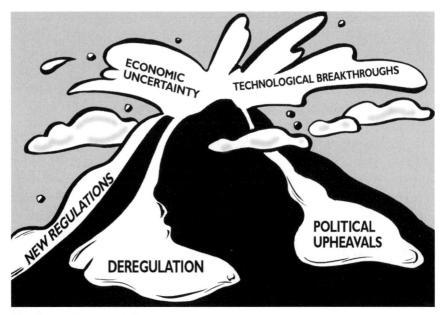

The Impact on Logistics

It is hard to understate the severity of those forces of change and trigger points for logistics operations. Twenty years ago, who could have imagined mergers valued at $80 billion or even $30 billion? Or a new book retailer that, in three years, went from scratch to $500 million in sales without building one physical store? Or a multibillion-dollar manufacturer (Cisco Systems) that in four years went from selling nothing online to booking most of its business over the Web? Twenty years ago, newspaper headlines for those stories would have been truly inconceivable.

What does all that mean for logistics managers? Under what kinds of performance standards will they operate, due to the confluence of the disruptive forces just discussed? Will two-hour inquiry responses suffice in the PC industry? Will two-day fulfillment cycles cut it in the book industry? How about six-week delivery times for customized automobiles? Or 97 percent order fill rates in the cellular phone business?

There is no blanket answer for every industry or even for every company within an industry. Some companies are willing to trade cycle time for rock-bottom prices. In 1998, the U.S. Postal Service still owned a 6 percent share of the more than 270 million packages shipped annually via courier service[28] —despite its inability to match the nationwide next-day delivery guarantee of FedEx and UPS.[29] Others create such strong emotional attachments with consumers that short-term supply chain inadequacies are overlooked. Getting a customized Cadillac in three weeks will not be enough to win many die-hard Mercedes and BMW owners who are willing to wait longer for the options—and cachet—that they desire.

Nevertheless, for long-term success, a company's supply chain must perform at a level that, at worst, approximates its nearest competitor. The danger of trailing too far is one of falling seriously behind. It is a multibillion-dollar lesson that UPS learned by letting FedEx get a jump on it through package-tracking technology in the 1980s.[30] With Internet-direct companies setting new standards in the minds of customers, most companies will not have the luxury of years to catch up to the competition.

With revolutionary technologies like electronic commerce and advanced planning applications beginning to reshape logistics practices, managers must not be lulled into thinking that today's performance standards will remain static. By exploiting technologies like the Internet and new software, unforeseen competitors can create entirely new customer expectations seemingly overnight—as Amazon has done in the book industry. It took a while for Barnes & Noble to realize that its competition was not just other booksellers with actual stores, but Internet sellers as well. Compaq does not worry only about PC makers that sell through dealers. Compaq is just as nervous about direct sellers like Dell, Gateway, and Micron. In all industries, companies should be creating futuristic scenarios by which they can envision new supply chains and their associated performance requirements. Companies must not wait for present or future competitors to do it for them.

How Logistics Measurement Must Change

Whether logistics managers compare themselves to their existing or to imagined competitors, the performance measures and standards for their operations are likely to change dramatically. Whole industry supply chains—not just the logistics operations of a single company in them—will become the new focus. Even the mightiest of retailers cannot be assured a sufficient supply of a hot video game if manufacturers underestimate demand and cannot make the product fast enough. If automobile manufacturers truly envision a business in which the majority of cars are built to order and not to inventory, they cannot afford to have key suppliers run out of parts. As Mike Mauer, Procter & Gamble's director of industry affairs and co-chairman of the Efficient Consumer Response Operating Committee, has said: "Trading partners working together toward systematic solutions, working across the supply chain, are going to yield better solutions than siloed approaches."[31]

The underlying premise of such industry-wide efficiency initiatives as just-in-time (JIT) in the automotive industry, Efficient Consumer Response (ECR) in the grocery business, Efficient Foodservice Response (EFR) in the prepared-foods industry, and Efficient Healthcare Consumer Response (EHCR) in the pharmaceutical and life sciences business is that companies throughout an industry supply chain must cooperate. In particular, they have to agree on standards in such areas as product identification, bar coding, and electronic communication. Then, they have to identify and systematically eliminate the waste and duplication of efforts and inventories that add incremental cost to the supply chain as a whole. Central to streamlining the flow of raw materials and finished goods from one end of the supply chain to the other is increasing the flow of information. If participants in the supply chain lack data on how each of them is performing, where a shipment stands, and where items are getting bogged down, it is nearly impossible to synchronize people, transportation, and warehouse resources. To improve logistics processes, access to information is now more important than access to capital.

The time has come to optimize whole channels between the production of goods and their consumption by consumers. In fact, it is a natural progression in the activities by which corporations have been improving their operations. No longer is internal functional improvement the only focus. Managers have been changing activities that cross functional boundaries—complete business processes—for the past decade.[32] While the work there remains unfinished, managers must simultaneously extend their improvement initiatives to the next level. As reengineering guru Michael Hammer has said, "The walls between companies generate far more overhead and delay than the walls between departments. ... The only relevant question is how all participants in the supply chain can unite to create greater value for the end consumer and do so at lower total costs."[33] While companies continue to seek and eliminate waste within their own processes, they also must continue to improve relationships with their trading partners to gain maximum cost effectiveness and, most of all, to establish and sustain earnings growth.

The New Focus of Competition: Supply Chain to Supply Chain

In the next decade, the challenge in logistics will be to make major improvements in logistics processes that cross company boundaries. Consider the following example in the PC industry. Even if a PC manufacturer with a traditional distribution network eliminates huge chunks of inventory costs and cycle time in the manufacturing and shipping of PCs to retailers' warehouses, it is still at the mercy of its trading partners. The PC manufacturer's suppliers must deliver components such as microprocessors, memory chips, hard drives, and computer terminals to its factories, and, as quickly as possible, the retailers must get the machines into the right stores, in the right quantities, and at the right prices.

In the mind of the end consumer, the manufacturer's cycle time and costs are irrelevant. It is the "product" at the end of the total supply chain that consumers compare against the likes of other PC makers that sell direct. In other words, it is the supply chain that Compaq and its suppliers and distributors/dealers can configure versus the supply chains within which Dell and Gateway operate. The winners will be those with the best-improved logistics of the entire supply chain.

The same goes for discount retailing. The basis of supply chain competition for these companies has come down to this: Which will be best at rooting out the greatest amount of inefficiency with the greatest number of key suppliers? Again, it is not Wal-Mart's logistics process versus Target's and Kmart's logistics processes. It is the new supply chain processes that Wal-Mart can configure with Procter & Gamble, Hallmark Cards, Michelin Tires, and others versus what Target and Kmart can do with *their* key suppliers.

Every day, it is becoming more apparent that companies no longer can focus solely on optimizing their own logistics operations to the exclusion of their suppliers' or customers' logistics operations. Instead, companies across an entire supply chain must work collaboratively to generate the greatest possible mutual gains and savings.

KEEPING SCORE: THE NEED FOR IMPROVED PERFORMANCE MEASUREMENT

Dramatic improvements in any business process require effective ways to gauge its performance. Such performance measures as on-time delivery, returns, customer complaints, finished goods inventory turns, and invoice accuracy are a logistics manager's tools for monitoring logistics operations, making effective decisions, and taking corrective action. Performance measures are the scorecard—the way to understand whether logistics operations are winning or losing the game.

The performance measures in use at many of today's logistics organizations are the natural outgrowth of a time when their companies focused on functional optimization. Warehouse managers were measured on number of items picked per hour or inventory carrying costs. Transportation departments were measured on truck utilization rates or shipping costs.

Although they once helped improve the performance of individual functional activities, today, such performance metrics actually can hamper a company, keeping it from making improvements across its own logistics processes or the extended supply chain. The problem is that measuring and optimizing the performance of such narrow logistics functions as warehousing, shipping, and customer service can wind up degrading the performance of the entire supply chain.

Certainly, it is important to measure the performance of the transportation function. But a company no longer can measure the transportation function in isolation from the other links in its logistics processes, which include everything from raw material sourcing and production scheduling to forecasting, order management, and customer service. Functional measures and associated goals must be aligned with the overall business strategies and process objectives to explicitly demonstrate the tradeoffs that exist. For instance, driving transportation costs to their minimum may impair order cycle time and consistency, increase damages, or generate more inventory. So while transportation costs may go down, customer satisfaction and overall logistics performance and costs will suffer.

It is dangerous today to base logistics measures on functional metrics. Even worse is having logistics measures that are not in harmony with a company's overall business strategy. Consider what

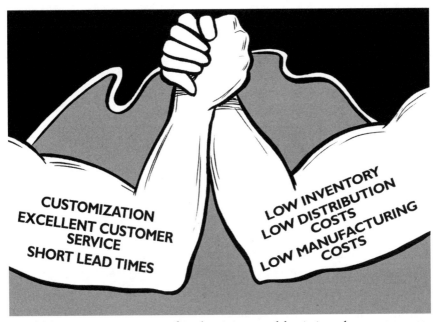

CUSTOMIZATION
EXCELLENT CUSTOMER SERVICE
SHORT LEAD TIMES

LOW INVENTORY
LOW DISTRIBUTION COSTS
LOW MANUFACTURING COSTS

would happen to Amazon if its business and logistics plans were not aligned. Amazon bases its entire business model on convenience and superior fulfillment capabilities. If the company could not quickly fulfill the orders it gets for hot-selling books, its business strategy would be for naught. Speedy delivery, proactive order status information, and service quality are part and parcel of Amazon's brand identity. If Amazon drove its logistics activities (and logistics providers) with measures focused solely on reducing delivery costs, it would cripple its ability to serve customers. To prevent such scenarios in their businesses, wise executives are fusing their logistics plan with their business strategies, ensuring that what is measured in the field is valued at the top of the organization.

To ensure that all measures (logistics or otherwise) are in synch with a company's market direction, more and more companies are driving all their corporate measurement activities to meet the needs of two of their most powerful constituencies: shareholders and customers. Shareholder success is measured through such calculations as economic value-added (EVA) or return on capital employed (ROCE). (Exhibit 1.4 and Exhibit 1.5 indicate two common methods for calculating ROCE.) Both measures calculate how much profit a company generates after subtracting the cost of equity capital required to finance its operations. The intent is to help managers

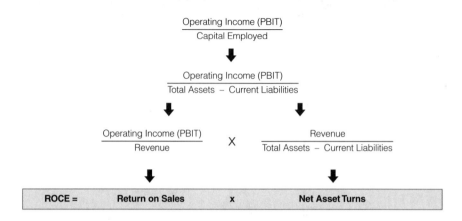

Exhibit 1.4 CALCULATING ROCE – METHOD ONE

$$\frac{\text{Operating Income (PBIT)}}{\text{Capital Employed}}$$

⬇

$$\frac{\text{Operating Income (PBIT)}}{\text{Total Assets} - \text{Current Liabilities}}$$

⬇   ⬇

$$\frac{\text{Operating Income (PBIT)}}{\text{Revenue}} \quad X \quad \frac{\text{Revenue}}{\text{Total Assets} - \text{Current Liabilities}}$$

⬇   ⬇

ROCE =	Return on Sales	x	Net Asset Turns

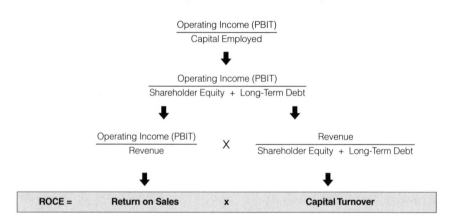

Exhibit 1.5 CALCULATING ROCE – METHOD TWO

$$\frac{\text{Operating Income (PBIT)}}{\text{Capital Employed}}$$

⬇

$$\frac{\text{Operating Income (PBIT)}}{\text{Shareholder Equity} + \text{Long-Term Debt}}$$

⬇   ⬇

$$\frac{\text{Operating Income (PBIT)}}{\text{Revenue}} \quad X \quad \frac{\text{Revenue}}{\text{Shareholder Equity} + \text{Long-Term Debt}}$$

⬇   ⬇

ROCE =	Return on Sales	x	Capital Turnover

understand whether investments in products, processes, and businesses will enhance or detract from shareholder value. Measures like EVA and ROCE are rapidly gaining the favor of CEOs and CFOs of many public corporations. Improvements in logistics have a direct and positive impact on those measures.

Customer-value measurements appear to be replacing utilization and productivity measures as the key drivers in decision making. That reflects the shift in power from "push" manufacturing to "pull" consumerism. Companies that focus on pleasing such channel inter-

CUSTOMER SERVICE OFFERINGS

COST REDUCTION

mediaries as wholesalers and retailers—in pricing, product configuration, packaging, delivery times, and service—without monitoring the needs of end consumers are playing a dangerous game. Similarly, logistics operations that measure only internal performance or performance with a channel partner—and not the end consumer—run the risk of falling behind in logistics capabilities.

To keep their organizations competitive, logistics managers need new performance measures that are linked to such corporate measurements as ROCE and customer value. And, because the focus of many supply chain improvement efforts necessarily will involve more than one company—and sometimes many companies—the new measures must be common to all participants in a supply chain.

The remainder of this book will outline an approach by which companies can define and implement the new measures that are necessary in today's dynamic, global, and interconnected business environment. The intent is to help logistics managers spur logistics performance both across their companies and across the greater supply chain, which includes their most important suppliers, customers, and, if need be, customers' customers. By mastering the critical step of measuring logistics performance that transcends emphasis on individual activities, logistics managers will go a long way toward positioning their companies to compete in a world that pits supply chains against supply chains.

WHAT IS NEXT?

As marketplace change accelerates, business strategies themselves will have to change fast enough for companies to respond to emerging market needs and competitive threats. With business strategy and logistics working hand-in-hand, changes in one must be reflected in changes to the other. Business strategy must drive logistics strategy and logistics measurement, which in turn will determine the measures used in specific logistics activities. If those linkages are weak, the business strategy has a high probability of failure.

Given the speed with which the marketplace is changing, performance measurements must generate data to help logistics managers make intelligent, informed decisions about their operations quickly in the face of changing business conditions. The only way changes can be anticipated, assessed, and made is through a linked set of performance measurements. The increasing complexity of logistics requires managers to make decisions based on facts—especially about the tradeoffs that must be made when a logistics process is optimized.

This book is, as much as anything else, a call to arms for all companies that rely on logistics as a core operation. It is *not* a book on how to redesign logistics processes, a topic covered by a number of other books. Instead, the focus is on the process measures and new measurement programs that managers must institute for new, efficient logistics processes to take hold—and continually improve.

ENDNOTES

[1] M. MacDonald, "From Supply-Chain Manager to CEO," *Logistics,* June 1998, p. 96.

[2] E. Nelson, "Logistics Whiz Rises at Wal-Mart," The Wall Street Journal, March 11, 1999, p. B1.

[3] KPMG Peat Marwick and MIT, "Global Supply Chain Benchmarking: The Consumer Markets Industry," 1997 (published separately).

[4] G. A. Mercer, "Don't Just Optimize – Unbundle," McKinsey Quarterly, 1994, No. 3, pp. 103-116. From 1980 to 1990, the average annual productivity improvement in auto manufacturing in the UK was nearly 80 percent greater than the average per annum productivity gain in distribution—6.6 percent (measured by number of cars assembled per production worker) vs. 3.7 percent (cars sold per retail employee), according to the UK Central Statistical Office, Department of Employment, and Sewells International. Distribution costs include logistics, dealer margins, incentives and allowances for advertising.

[5] Ibid.

[6] J. Fuller, J. O'Conor, and R. Rawlinson, "Tailored Logistics: The Next Advantage," Harvard Business Review, May-June 1993, pp. 87-98.

[7] McKinsey & Co. analysis of data from Discount Merchandiser magazine, Profound Inc., IMB, and industry estimates, as detailed in 1997 No. 4 issue of the McKinsey Quarterly. Mass retailers were defined as having at least 10,000 square feet of store space, at least $1 million in per-store annual sales, low margins, departmentalized, and having many self-service sales techniques.

[8] Ibid.

[9] J. Castrillo, R. Forn, and R. Mira, "Hypermarkets May be Losing Their Appeal for European Consumers," McKinsey Quarterly, 1997, No. 4, pp. 194-200.

[10] Lou Pritchett, in a keynote speech to the Supply Chain Council Conference, September 1998.

[11] Whirlpool CEO David Whitwam's letter to shareholders in Whirlpool Corp.'s 1997 annual report.

[12] K. Barth, N. Karch, K. McLaughlin, and C. Smith Shi, "Global Retailing: Tempting Trouble?" McKinsey Quarterly, 1996, No. 1, pp. 116-125.

[13] Forrester Research Inc. press release, November 19, 1998. The company projected $7.8 billion in online retail sales in the U.S. in 1998 for goods other than automobiles.

[14] M. Zane, "E-tailers Tell Tales of Hot Holiday Sales," *ZDNet* online, December 29, 1998.

[15] O. Thomas, "Wal-Mart vs. the Wal-Mart of the Web," Red Herring Online, November 10, 1998.

[16] D. Gordon, "Books Caught in the Web," Newsweek, November 23, 1998, p. 85.

[17] G. McWilliams, "Compaq Says Sales of New PC Top $1 Million a Day," The Wall Street Journal, February 1, 1999.

[18] Reuters, "Compaq Forms Compaq.com Internet Product Sales Unit," February 1, 1999.

[19] S. Thurm, "Leading the PC Pack," The Wall Street Journal, December 7, 1998, special report on the Internet, p. R27.

[20] Reuters, "Nike Begins Selling Products Directly on Internet," February 9, 1999.

[21] S. Kravetz, "Mattel Revamps Retail Plan to Reduce Its Dependence on Traditional Outlets," The Wall Street Journal, February 17, 1999, p. B8.

[22] Associated Press, "Sales Soar, but Not All Shoppers Are Pleased with E-Commerce," The Wall Street Journal, January 18, 1999.

[23] Ibid. From Jupiter Communications survey of 2,300 online holiday shoppers.

[24] Forrester Research press release, November 5, 1998.

[25] S. Tully, "How Cisco Mastered the Net," Fortune, August 17, 1998.

[26] A. Hardin, "Eaton Corp. Looking to Expand e-Commerce," Crain's Cleveland Business, October 5, 1998.

[27] T. Gerdel, "LTV to Sell Excess and Damaged Steel on Web Site," The [Cleveland] Plain Dealer, August 19, 1998.

[28] G. Jaffe and M. Brannigan, "Possible FedEx Walkout Threatens to Disrupt Holiday," The Wall Street Journal, November 12, 1998, p. B8. The authors cited market share data on the overnight package delivery market from The Colography Group, Atlanta.

[29] D. Blackmon, "UPS to Guarantee On-Time Ground Delivery," The Wall Street Journal, April 10, 1998, p. A3.

[30] C. Hawkins and P. Oster, "After a U-Turn, UPS Really Delivers," Business Week, May 31, 1993. The article said UPS had spent about $2 billion in the early 1990s on package-tracking technology.

[31] R. Mathews, "ECR/EFT: The Next Steps," Progressive Grocer, September 1, 1997, p. 35.

[32] This point was driven home in the Council of Logistics Management's 1991 book, Improving Quality and Productivity in the Logistics Process. The authors noted the distinction between making improvements in logistics tasks within functional silos and making changes across functions in end-to-end logistics processes.

[33] This quote was taken from a program description of a 1998 Hammer and Company conference led by Michael Hammer on supply chain reengineering, "Transforming the Supply Chain: Integrating to Serve the Final Customer."

2

THE PAST AND CURRENT
STATE OF LOGISTICS

Logistics managers who have been in the profession for any length of time must feel like 18th century American colonists, who had to pay continually higher taxes to England: What they gave yesterday is not good enough today, and what they give today will not be good enough tomorrow. Substitute the word "performance" for the word "taxes" and "the company" for "England" and that pretty much summed up the expectations placed upon the logistics organization since the early 1960s.

What was considered acceptable performance 40 years ago—the time to fill orders, how many items could arrive damaged, how often the goods got there on time, and other metrics—would today put most companies out of business. The standards of performance, as set by the marketplace, have risen tremendously for logistics professionals. Even the performance standards of a decade ago are as dated as an old newspaper. In some fast-moving, highly competitive industries, last year's performance targets are already old hat.

Measuring performance has become increasingly important in logistics. The logistics performance standards that today's companies must meet have outstripped those of nearly every other corporate function during the past four decades. It was not like that 40 years ago, when manufacturing efficiencies and mass marketing effectiveness drove companies to market success. American automobile manufacturers, for instance, did not have a great incentive to measure logistics performance in the 1960s. All they had to do was continue to find ways to speed the production lines (to lower the per-unit cost of cars) and use the national media to announce that their cars were now within finan-

Definition of Terms

For the purpose of a common ground of understanding and discussion, the following definitions are used for various logistics and business terminology in this book.

1. **Task:** a coherent piece of work that can be assigned to an individual or small team and completed in a reasonably short amount of time.

2. **Activity:** a collection of tasks that have a common purpose, produce a common output, or address a common theme.

3. **Function:** a grouping of related activities contributing to a combined result, where trade-offs between the tasks and activities can be made under unified management.

4. **Process:** a series of linked, continuous, and managed tasks and activities that contribute to an overall desired outcome or result. Processes have a specific starting point and ending point and often, but not always, cross functional boundaries. Customers of the process are always at the end point of the process, and they are also often at its starting point.

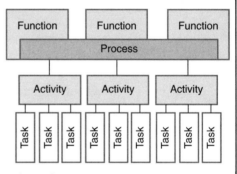

5. **Integration (as applied to Process):** the uniting, combining, or incorporation of two or more functions within a company, or two or more processes between two or more companies into a compatible or unified process. This presupposes that joint definitions and agreements concerning the separate functions and processes have been defined and articulated between all parties.

6. **Logistics:** that part of the supply chain process that plans, implements, and controls the efficient flow and storage of goods, services, and related information from the point of origin to the point of consumption in order to meet customers' requirements. (Council of Logistics Management, 1998)[1]

7. **Supply Chain:** a set of three or more organizations directly linked by one or more of the upstream and downstream flows of products, services, finances, and information from a source to a customer. (Supply Chain Research Group, University of Tennessee, 1999)[2]

were now within financial reach of more consumers. Similarly, large consumer products companies like Procter & Gamble and Kellogg had little need to optimize logistics. Instead, their goal was to pack their customers' warehouses with as much product as possible—and leave it to the retailers to figure out how to get it into consumers' hands. But as Chapter 1 discussed, today's business conditions are different. The performance demands on logistics managers are an order of magnitude greater today than four decades ago.

The performance requirements did not change overnight. Rather, they have evolved, slowly at first, and then ever more rapidly in concert with new trends in markets, technology, regulations, competition, and other elements that affect both the way companies organize their logistics operations and the way those companies measure performance. Putting those trends in perspective helps companies prepare for the great changes ahead.

Chapter 1 reviewed five forces and several "trigger points" that are having significant impact now—and will have in the future—on companies' logistics operations. Those forces are derivatives of a number of larger market elements that have evolved since the 1960s. Chapter 2 will briefly describe the elements and how they have played out during the past four decades. It also will review how these elements have increased performance standards for companies' logistics operations, and will discuss what those standards mean for logistics operations and logistics measures: How did logistics operations improve to meet rising performance demands? What role did measurement play in such improvements? What operations did they measure, and how did they measure them?

The chapter then will explore the state of logistics measurement today to determine what those market elements have wrought at the change of the millennium—and how today's companies are responding to the challenges.

MARKET ELEMENTS

Six major market elements, individually and together, have challenged—and, in some cases, enabled—manufacturers, distributors, and retailers to achieve progressively better levels of logistics performance. They are: competition, customers, technology, regulations, shareholder demands, and suppliers.[3]

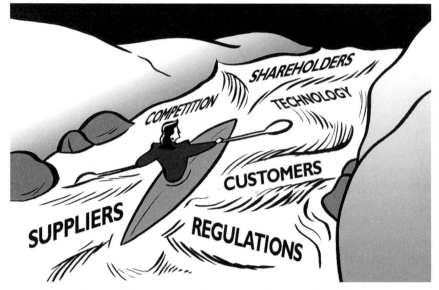

- *Competition.* When a product manufacturer has little competition, customers—whether retailers or consumers—have little choice. More or less, they must accept the manufacturer's terms and conditions: the prices they set, the delivery schedules they follow, the customer service they provide. Such manufacturers have little incentive to bend over backward to get products shipped on time, without damage, and at low cost. However, when competition is fierce, products become harder to differentiate, and manufacturers must provide far better service to get and retain the business. Measuring and monitoring one's performance becomes important.

- *Customers.* Changes in customers—of manufacturers, distributors, and retailers alike—have had a powerful impact on logistics operations and measurement. Customers have much more buying clout and knowledge about what they are buying, and they have become global. When customers are small, they individually account for a small slice of a manufacturer's total sales, and thus they have little bargaining power. In many sectors, however, retail customers have grown substantially, as described in Chapter 1. They have forced manufacturers to become far better at delivering the goods—when, where, and in what form they are needed. In addition, customers now are spread all over the globe. For makers of everything from soft drinks to software, the entire world is the market. Operating far beyond one's "home turf" has introduced new complexities for logistics managers. In some cases, it may become necessary to forge logistical alliances to cover the expanded territory.

- *Technology.* Information technology has become a powerful tool for improving every aspect of a business, especially its logistics operations and measurement. Technologies that dynamically reconfigure logistics resources have advanced at a truly astonishing rate: They can track and speed the flow of raw materials and final products through the distribution chain, manage transportation more effectively, and optimize planning and scheduling. Those advances also have allowed managers to capture, store, and manipulate data in ways that were impractical or impossible a few years ago, enabling managers to measure and manage far more efficiently and effectively.

- *Regulatory environment.* Deregulation has been a key factor in making transportation providers more responsive to the needs of manufacturers and retailers. Prior to the 1970s, the selection of transportation options available to U.S. shippers was far more limited than it is today. Also, pricing for such transportation as truck, rail, and other shipping services was fixed by regulatory fiat. The deregulation of U.S. transportation industries created substantial competition among established transportation providers and enabled new transportation companies to join the fray. More recently, the lifting of trade barriers through such programs as the North American Free Trade Agreement (NAFTA), and revisions to such legislation as the Ocean Shipping Reform Act of 1998, will continue to redefine the business landscape.

- *Shareholder demands.* In the 1990s, boosting shareholder value became one of the most significant forces of change for logistics. How did that happen? A big factor has been institutional investors' ownership of large public companies. Large pension fund and mutual fund managers are highly influential with the top management at many large companies. If major shareholders believe a company is under-performing financially, they pressure the board and management to take action—cut costs, increase revenue, sell off unprofitable or declining businesses, or even sell the entire company to another that offers an attractive price. Logistics is both a major cost area and a potential source of significant shareholder value. As such, it continues to be targeted for improvement.

- *Suppliers.* Just as customers can be found nearly everywhere on the globe, so can suppliers. For a growing number of manufacturers of automobiles, chemicals, pharmaceuticals, clothing, telecommunications equipment, and many other products, global sourcing has become an established practice. There are strong incentives for scouring the globe for low-cost, world-class suppliers. From the mid-1930s to the mid-1980s, U.S. industrial companies saw the average cost of manufacturing-related goods and services jump from 20 percent of sales to 56 percent of sales.[4] As manufacturers' margins continue to get thinner, a better, cheaper supplier increasingly is just a few clicks of a computer mouse away. The ability to source supplies effectively from anywhere in the world has improved dramatically in recent years due to the Internet, more effective transportation systems (FedEx and UPS, for example, have become global distributors), and lower trade barriers. However, global sourcing from widely dispersed suppliers—in countries of disparate cultures, currencies, and political and economic systems—poses major problems in monitoring quality, delivery, and other performance metrics. Among those problems are the logistical needs to get products around the globe, to the point of use, in the most effective manner.

So, how have those elements affected logistics and logistics measurement during the past four decades? They have in the many ways—both positive and negative—that are detailed on the next few pages.

These descriptions of each decade's state of logistics are broad statements. It is not suggested that these conditions existed in every company or in every industry during that time period. (In fact, some companies in the 1970s were more advanced in logistics than others are today.) The intention merely is to characterize the general state of logistics during the past 40 years, illustrating how the need for effective logistics measurement has intensified.

The 1960s: The Days of Little Measurement

The U.S. retail landscape of the 1960s was far different from what it is today. Sears, J.C. Penney, F.W. Woolworth, and a few other chains were the only national retailers. Consumers did much more of their shopping at independent regional and local retailers. Warehouse stores and "category killers" did not exist. Supply chain power rested with manufacturers, which spent unfathomable sums of money mass-marketing consumer products. Manufacturers effectively dictated to retailers what they could sell. They focused their improvement efforts on manufacturing, on boosting the economics of making the goods. Gaining price advantage was the way to compete.

Retailers and consumers were relatively uninformed about their purchases. Retailers' in-store "technology" was the basic cash register. Mainframe computers at corporate headquarters were relegated to chores like tracking accounts payable and receivables and getting the payroll out.

Here is how the late Sam Walton described the Wal-Mart of the 1960s in his autobiography:

> "We didn't have systems. We didn't have ordering programs. We didn't have a basic merchandising assortment. We certainly didn't have any sort of computers. In fact, when I look at it today, I realize that so much of what we did in the beginning was really poorly done. ... In addition to no basic merchandise assortment, we had no real replenishment system. ... We had no established distributors. No credit. Salesmen would just show up at our door, and we would try to get the best deals we could. Sometimes it was difficult getting the bigger companies—the Procter & Gambles, Eastman Kodaks, whoever—to call on us at all, and when they did they would dictate to us how much they would sell us and at what price. P&G gave a 2 percent discount if you paid within 10 days, and if you didn't, man, they took that discount right off. I don't mind saying that we were the victims of a good bit of arrogance from a lot of vendors in those days. They didn't need us, and they acted that way."[5]

Manufacturers were not faced with the kind of global competition they have today. "Made in Japan" did not mean quality, and U.S. nationalism was strong. With little incentive from their competitors or customers to improve logistics, manufacturers' logistics measurement activities were few and far between.

The 1970s: A Shift in the Power Base

If the 1960s could be characterized as an era of tranquility for logistics, the 1970s would have to be termed the decade when "the dam broke." Foreign competition for U.S. manufacturers made inroads. Two oil embargoes ushered in a flood of foreign goods, ranging from fuel-efficient cars and semiconductor chips to consumer electronics and textiles. Many U.S. industrial giants were challenged on their home turf, often for the first time, by foreign competition, which frequently enjoyed price advantages. U.S. manufacturers, by now bloated, slow to react, and rigid in their thinking, were forced to redouble their efforts to slash costs.

Manufacturers began to lose some of their power in the supply chains. With low-cost competition invading, an increasing number of products were becoming commodities. U.S. manufacturers began seeing customer service as a way to compete. However, it was customer service from a manufacturer's perspective, not from a customer's perspective. For example, manufacturers measured how often they shipped their goods on their promised ship dates—not whether the goods were received when the customer wanted them or whether they met the customer's quality standards.

As in the 1960s, much of the cost of moving goods from manufacturers to retailers was, in part, fixed: Transportation services such as rail and trucking were heavily regulated. Transportation comprised as much as 70 percent of a manufacturer's logistics expenses, compared with 57 percent today.[6]

Soaring fuel prices and high borrowing costs forced companies to track transportation and inventory expenditures. A 10 percent jump in those costs could wipe out profit margins altogether, especially in thin-margin businesses like grocery retailing. To make their supply lines more efficient, manufacturers began overhauling warehouse layouts and route structures. Measurement similarly emphasized costs and functions. But improvement was inwardly focused; it emphasized improving a particular warehouse or route. For example, a research effort published in 1978 by the Council of Logistics Management (known then as the National Council of Physical Distribution Management) focused entirely on productivity improvement in transportation.[7]

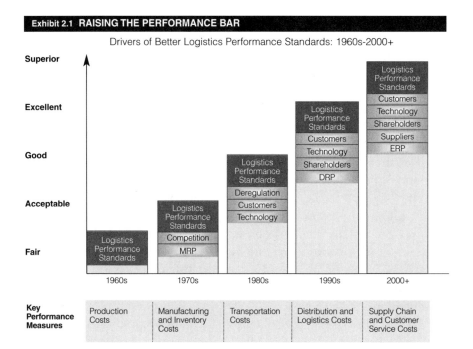

Exhibit 2.1 RAISING THE PERFORMANCE BAR

Drivers of Better Logistics Performance Standards: 1960s-2000+

Performance	1960s	1970s	1980s	1990s	2000+
Superior					Logistics Performance Standards
					Customers
Excellent				Logistics Performance Standards	Technology
					Shareholders
				Customers	Suppliers
Good				Technology	ERP
			Logistics Performance Standards	Shareholders	
				DRP	
			Deregulation		
Acceptable		Logistics Performance Standards	Customers		
			Technology		
		Competition			
Fair	Logistics Performance Standards	MRP			

Key Performance Measures	Production Costs	Manufacturing and Inventory Costs	Transportation Costs	Distribution and Logistics Costs	Supply Chain and Customer Service Costs

The 1980s: The Other Shoe Drops

By the 1980s, soaring inflation and interest rates, deregulation of trucking and railroads, foreign competition, rising demands and power of big shareholders, and consolidating retail environments put even greater pressure on companies to improve logistics. Many began earnest efforts to measure their logistics effectiveness, focusing on physical distribution activities.

Deregulation led to unprecedented price and service competition among trucking companies and railroads. It also exposed the operating inefficiencies and over-capacity that had been concealed in the previous environment of price regulation. With those restrictions removed and free-market pricing of transportation allowed, the only carriers that survived in the short term were those willing to sit down with shippers and make major rate and service accommodations. Many carriers went out of business, unable to cope with decreasing revenue and high operating costs.

The most progressive manufacturers and distributors aggressively exploited the decade's technology. In the 1970s, to communicate information about inventory and shipments from their distribution centers, some manufacturers used teletype machines, entering data from handwritten forms. In the 1980s, they began using electronic bar code scanning to track vehicles and product shipments. By the late 1980s, the use of uniform product codes (UPC) became widespread in retailing. Through electronic data interchange (EDI), companies adopted far more efficient ways of sending orders and information on supply conditions. EDI also forced suppliers and their channel partners to sit down together, understand their mutual requirements, standardize their practices, and agree to some extent on definitions for terminology such as "customer," "shipment," and "invoice."

With the rise of the PC, retailers were able to harness affordable in-store computer power for tracking what was selling—where and when—on a daily basis. Regional merchants like Wal-Mart used computers in inventory management to gain operating efficiencies and expand their geographic reach. Information on customer demand was a major factor in shifting the balance of power from the manufacturer to the retailer.

By the late 1980s, consolidation in retail channels meant more power in fewer hands. So-called "superstores" began to dot the countryside. Hundreds of local stores and regional chains went bust as the big retailers successfully leveraged their large volumes to twist manufacturers' arms for better prices and better delivery terms.

Finally, both manufacturers and retailers had a significant and enduring incentive to improve logistics operations. Many of them instituted quality programs in manufacturing or distribution. Others looked at making improvements in end-to-end logistics processes—not just discrete functions or smaller activities. By the end of the decade, logistics was recognized as a process that included purchasing, materials management, and physical distribution.[8]

The 1990s: Technology to the Rescue

Corporate CEOs in this decade were under tremendous pressure to generate strong earnings and enhance their stock price—to "increase shareholder value," as it became known. Logistics processes were the targets of continual cost-cutting and improvement.

By the 1990s, manufacturers were facing even greater global competition, ushered in by, among other things, free-trade agreements with Mexico and Canada (NAFTA). Competition in product category after product category became more intense, as companies such as Coca-Cola, Pepsi, and Kmart began shedding sideline businesses to focus on their core products or businesses. Companies reengineered their business processes to get closer to customers and suppliers and to break through their internal barriers. They dramatically reorganized their operations in ways that truly exploited information technology, rather than just automating old, inefficient operations as they had in the past.

Information technology was revolutionizing manufacturing and logistics. Manufacturing moved from standard long-run production to modular customized assembly. Suppliers had to increase the flexibility of their logistics, as manufacturers—to reduce inventory costs and the risk of obsolescence—increasingly postponed production until they had orders in hand. Supply chain optimization software, enterprise resource planning software, hand-held computers, satellite tracking, and the Internet gave companies powerful tools for overhauling their logistics chain and monitoring the movement of goods, people, and other resources within it. The Internet was enabling new standards for the electronic exchange of data among suppliers, distributors, and retailers.

Information technology was revolutionizing the shopping experience for consumers as well. The emergence of the World Wide Web set off a wave of online storefronts offering books, music, flowers, automobiles, vacations, stereos, wine—virtually every product available on store shelves.

Driven by continuing market pressures to increase shareholder value and return on assets, many companies sold their private truck fleets and outsourced their transportation, giving rise to a new player: the third-party logistics provider (3PL). With their survival totally dependent on logistics excellence, those companies further exploited technology to improve their logistics processes. To prove their value to customers, they aggressively used technology to measure their performance.

In addition to pressure from those far more knowledgeable and demanding consumers, manufacturers were staring at immense buying power of mega-retailers. Companies that crossed swords with powerful retailers often found themselves severely wounded, locked out of major distribution channels.

As the year 2000 approached, logistics processes were faster, more efficient, and of higher quality than ever before. In fact, quality became a standard of performance, not an option. Measurement followed the shift from improving functions to improving processes.

THE STATE OF LOGISTICS MEASUREMENT TODAY

As the new millennium begins, making large-scale improvements in logistics processes is no longer an option, it is a necessity. In some instances, wholesale transformation will be required, with new global perspectives. Consequently, measuring performance moves to center stage. The survey and case study research[9] conducted for this book found many companies measuring their logistics operations. Most companies that responded to the survey were measuring performance within their organizations in customer service, order fulfillment, procurement, and other logistics areas. A smaller number of companies were measuring logistics performance with customers and/or suppliers. Few, if any, were measuring full supply chain network performance.

The research also found a strong association between how well a company's logistics operations performed and the extent to which it measured that performance. Companies that said their logistics operations had a major advantage over the competition were more likely to measure logistics processes than companies whose logistics were lagging behind. For example, Graybar Electric Company Inc., a distributor of data communications and electrical equipment, has, in part through an intensive measurement program, improved on-time delivery and reduced the number of out-of-stock items for Texas Instruments Inc., one of its major customers. Transportation manager Caliber Logistics tracks nine logistics measures in helping an automotive replacement-parts division improve its performance with automobile dealers. And 3M, Motorola, and Modus Media have vastly improved logistics performance through measurement. The latter three programs will be explored in detail in Chapter 7.

Apart from those innovative programs, however, the research found many other companies with far fewer measurement programs in action. In addition, measuring one's performance across the supply chain—with customers and suppliers—is much less common than measurement within a company's four walls. In fact, the research found that logistics measurement is happening much less frequently than one might imagine. And where it was happening, it was less advanced than might be expected. While companies have made great progress in reengineering their business processes and using information technology to alter the way work is performed, they have been much slower to measure those processes and their associated activities.

The survey, conducted as part of the research for this book, explored a wide range of logistics measurement issues:

- The perception of logistics in the organization

- The software packages, technologies, and business practices in use or being implemented in logistics

- Company supply chain relationships with customers and suppliers

- The performance measures each company used and their importance

- The degree to which certain measures were mutually defined with customers or suppliers

- Company performance in key logistics activities versus its competitors' performance

- Company overall business and logistics strategy

- The facilitators and inhibitors of measuring logistics performance—both within their organization and with supply channel partners.

Surveys were mailed to the most senior logistics executive of more than 3,100 companies. (See Appendix for survey details. Not all respondents answered every question in the survey; therefore, unless indicated otherwise, response percentages are based on the number of respondents who answered each particular question.) The results provide insight into where companies' measurement efforts are focused—and where they are lacking.

Measurement Is Internally Focused

One section of the survey was designed to characterize the nature of logistics measurement in business—that is, the degree to which companies were measuring internally and externally, with suppliers and customers. To determine that, logistics executives were asked to indicate the type of measurement activities they were conducting both within their companies, and with suppliers and customers, in six key areas: sourcing/procurement; planning, forecasting, and scheduling; order fulfillment; transportation/distribution; warehousing/storage; and customer service. Respondents were asked to classify the nature of measurement programs in one of four ways: awareness, measurement, coordination, or integration (Exhibit 2.2).

Exhibit 2.2 THE NATURE OF LOGISTICS MEASUREMENT

	Intracompany	Intercompany
Integrate	Measuring **intracompany** cross-functional processes using measures that are both **functional and financial** in nature. Estimating costs/benefits and implementing initiatives.	Measuring **intercompany** cross-functional processes using measures that are both **functional and financial** in nature. Estimating costs/benefits to improve, **reaching agreement**, and implementing initiatives that impact **both companies**.
Coordinate	Identifying underlying factors for performance against measures, estimating **costs/benefits** to improve performance, and **implementing initiatives.**	Identifying underlying factors for performance against measures, estimating costs/benefits to improve, and **reaching agreement** to implement initiatives that impact **both companies**.
Measure	Measuring functional activities **within the company**, reconciling definitions of measures, and comparing to average and/or best-in-class benchmarks.	Measuring functional activities occurring **between two companies**, reconciling definitions of measures, and comparing to average and/or best-in-class benchmarks.
Aware	**Awareness** of logistics functions and the potential benefits of logistics management for **the company**.	**Awareness** of logistics functions and the potential benefits of supply chain management for **both companies**.

Awareness, the most basic level, means that the company knows that effective management of key logistics functions and processes can have a substantial impact on its organization and trading partners. Companies at that stage know which activities they must measure to boost performance.

One cell up the scale is *measurement*. Companies at this level are measuring functional activities, either internally or with trading partners, are reconciling definitions of measures, and may be comparing their measures to industry benchmarks, averages, or best-in-class metrics that compare their performance to industry peers. In other words, such companies have a very good understanding of the performance of a specific function or activity.

At the next level, *coordination*, companies not only are measuring, they also are beginning to understand the impact of those measures on the organization or trading partners. Here, companies are able to identify costs and benefits of specific functions or processes, and that helps them to devise ways to improve performance. They also are starting to implement those performance initiatives—either cross-functionally or with trading partners. Companies at the coordination level can identify and understand the trade-offs that must be made among activities to contribute to the greater good of the process.

The highest level in the model is *integration*. Companies at this stage have reached the point at which their measures and processes are tied closely together. Measures at this level transcend functional to the financial, meaning that the monetary impact of specific processes and activities is visible and attributable. This term is used frequently throughout the book to characterize companies whose measurement programs are in high gear, either across logistics functions in their organizations or with suppliers and customers.

Respondents clearly indicated that they focused *internally* (measuring their company's logistics performance) more than *externally* (working with customers and suppliers to define measures, share information, and make improvements). Approximately twice as much measurement activity is occurring within companies as between companies and their customers/suppliers (Exhibit 2.3).

For example, some 12 percent of the companies indicated they were "unaware" of measurement activities in customer service between their companies and their customers or suppliers. That number jumped to 27 percent when it came to sourcing/procurement. In contrast, only 5 percent of the companies said they were fully integrated in measurement programs with customers or suppliers in customer service. However, companies that claim advantage or major advantage in logistics process areas are more likely to be integrated in their measurements, and those that are integrated in the measurements in one area tend to be integrated in most, if not all, processes.

An important caveat: Integration is not necessarily more desirable than coordination or measurement. For example, due to the transactional nature of purchasing commodities such as flour, sugar, and salt used in the production of its crackers and cookies, Nabisco's raw materials procurement process would be most appropriate in the

Exhibit 2.3 **LEVELS OF INTEGRATION BY CAPABILITY**

Within Company

■ Unaware or Aware	
Measure	
▩ Coordinate or Integrate	*Source:* CSC / University of Tennessee Logistics Survey 1998

Between Company and Trading Partners

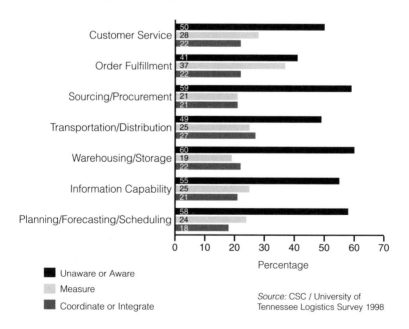

■ Unaware or Aware	
Measure	
▩ Coordinate or Integrate	*Source:* CSC / University of Tennessee Logistics Survey 1998

measurement level. However, because of the company's involvement in the industry's Collaborative Planning, Forecasting, and Replenishment (CPFR) initiative, its planning, forecasting, and scheduling process, by definition, would need to be in the integration cell to be most effective—at least for its key customers participating in the CPFR initiative.

Logistics Measurement Is Not a Top Issue

Survey respondents also were asked to indicate the three most important logistics issues facing their organizations (Exhibit 2.4). Only 16 percent ranked logistics measurement within their company among their top three issues. Logistics measurement between the company and customers or suppliers ranked 10th in importance.

And yet the four most important logistics issues—controlling costs, optimizing information technology, improving customer ser-

Exhibit 2.4 CRITICAL ISSUES OF LOGISTICS MANAGERS

(Percentage of respondents ranking it among their three most important issues.)

1	Cost control/cost reduction	55%
2	Information technology utilization/optimization	48%
3	Improving customer service processes	38%
4	Cycle-time reduction	28%
(TIE)	Strategic alliances with customers/suppliers	28%
6	Changing organizational structure	17%
7	Logistics measurement within the company	16%
8	Expanding distribution into new channels/markets	15%
9	Quality improvement	12%
10	Logistics measurement between company and customers/suppliers	11%

Source: CSC / University of Tennessee Logistics Survey 1998

vice, and cutting cycle time—all rely on measurement. To cut costs, companies have to track their spending on various tasks, functions, and other activities. Improving how information technology is used, in part, requires quantifying the payback of technology investments in place. Better customer service cannot be achieved unless companies know how well they are performing for customers in the first place. And to cut time out of a business process, companies must understand just how much time it takes to accomplish each activity in the process. Logistics measurement is not a universal practice. However, it will play a key role in resolving the most important issues facing logistics managers.

Fundamental Measures Are Missing

In light of today's competitive necessity of having the goods—whether they are cereal boxes on a supermarket shelf or windshields in an automobile assembly plant—in the right place at the right time, one would expect that nearly every company measures at least some aspects of its logistics operations. And with the much-ballyhooed industry-wide initiatives for reducing costs, cycle times, and errors, it would seem that logistics measurement would be accepted business practice in every company.

That, however, is not the case (Exhibit 2.5). While the majority of survey respondents do measure some aspect of their logistics performance, a surprising number—20 percent—do not track on-time delivery or order fill rates. Even when order fill, line fill, and case fill are combined, only 82 percent indicated that they measure any one of the three. Those are fundamental (and relatively simple) measures that are critical to customers. Some 39 percent do not track overall customer satisfaction, 38 percent do not measure order cycle time, and 48 percent do not calculate invoice accuracy. Logistics cost per unit versus budgeted cost—which was ranked as a very important measure—was tracked regularly by only 52 percent of the respondents.

Process-Based Measures Are Growing

While many of the logistics measures in use are still largely functional in nature, a number of respondents are beginning to use process-based measures. Some 79 percent measure on-time delivery, while 62 percent track order cycle time, and 80 percent monitor finished goods inventory turns. Cash-to-cash measures—the time from when a company has to pay for materials, labor, and the like, until it receives payment from the customer—are used in 32 percent of the respondent companies. Other process-based measures are common as well: days sales outstanding (59 percent), cost to serve (37 percent), and processing accuracy (45 percent). It should be pointed out that most previous research in this area was focused on functional, utilization, and productivity measures. The results reported here indicate the growing use of process-based measures, an area that should receive continued emphasis.

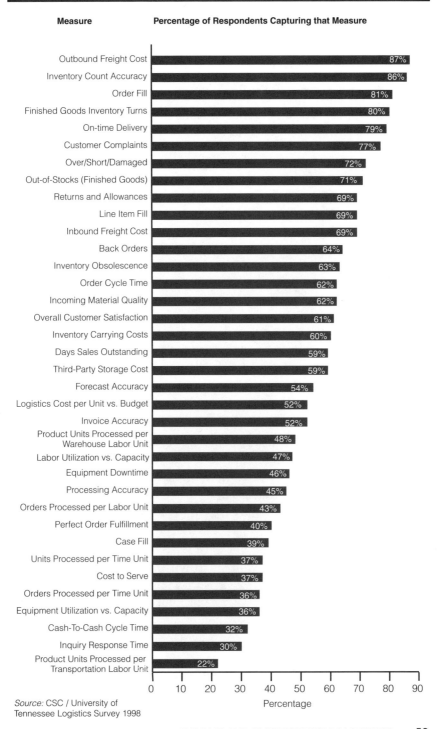

Exhibit 2.5 MEASURES CAPTURED ON A REGULAR BASIS WITHIN THE COMPANY

Measure **Percentage of Respondents Capturing that Measure**

Measure	Percentage
Outbound Freight Cost	87%
Inventory Count Accuracy	86%
Order Fill	81%
Finished Goods Inventory Turns	80%
On-time Delivery	79%
Customer Complaints	77%
Over/Short/Damaged	72%
Out-of-Stocks (Finished Goods)	71%
Returns and Allowances	69%
Line Item Fill	69%
Inbound Freight Cost	69%
Back Orders	64%
Inventory Obsolescence	63%
Order Cycle Time	62%
Incoming Material Quality	62%
Overall Customer Satisfaction	61%
Inventory Carrying Costs	60%
Days Sales Outstanding	59%
Third-Party Storage Cost	59%
Forecast Accuracy	54%
Logistics Cost per Unit vs. Budget	52%
Invoice Accuracy	52%
Product Units Processed per Warehouse Labor Unit	48%
Labor Utilization vs. Capacity	47%
Equipment Downtime	46%
Processing Accuracy	45%
Orders Processed per Labor Unit	43%
Perfect Order Fulfillment	40%
Case Fill	39%
Units Processed per Time Unit	37%
Cost to Serve	37%
Orders Processed per Time Unit	36%
Equipment Utilization vs. Capacity	36%
Cash-To-Cash Cycle Time	32%
Inquiry Response Time	30%
Product Units Processed per Transportation Labor Unit	22%

Percentage axis: 0 10 20 30 40 50 60 70 80 90

Source: CSC / University of Tennessee Logistics Survey 1998

Cost to Serve

Activity-based costing techniques enable companies to determine the actual cost of services provided throughout the supply chain to individual customers or segments of customers. The calculation of "cost to serve" includes more than just the cost of distribution. In this context, cost to serve includes virtually all non-manufacturing costs directed at individual customers and segments, and includes the following general categories:

- **Cost of services:** Various event-driven order capture and fulfillment costs.

- **Order-driven costs:** Costs incurred every time an order occurs irrespective of the size of the order. Electronic orders have clearly different cost structures than telephone or fax orders.

- **Order fill costs:** Costs incurred to assemble the customer order. Care must be taken in individually developing the cost of this group, as costs vary significantly by customer or segment.

- **Freight costs:** Often the largest single cost component is the cost of freight between the distribution center and the ultimate ship-to location.

- **Cost of coverage:** Investment of resources in "covering" an account. Particularly illuminating is the cost of time spent in activities that are administrative, and play no direct part in demand creation.

Key Cross-Company Measures Are Not Being Captured

While a surprising number of companies do not measure processes with customers or suppliers, the majority of companies do. And what they measure is valued highly by customers: on-time delivery, order fill rates, and accurate invoices. Still, only 60 percent of logistics managers reported that they worked jointly with customers to define those key measures or that they are using customer-defined measures (Exhibit 2.6). Case-study interviews with 22 companies uncovered no examples in which more than two companies were working together to measure logistics processes jointly. It appears that the overriding majority of inter-company logistics measurement programs involve two companies—a manufacturer and a key supplier or customer—but not a manufacturer *and* a key supplier *and* a key customer.

Clearly, most companies have opportunities to make significant and immediate progress by working jointly with important customers

Measure	% of Customers Using Measure	% Say Important or Very Important	How are measures defined?		
			Jointly	By Customer	Total Defined
On-time Delivery	86	91	31	29	60
Order Fill	75	88	25	33	58
Invoice Accuracy	69	77	28	30	58
Performance to Request Date	66	82	22	32	54
Order Cycle Time	63	78	25	25	50
Customer Service Performance	63	79	24	28	52
Stock-outs/Back Orders	62	84	26	29	55
Over/Short/Damaged	61	73	25	32	57
Performance to Commit Date	55	84	22	30	52
Line Item Fill	55	84	29	29	58
Returns and Allowance Handling	44	63	24	26	50
Freight Cost	44	68	31	21	52
Inquiry Response Time	36	63	25	27	52
Case Fill	32	77	24	29	53
Forecast Accuracy	16	55	25	19	44

Source: CSC / University of Tennessee Logistics Survey 1998

to define key measures of performance. As retailers begin to focus on specific consumer bases, the need to have logistics measures that show the direct impact of logistics on those consumers also will become increasingly important.

Technology Is an Enabler and a Barrier

Less than 60 percent of the survey respondents claimed a competitive advantage in any of seven logistics processes and capabilities (Exhibit 2.7). Information technology capability and planning were considered by the largest percentage of respondents as areas in which they were at a competitive disadvantage. However, companies that are more integrated in measurement activities with their customers and/or suppliers and claim a major advantage by process are more likely to use technology to create that advantage.

Key Tools and Technologies for Effective Measurement

Interviews with 22 companies revealed a number of logistics managers who had begun their measurement programs very mod-

Exhibit 2.7 **COMPARISON OF CAPABILITIES VERSUS COMPETITORS**

	Major Advantage	Advantage	Parity with Competitors	Disadvantage	Major Disadvantage	Not a Factor
Sourcing/ Procurement	9%	28%	45%	10%	1%	7%
Planning/Forecasting/ Scheduling	8%	20%	45%	19%	4%	5%
Order Fulfillment	17%	31%	41%	9%	1%	2%
Transportation/ Distribution	18%	36%	37%	8%	0%	1%
Warehousing/ Storage	13%	30%	41%	12%	1%	4%
Customer Service	19%	40%	32%	7%	1%	1%
Information Capability	14%	30%	38%	22%	5%	1%

Source: CSC / University of Tennessee Logistics Survey 1998

estly. Many, in fact, initially used little more than a simple spread-sheet to calculate one or two measures of performance. Motorola, for example, first tracked its scheduled shipping dates and compared them with the shipping dates requested by customers. (See Chapter 7 for more information on Motorola.) Use of such basic tools can, indeed, improve performance. However, taking performance measurement to the next level requires more sophisticated tools, in both technology and management. While a great number of survey respondents were using or planning to use such tools, a sizable percentage were not using them or planning to use them (Exhibit 2.8).

As an example, about 11 percent of the survey respondents had implemented activity-based costing (ABC) practices—a key management tool in performance measurement. Another 9 percent had ABC practices underway, while 24 percent had plans to institute them. However, the majority of companies (56 percent) had no plans to implement ABC. Measuring the actual cost of various logistics activities requires ABC (or other related cost accounting techniques). ABC is a financial analysis technique that allocates costs to specific activities and zeroes in on the profitability of customers, routes, and other key elements. ABC takes aggregated costs of such activities as shipping, loading, warehousing, and stocking shelves and allocates them to individual products and categories. When results were compared

Exhibit 2.8 KEY TOOLS AND TECHNOLOGIES FOR EFFECTIVE MEASUREMENT

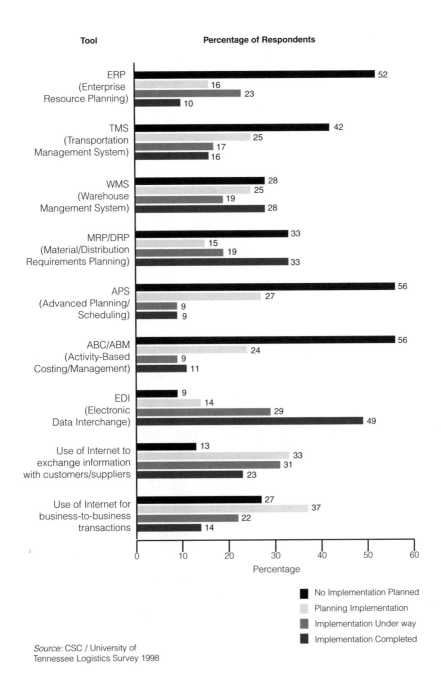

Tool

Percentage of Respondents

ERP (Enterprise Resource Planning)
- 52
- 16
- 23
- 10

TMS (Transportation Management System)
- 42
- 25
- 17
- 16

WMS (Warehouse Mangement System)
- 28
- 25
- 19
- 28

MRP/DRP (Material/Distribution Requirements Planning)
- 33
- 15
- 19
- 33

APS (Advanced Planning/ Scheduling)
- 56
- 27
- 9
- 9

ABC/ABM (Activity-Based Costing/Management)
- 56
- 24
- 9
- 11

EDI (Electronic Data Interchange)
- 9
- 14
- 29
- 49

Use of Internet to exchange information with customers/suppliers
- 13
- 33
- 31
- 23

Use of Internet for business-to-business transactions
- 27
- 37
- 22
- 14

Percentage

■ No Implementation Planned
▫ Planning Implementation
▪ Implementation Under way
■ Implementation Completed

Source: CSC / University of Tennessee Logistics Survey 1998

for the first four categories as a group, only four respondents (1.1 percent) indicated implementation was complete for all four. Conversely, only 23 respondents (6.5 percent) indicated "No Implementation Planned" for all four.

Most companies had committed to major technology investments that will enhance their ability to measure logistics performance. For instance, more than three-quarters (78 percent) of the respondents had implemented, were implementing, or were planning to implement scanning/point-of-sale systems, an important tool for collecting data on the movement and sale of goods. The majority of respondents reported using or planning to use warehouse management and transportation management information systems. Nearly half (48 percent) had committed themselves to costly and difficult-to-implement enterprise resource planning systems (ERP). The vast majority were planning or already using EDI or Internet systems to exchange information with customers or suppliers. Some companies, like 3M, had discovered the importance of technology to measurement. By tapping into 3M's sophisticated data warehouse and Web site, its customers can check order status and inventory availability.

Respondents who claimed advantage or major advantage are more likely to have implemented or are planning to implement key enabling technologies. Also, the gap between companies that use technology to gain advantage and those that do not is large.

What Helps or Hinders Measurement?

Why have some logistics organizations established a cult of measurement while others scarcely can find the time to track their performance? What factors are behind those that measure heartily and those that hardly measure? The two biggest factors helping or hindering the measurement of logistics activities are the support of upper management and access to I/T resources and information. Both were identified most frequently as either a "very significant enabler" or "very significant barrier" to the development and use of logistics measures within an organization (Exhibit 2.9).

Upper management support was cited as an enabler far more often than as a barrier and showed a substantially larger gap between the two than did any other factor. In fact, the research shows that logistics measurement programs pay off in companies whose top management demand fact-based decision-making.

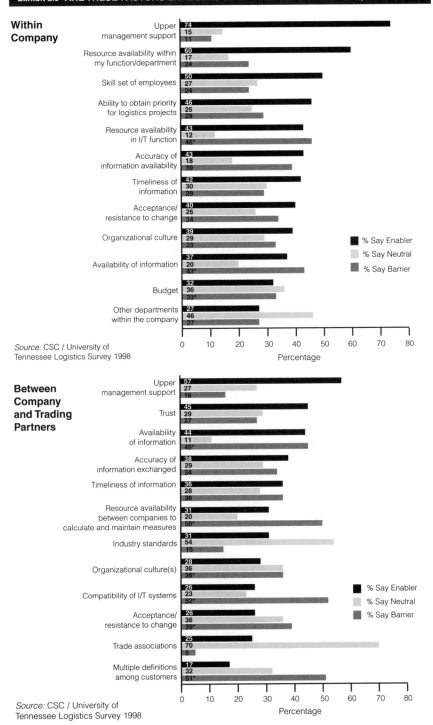

Exhibit 2.9 ARE THESE FACTORS ENABLERS OR BARRIERS TO MEASUREMENT?

Within Company

Factor	% Say Enabler	% Say Neutral	% Say Barrier
Upper management support	74	15	11
Resource availability within my function/department	60	17	24
Skill set of employees	50	27	24
Ability to obtain priority for logistics projects	46	25	29
Resource availability in I/T function	43	12	46*
Accuracy of information availability	43	18	39
Timeliness of information	42	30	29
Acceptance/resistance to change	40	26	34
Organizational culture	39	29	33
Availability of information	37	20	43*
Budget	32	36	33*
Other departments within the company	27	46	27

■ % Say Enabler
▨ % Say Neutral
▨ % Say Barrier

Source: CSC / University of Tennessee Logistics Survey 1998

Percentage

Between Company and Trading Partners

Factor	% Say Enabler	% Say Neutral	% Say Barrier
Upper management support	57	27	16
Trust	45	29	27
Availability of information	44	11	45*
Accuracy of information exchanged	38	29	34
Timeliness of information	36	28	36
Resource availability between companies to calculate and maintain measures	31	20	50*
Industry standards	31	54	15
Organizational culture(s)	28	36	36*
Compatibility of I/T systems	26	23	52*
Acceptance/resistance to change	26	36	39*
Trade associations	25	70	5
Multiple definitions among customers	17	32	51*

■ % Say Enabler
▨ % Say Neutral
▨ % Say Barrier

Source: CSC / University of Tennessee Logistics Survey 1998

Percentage

In the minds of logistics professionals, the most significant barrier to logistics measurement is unavailability of I/T resources. Ranking close behind are the unavailability of accurate information and the unavailability of information, period. It is interesting to note that in all cases, the frequency with which these factors are named as enablers is as high or higher than the percentage that named them as barriers.

Some Measures Are Good, Some Are Bad

Most companies surveyed reported that their logistics measures were good. A minority questioned their value (Exhibit 2.10). For example, 71 percent said their measures accurately captured the events and activities they were designed to track. Two-thirds (67 percent) agreed or agreed strongly that the benefits of their measures outweighed the cost of collecting, analyzing, and reporting them. And 67 percent said their measures were interpreted similarly by external users, were repeatable, and were comparable across time, location, and divisions. However, their responses to survey questions do not address the validity of the measures themselves. Less than half of the survey respondents (46 percent) said their measures minimize incentives for counterproductive acts or game-playing and are presented in a useful form.

One company that said its measures had become counterproductive was a large food distributor. Its largest customer measures that distributor's performance by on-time delivery, delivery reliability, delivery accuracy, damaged goods, and other metrics. The company defined those measures more than a decade ago. They have been expanded and enhanced since then, and they have contributed greatly to the customer's success. However, the measures monitor such discrete activities in the overall supply chain as number of cases transported per mile and labor hours per truckload. Inadvertently, those measures directed both companies to look for improvements in isolated pieces of the supply chain, and now they pose a barrier to looking at the entire process and thinking of ways to make breakthrough improvements. The distributor is trying to look at the overall supply chain—from the restaurants back to the food producers—to improve performance and cut costs. However, the customer will have to agree to lower performance in certain measures in order to enjoy lower total cost across the supply chain.

Exhibit 2.10 QUALITY OF LOGISTICS MEASURES USED

The logistics measures we use...	% Who Agree	Neutral	% Who Disagree
...*accurately* capture the events/activities being measured	71	7	22
...are interpreted similarly by *internal* users	68	9	22
...internally have significant *benefits that outweigh the costs* of data collection, analysis, and reporting	67	16	17
...are readily *understandable* by decision-makers	66	13	20
...minimize incentives for counter-productive acts or game-playing	46	26	28
...*promote coordination* across functions and divisions	34	20	46*

* disagreement is greater than agreement

Source: CSC / University of Tennessee Logistics Survey 1998

PUTTING MEASUREMENT IN MOTION

In summary, the research shows a significant amount of logistics measurement activity. However, although the majority of companies measure logistics at some level, true performance measurement is by no means a universal practice. Companies that do measure logistics often lack the organization-wide cooperation necessary to measure and improve end-to-end logistics processes—not just discrete functions. And cooperation across three or more companies that depend on each other in a larger industry supply chain is virtually non-existent. Yet it is just that kind of cooperation that will be needed for supply chain participants to make the enormous improvements that tomorrow's customers will demand.

In a growing number of industries, an effective logistics measurement program no longer will be a luxury—a nicety that gets shoved aside by the daily demands of getting goods to market. As discussed in Chapter 1, this is particularly true for companies with high cost structures, products that are getting harder to differentiate, customers that are becoming more powerful and knowledgeable, global markets that are beckoning, and supply lines that electronic commerce is starting to reconfigure.

The next chapter will examine the reasons for measuring any business activity—but particularly those in logistics—and explain the internal and external rewards for those companies that measure correctly. Also discussed will be how measurement programs often get started, how they can take wrong turns, why they are difficult to execute—and what penalties are leveled on those companies that do not measure.

ENDNOTES

[1] Presented at the annual business meeting of the Council of Logistics Management in Anaheim, CA, October 1998. The definition is also posted at the CLM homepage: www.CLM1.org.

[2] J. T. Mentzer, W. DeWitt, J. S. Keebler, S. Min, N. W. Nix, C. D. Smith, and Z. G. Zacharia, "A Unified Definition of Supply Chain Management," Working Paper, The University of Tennessee, 1999.

[3] G. Armstrong and P. Kotler, *Marketing: An Introduction*, Prentice Hall, 1997, p. 14. We have derived these market forces from several strategic frameworks, most notably Philip Kotler and Gary Armstrong's depiction of the main forces in a marketing system.

[4] M. Keough, "Buying Your Way to the Top," *McKinsey Quarterly*, 1993, No. 3, pp. 41-62. The author cited statistics from the U.S. Census Bureau's 1985 Annual Survey of Manufacturers, Government Printing Office, 1987, pp. 1-8.

[5] S. Walton, with J. Huey, *Sam Walton: Made in America*, Doubleday, 1992, pp. 50-51.

[6] 9th Annual State of Logistics Report, "We, The People, Demand Productivity," Robert V. Delaney, Cass Information Systems, June 1, 1998, National Press Club, Washington, DC.

[7] Council of Logistics Management, *Measuring Productivity in Physical Distribution: The $40 Billion Gold Mine*, 1978.

[8] A.T. Kearney Inc., *Improving Quality and Productivity in the Logistics Process—Achieving Customer Satisfaction Breakthroughs*, Council of Logistics Management, 1991, Introduction, p. viii-ix.

[9] For an explanation on the selection of companies and methodology used for the case study interviews, please refer to Appendix C. For an explanation on the survey, please refer to Appendix D.

3

THE CASE FOR
MEASUREMENT

Data rich, information poor. Those four words could describe many companies today, particularly those that have invested heavily in information technology, reengineering, and various cost-cutting measures. Companies in that category consume reams of paper, generating reports on production, overhead costs, deliveries, customer satisfaction, and a host of other measures of performance. And, in today's fast-paced business environment, by the time those reports have been compiled and delivered, their information is outdated. In highly bureaucratic companies, those reports might never make it very far from the office or the departmental "silo"—e.g., the functions of manufacturing, warehousing, distribution, sales, marketing, and so on—that generates them in the first place.

Some companies are data rich but information poor because they measure the wrong things. Consider, for instance, a company that produces and markets ice cream. It devotes a significant amount of time, money, and effort to measuring how full the cartons are after workers fill them and how full trucks are when they leave the shipping dock. But it spends next to nothing to determine whether deliveries are made on time, if the packages have been damaged in shipment, or how much product is being retained. Is that company measuring what its customers care about?

Other companies are rich in neither data nor information. They have resisted investing in those high-tech, multimillion-dollar "solutions in search of a problem." Certain executive factions argue that the company has so many other issues that demand resources and attention. Spending money to measure this shift's production or that carrier's ability to get company products to its customers on time is a luxury that the company can do without, at least for the moment. After all, they reason, only a handful of other companies in the industry are earmarking large sums of money to measure productivity or efficient distribution.

Some executives are nagged by the possibility that the collection and dissemination of data may prove threatening to them personally. Business leaders and managers are held accountable for all sorts of measures—shareholder equity, annual revenues, profits and losses, total quality, customer satisfaction, and so on. The less said or known, the better—or so the thinking goes.

None of the preceding scenarios is tenable in today's competitive environment. Still, each scenario contains real-life assumptions that may be keeping companies from developing *purposeful* and *effective* logistics measurements critical to their success.

> **Logistics measurement is no longer just a "nice thing to have." It is an essential element in maintaining or increasing every company's competitive advantage. Measurement builds trust and enables companies from one end of the supply chain to the other to work collaboratively and productively toward mutually beneficial goals. This is, in essence, the case for measurement.**

But before an argument is built for that position, it is necessary to review some of the major barriers that may be standing in the way. These barriers could prevent any company from realizing its full potential and interfere with the creation of the conditions under which its suppliers and customers also become winners.

WHAT ARE THE BARRIERS TO MEASUREMENT?

Why is logistics not being measured by everyone? Why is it not ranked higher in the opinions of the people surveyed? The research into the histories of real-life companies revealed that even in some of the best organizations, measurement is spotty and less than fully productive. These examples, and managers' descriptions of their own experiences, have isolated five major barriers people face in creating and institutionalizing logistics performance measurements:

- Measurement is difficult

- The links between measurement and strategy are often unclear

- Functions and processes are complex and often misaligned

- People being measured may be resistant to sharing information

- There is a significant lack of consensus on definitions of terms

Measurement Is Hard Work

Many of those surveyed did not rank logistics measurement among their three most important issues, perhaps believing it to be difficult and costly. Of course, it can be both. "How much will it cost?" they ask, with skepticism. "What resources—people, facilities, money—must we devote to collecting, storing, analyzing, interpreting, disseminating, and trying to make sense of the results?"

No one can promise that logistics measurements automatically will cut costs across the board or even within certain company functions or divisions. It is a safe bet that companies will incur extra costs involved in gathering and processing the data they decide to collect and use to evaluate how efficiently their logistics processes work. However, survey results showed that more than 65 percent of the respondents agreed that the internal logistics measures they already use do have significant benefits that outweigh the cost of data collection, analysis, and reporting.

A successful program of measurement requires commitment and vision from top management, who must promote it internally and externally. People have to be persuaded to accept both the discipline of measurement and the validity of using the results to evaluate current business processes and performance in all activities across the supply chain. With everyone in agreement on what is measured, how it is to be measured, and what to do with the results, managers will have to convince their own employees to learn to live by the numbers. But it does not stop there: Management also must reach consensus with the company's key trading partners—the leading suppliers and customers—about what is measured and for what purpose.

Not only is it sometimes difficult to get people to agree on what should be measured, it can be hard to persuade them to accept measurements once developed. Practically everyone who has hit middle

age will testify to having questioned the accuracy of the scales at the doctor's office: "I cannot weigh that much; there must be something wrong with those scales!" The tendency to dispute measures, especially when the measures are displeasing or threatening, is a thoroughly human response. Therefore, it should come as no surprise that whatever logistics measures companies decide to use, some people, both internal and external to those companies, will question how the measure is taken and how it is to be interpreted.

Measures Are Not in Synch With Corporate Strategy

One of the major barriers to logistics measurement is often the lack of clear corporate goals and strategies. It is important to stress that all measures are not created equal—some are more important than others. The identification of key measures depends more on what individual companies are trying to accomplish than on anything inherently good or bad about the measurement itself.

"What gets measured gets managed." That simple bromide has importance for logistics managers. If a company builds a low-cost logistics system but does not measure what customers value—say, for example, on-time delivery and complete orders—it will have little idea about how it is truly performing for those customers. If customers value speed and accuracy as much as price, they will turn to other suppliers. With nothing but incidental and anecdotal data—for instance, customers that respond angrily to late and incomplete shipments—companies that do not measure what customers value will find it difficult to monitor and rectify their customers' growing disenchantment. Perhaps Lewis Carroll, in *Alice in Wonderland*, best captures the plight of those who lose their way because they lack direction:

> "Would you tell me please which way I ought to go from here?" asked Alice.
> "That depends a good deal on where you want to get to."
> "I don't really know," replied Alice.
> "Then it doesn't matter which way you go," said the cat.

Without information on whether it is winning or losing the daily battle of performing for customers, how can a company decide which path of improvement to take? Simply having logistics measures is not enough. One of the most important messages of this book is that any old measures will *not* do. Each company's logistics measures must be in line with its overall strategic direction. The logistics measures of a company whose strategy is providing excellent customer service rather than being the low-cost provider had better reflect that strategy. Measures such as on-time delivery (as defined by the customer), invoice accuracy, inquiry response time, and customer service performance become crucial.

The failure to communicate changes in strategy clearly can have severe consequences. In 1996, aiming to increase customer traffic, Kmart decided to augment its core discount assortment with convenience merchandise—the now famous "pantry" strategy. Consequently, the modest revenue growth planned for the following year masked what was a major increase in actual product volume. Unfortunately, planning activities did not accurately translate the lower value per unit. Unit growth turned out to be more than 12 percent—an increase of more than 40 *million* cartons. Needless to say, Kmart's distribution centers were not prepared for that increase, and the normally high holiday-season volume turned into an avalanche. Logistics managers scrambled to expand operating capacity by adding work shifts, going from 12 shifts per week to 19 per week. They instituted cross-docking procedures as fast as they could, and they used temporary third-party logistics providers to ease the congestion. If the increase in unit volume had been understood, Kmart's logistics managers might have been able to handle the holiday crush. Instead, the company suffered long delays and out-of-stocks on many items.

There Are Many Conflicting Measures

When faced with decisions about complex functions and processes, managers have to resist the temptation to measure "everything that moves." The survey data suggests that the top performers of a given process actually use fewer measures than the total sample. The temptation to use more measures is strongest perhaps when management is not clear on which measures best reflect the overall performance of the company. The hope is that by measuring as much as possible, management will have the data if and when it is ever needed. The problem is compounded when internal departments or silos fail to align their processes and incentives, producing the conditions under which the good effects of logistics measurement can be lost or seriously diluted. One side of the company does not know (or care) what the other side is doing, as long as everyone continues to receive paychecks and bonuses.

One retailer, which will remain anonymous, illustrates the problems that result when managers independently set logistics measures. The person in charge of procurement continually reviews inventories across the entire system, looking for ways to reduce levels of stock. Reporting to a different division head, a store manager is unconcerned with such measures; he is evaluated on sales and stock-outs (fewer is better), not on inventory turns. He wants to be sure that there is stock in the warehouse whenever he needs it. The barriers to implementing effective process measurements in this company are largely internal and are based on current corporate structure and inconsistent performance incentives.

That scenario plays out in many companies, particularly manufacturing firms. Each of the company's departmental silos has its own performance measures, some of which conflict when end-to-end process improvement is the goal. For example, manufacturing managers typically desire plenty of raw material inventory to support long production runs, which are more efficient than short runs. The

Exhibit 3.1 THE BASIS OF EFFECTIVE DECISIONS IS THE QUALITY OF CORE DATA

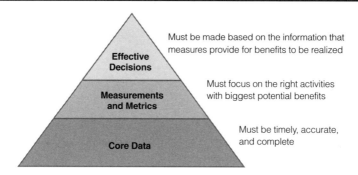

Effective Decisions — Must be made based on the information that measures provide for benefits to be realized

Measurements and Metrics — Must focus on the right activities with biggest potential benefits

Core Data — Must be timely, accurate, and complete

sales organization wants a high level of finished goods inventory to hedge against spikes in demand. Finance, however, wants to squeeze costs, a goal that requires keeping inventory and other assets to a minimum. With each function optimizing its own operations and focused on its own performance measure, the company as a whole cannot achieve its greater potential.

There Is Resistance to Providing Data

Using logistics measures in restructuring an organization and changing a corporate culture are delicate operations, neither to be undertaken lightly nor implemented with a heavy hand. Logistics measures may appear ominous to the uninitiated, with each worker's productivity measured with a stopwatch and rewarded with a stroke or a strap. After all, it is easier to blame the carriers for late deliveries than to hold oneself accountable for issuing orders on time. Furthermore, because measuring can illustrate problems that may not be fixed easily, certain managers may choose to keep those problems under wraps. Companies that are serious about measurement have long fought the stereotyped image of backroom logistics, bean-counters, and the negative associations with scientific management. They seek to elevate logistics measurement to a prominent position in the executive suite, where decisions about corporate strategy are made.

There Is Disagreement Over Key Terms

Measurement of any sort relies on precise definitions of terms. That is one reason why measurement is so difficult in the first place. Not every company will agree with all the others in its industry about what constitutes "performance," for instance. Some manufacturers consider that shipments are "on time" if the goods leave their factories or warehouses on the predetermined dates. "If I get it off my dock when I told you I would, I'm doing a great job." That measure does not do customers any good. All they care about is when they take possession of the goods.

"Complete order" is another logistics measure suppliers and customers often define differently. To the customer, that may mean receiving all the products in one shipment on a certain date; to the manufacturer, it may mean delivering the products in multiple shipments within a given time period. A third measure that leads to numerous arguments is "order fill." The supplier promises the customer 100 percent order fill. To fulfill that promise, the supplier waits until it has all the products to complete the entire order and then ships everything. But it takes two weeks instead of the two days the customer had expected. To the supplier, the order has been filled; to the customer the order has been filled late, and that is the same as an unfilled order.

Here is a good example: A food products distributor receives orders from two customers, each with 20 lines on the order. He is able to supply 19 of the 20 items to each company, and considers his fill rate to be 95 percent in both cases. The first customer, a grocer, receives the first order and is slightly disappointed that he did not receive one item. However, the grocer is able to stock his shelves and sell the other 19 items. The second customer, a food service company, needed all 20 items to make the soup planned for the next day's menu. The order fill rate was 0 percent in that company's eyes, and chances are good that it will be looking for a new supplier if service does not improve.

Lack of a common understanding of fundamental measurement terms is complicated further when multiple customers of a single company have different definitions or requirements. Managers across companies must work together to gain a clear understanding of terms.

THE BENEFITS OF MEASUREMENT

Why should companies measure? That is the question many managers pose, and it is hard to change the attitudes behind it. A plant manager for a major food manufacturer, when asked about the met-

What Is Supply Chain Management?

If the difference between logistics and supply chain is confusing, discussions about the phenomenon of "supply chain management" (SCM) can be thoroughly bewildering. The problem, according to the Supply Chain Research Group (1999) at the University of Tennessee, is one of trying to define two concepts with one term, i.e., supply chain management. The idea of viewing the coordination of a supply chain from an overall system perspective, with each of the tactical activities of distribution flows viewed within a broader strategic context (what has been called SCM as a management philosophy) is more accurately called a **Supply Chain Orientation**. The actual implementation of this orientation, across various companies in the supply chain, is more appropriately called **Supply Chain Management**.

This perspective leads to the definition of one of these crucial constructs. **Supply Chain Orientation** is defined as "the recognition by an organization of the systemic, strategic implications of the tactical activities involved in managing the various flows in a supply chain." Thus, a company possesses a supply chain orientation (SCO) if its management can see the implications of managing the upstream and downstream flows of products, services, finances, and information across their suppliers and their customers.

Furthermore, this does not mean the firm with the SCO can implement it. Such implementation requires an SCO across several companies, directly connected in the supply chain. The firm with the SCO may implement individual, disjointed supply chain tactics (such as Just-In-Time delivery or Electronic Data Interchange with suppliers and customers), but this is not Supply Chain Management unless those tactics are coordinated (a strategic orientation) across the supply chain (a systemic orientation).

Supply Chain Management is *the implementation of a supply chain orientation across suppliers and customers.* Companies implementing SCM first must have a supply chain orientation. In other words, a Supply Chain Orientation is a management philosophy, and Supply Chain Management is *the sum total of all the overt management actions undertaken to realize that philosophy.*

Supply Chain Management, then, is defined as "the systemic, strategic coordination of the traditional business functions and the tactics across these business functions within a particular company and across businesses within the supply chain, for the purposes of improving the long-term performance of the individual companies and the supply chain as a whole."[1]

rics that would be reported to corporate management, stated, "We can always create the data." As noted in Chapter 2, the survey of logistics managers revealed that a majority ranked logistics measurement within their company relatively low in a list of issues and problems they considered most pressing—seventh on a list of 13 items. Many people apparently still consider logistics measurement a backroom activity and give it little credence when it comes time for business leaders to map out a set of strategies to reach next quarter's or next year's goals. However, logistics measurement is needed to determine if initiatives on the top of that list are succeeding.

As the companies highlighted in this chapter demonstrate, logistics measurements come in all sizes and shapes, and there is no single generic measure that fits all companies or situations. That is both a blessing and a curse: It is essential for managers to determine exactly which measures are appropriate within their companies and with their trading partners, and to define measurement terms accordingly. What constitutes "on-time delivery" for a medical supply distributor such as Owens & Minor, for instance, may differ markedly from the time frame assigned to that measure by a fast-food distributor such as Sysco or a manufacturer of electrical components such as Hewlett-Packard.

It is clear, then, that business leaders and managers should not adopt a "template" of measurements and try to force their companies' unique processes, strategies, and cultures to fit that pattern. Instead, they can follow a carefully constructed plan that calls for the involvement not only of each company's administrative leaders but also of everyone internal to the company and all trading partners who have an interest in the outcomes. Furthermore, the case studies presented in this chapter demonstrate that every company's stakeholders include members of a company's supply chain as well as intermediate customers and end users—and all stakeholders have specific reasons, whether or not they are aware of them, for embracing certain measures.

So why measure? Here are eight very good reasons:

- Objective data provides support for improvement initiatives

- Effective measures are critical to success

- If a company depends on a process, it has to know its condition

- Measures help illustrate what should and should not be done now

- Measures help companies determine how to stay competitive

- Measures can help improve a company's culture

- Measurements help companies confirm their value to customers

- Measurement is the only way to control the logistics process.

Measures Provide the Basis for Process Improvement

Many logistics managers instinctively know when their logistics infrastructure needs an overhaul, particularly if their company acquires a product line or business that will funnel its products through the distribution system. However, making the case for eye-popping investments in new warehouses, information systems, and equipment can give logisticians ulcers. Logistics measurement provides decision-makers with something they cannot get from tea leaves, opinion polls, or informal discussions by the water cooler: namely, empirical evidence. There simply is no substitute for hard-and-fast data, provided that companies have the right data and use it properly in framing an argument.

In process improvement, the role of logistics is fundamental. The way to think of its role is to visualize a business process like logistics in a larger perspective—the context of a larger "business system."[2] A company's business system comprises five critical elements: business processes, jobs and organization structure, measurement and other management systems, corporate values and beliefs, and information technology. A well-designed business process defines the new way work will get done; in logistics, that means the flow of raw materials and/or finished products from production to consumption.

Redefining work and work flows requires a company to determine how the tasks that make up the new business process—the jobs, reporting relationships, and other elements of organization structure—will be organized. In turn, the reorganization of work into new processes and new jobs requires new metrics for measuring and rewarding performance. Such measures (and the rewards for meeting, missing, or exceeding those measures) drive the performance of individuals. In turn, the performance measures, incentives,

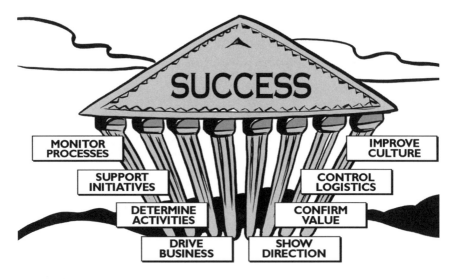

and other management systems support the organization's values and beliefs. Information technology, then, must be built to support the new way that work will be organized and to help the company track the performance of activities in the business process. Such a business system is self-reinforcing: All elements of the system must be in harmony for any business process—whether in logistics, marketing, or manufacturing areas—to perform well.[3]

Ensuring that business processes, once redesigned, continue to perform according to marketplace standards requires measuring them. This connection cannot be emphasized enough:

> **Improving business performance requires improving the way work is done in a business activity; and that, in turn, requires measuring and continuing to measure the appropriate dimensions of that activity to make further improvements.**

Effective Measures Are Critical to Success

In today's super-connected business environment, people are learning that there is much to be gained from sharing information to improve the way companies work together within a supply chain. A simple supply chain diagram can be drawn to spotlight any member at any time in the process of gathering raw materials or components and producing, marketing, and distributing products—eventually to an end user as the final link in that chain (see page 83).

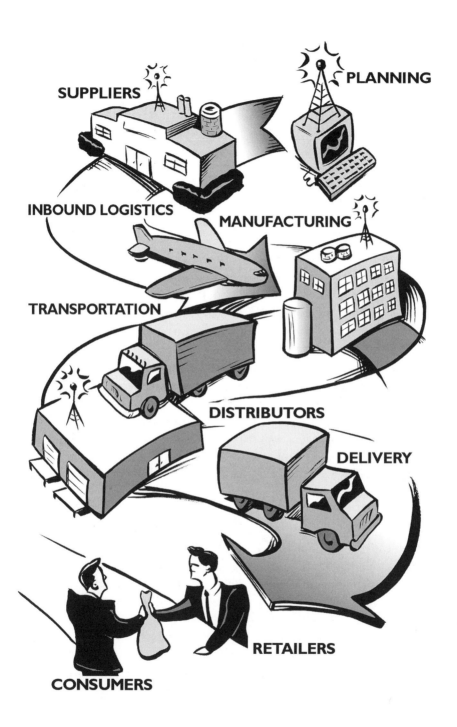

SUPPLIERS

PLANNING

INBOUND LOGISTICS

MANUFACTURING

TRANSPORTATION

DISTRIBUTORS

DELIVERY

RETAILERS

CONSUMERS

Having done so, managers are in a position to evaluate just how closely the company's performance matches predetermined goals or outcomes. It is surprising to find that many companies today do not systematically capture the data relevant to that performance, and thus they have only an intuitive sense of just how well they are doing. Their customers may tell them one thing; their suppliers, another; and on either side, the links in the supply chain get weaker and weaker. Logistics measurements, combined with a willingness on the part of company managers to share their data, are capable of making the links in the supply chain much more resilient to external or internal threats.

Consider the case of Paging Network Inc. (PageNet), the leading U.S. independent provider of paging and wireless messaging services. With operations centered in North America, PageNet continues to look for ways to expand its market globally. One of PageNet's biggest suppliers is Motorola. When PageNet was negotiating new prices with Motorola, Motorola declined to lower prices, requesting instead a review of those areas of the business in which its costs were increased by PageNet's business policies.

Although Motorola refused price concessions on one hand, it extended the other hand to PageNet's managers, offering to help them discover where they could work together to reduce the overall costs and share the benefits. Motorola previously had required 120-day lead times on orders, but it had accepted changes up to 30 days before the scheduled ship date. PageNet had decentralized pager purchasing and used "booking orders" to hold space in Motorola's production schedule.

Managers from both companies showed a sincere willingness to learn how to make their part of the supply chain work more efficiently and productively. Working in tandem, they hammered out a set of guidelines specifying a zero tolerance for changes, but reducing the order lead time to 30 days. To satisfy PageNet's needs for additional flexibility, Motorola officials agreed to allow a small percentage of orders to be expedited, even though they fell within the 30-day limit. They further worked out provisions for "on-time delivery," including policies for substitutions in the case of deliveries that could not be made according to schedule. And the two companies agreed to work with a six-month rolling forecast of PageNet's needs, without a firm commitment to order.

The point here is simple: To improve business performance significantly, companies must formulate common goals and objectives with trading partners. To build trust and control their relationship, they must agree on a shared set of logistics measures that accurately show where work is done, how well it is accomplished, and by whom.

Measures Let Companies Monitor Their Performance

This is a fairly simple idea, yet it is surprising how often it is ignored. Most people, for example, rely heavily on their cars to help them get through everyday life. They would be rendered virtually helpless should the cars fail. But how many people are as diligent as they should be about getting regular maintenance performed on their vehicles? For most, it is easy to assume the attitude that if it is running, everything is OK. Yet without regular checkups, it is impossible to confirm that a car is in good mechanical shape (or worse, uncover a potential disaster in the form of a cracked engine block or blown transmission).

The same can be said for logistics. Companies are so reliant on logistics that they would be in deep trouble if their logistics operations shut down. Yet, most senior managers have a very incomplete view of how their operations are running.

For an example of a complete view, consider St. Louis-based Graybar, one of the largest distributors of data communications and electrical products in North America. Graybar distributes more than 800,000 components for electrical and communications uses. In addition to the general public, its customers include small electrical and communications/data contractors as well as huge corporations in multiple industries. One of those customers is Texas Instruments (TI).

TI had 17 stockrooms dedicated to maintenance, repair, and operating supplies (MRO) in 13 facilities. Each stockroom was operated as an individual cost center. The company outsourced its facilities MRO purchasing to Graybar, which literally moved "inside" TI where it could control the stockrooms more effectively. TI kept close watch on the results, as Graybar shared data showing a significant reduction in the cost of procuring the goods and supplies. Prior to the partnership with Graybar, each TI stockroom added an overhead cost, ranging from 18 percent to 35 percent, to the purchase price of each item it "sold" internally to another TI department—just to break even. That is, if the stockroom purchased an item for $1.00, it had to sell it to the shop floor, for instance, at a price ranging between $1.18 and $1.35. As the partnership with Graybar progressed, however, TI saw those margins reduced to about 3 percent.

Several additional benefits of this "in-plant" arrangement have been realized. Stock-outs, which had previously ranged in the neighborhood of 9 percent, have been reduced to less than 3 percent. On-time delivery is at an admirable 99 percent, and Graybar's "customers"—the mechanics who use the stock rooms—report a high degree of satisfaction with the service they receive; in fact, satisfaction ratings have increased 35 percent to a current level of 94 percent. The savings in terms of reduced margins have been enormous, but the added value of satisfaction and efficient delivery render this example even more persuasive. The Graybar/TI partnership has engendered a deep sense of trust between the two companies and has become so successful that it now is entering a new phase for the supply of production materials.

Measures Help Companies Determine What They Must Do to Perform Well

It is easy to be swayed by opinions and advice on what companies must do to compete in today's volatile world: "Implement ERP to integrate decision-making across the company." "Design customer-specific logistics services to lock in important customers." "Standardize services and products for all customers to lower total cost." But how do companies know what advice to take and what to ignore? How do they decide what programs or initiatives are necessary to boost their business performance today—right now—and what is irrelevant, unnecessary, or just plain ineffective?

With a stated goal of being one of the top three computer companies in the world by the year 2000, Compaq Computer Corp. is determined to understand how to satisfy commercial and consumer customers in the highly competitive PC industry. As a part of that strategy, the company launched in 1994 a group to understand the unique needs of government agencies, educators, and administrators. Compaq's Government, Education, and Medical Group then formed an alliance with Ingram Micro, the largest worldwide wholesale distributor of computer products and services. Ingram Micro performs a variety of services, ranging from pick-pack-ship to hardware reconfiguration and software loading, including inventory management.

To plan and control its business better, both now and into the future, Compaq has initiated several measurement programs. Two key areas for measurement are:

- *Short-range operational objectives.* Compaq and Ingram Micro have a scorecard for the contractual measures that show how well the alliance is performing on a daily basis. Those measures include utilization of contractual capability, order cycle time, quality audits, on-time delivery, posting of receipts for inventory, and electronic reporting of daily, weekly, and month-end results. To determine root cause in any problem areas, Ingram Micro measures additional areas that roll up to those measures.

- *Long-range strategic planning objectives.* Compaq has a scorecard for the supply planning process and measures specific activities to gain information and knowledge for its continuous improvement initiatives. Key measures here include short-term and long-term forecast accuracy, capacity utilization, inventory turns, and replenishment cycle time. By accumulating information in those areas, Compaq will be in a stronger position to determine which new channels of distribution are appropriate to its business, even as the business continues to change and evolve.

Following the lead of Compaq and Ingram Micro, logistics managers should think of measurement when they contemplate how to boost performance, both short- and long-term. Measurement can identify a company's best customers, their needs, and what satisfying those needs could mean for the company's (and the customers') bottom lines. Measurement also helps the company see where it needs to go in the future.

Measures Can Help Companies Determine How to Stay Competitive

One of the advantages of effective measurement programs is that they not only help companies boost performance in the short term, they also can help point the way to future competitive advantage. In fact, a handful of leading companies are using measures to help them define immediate performance goals as well as longer-term, strategic objectives that, if achieved, will enable them to take a significant position in a market or industry.

This is precisely what management at International Paper Company (IP) has done in an attempt to solidify its position with its customers in an industry where many companies fall without making any noise. Based in Purchase, New York, IP makes much more than just paper for writing and printing. It is also a leading distributor of paperboard, packing, and cartons, as well as many other products such as chemicals, oil, and gas. Among its far-flung operations, IP has nine facilities that supply corrugated packaging to 83 locations owned and operated by poultry producer Tyson Foods Inc. Although Tyson is Arkansas-based, the company has facilities in more than 20 states and several foreign countries. Consequently, the logistics problems IP faced in securing Tyson as a customer and delivering cartons on time were a good deal more complex than one might first expect.

In the early 1990s, IP bid on a contract to supply Tyson with paper cartons, and it won approximately one-third of Tyson's orders. Since then, that portion has increased to about 65 percent of Tyson's needs, but IP would like to win an even greater share of the business. To reach that goal, IP is putting its eggs in the basket of partnership and total cost measurement. Here is how:

- IP has learned how to be more flexible and agile in accommodating Tyson, which frequently makes changes to its orders. Tyson has to make quick decisions about which "product" to get out once it has determined such vital information as the average weight of the birds being processed. Consequently, within the course of a single day, orders change seemingly at a moment's notice.

- Many of Tyson's 83 facilities are recent acquisitions, not operating under centralized purchasing control. That is, each facility is responsible for its own profits and losses. Accordingly, to increase margins and reduce costs, each location is looking for the best deal. Tyson is working to use total cost measures to help each facility make decisions and to obtain the best service and cost possible.

- IP acknowledges that Tyson managers are understandably reluctant to name a sole supplier of its packaging materials. The problem is complicated by the fact that many of the 83 Tyson facilities are decentralized: IP is thus more vulnerable to local packagers that can try to undersell it on selected individual items. Tyson managers, in contrast, are faced with the problem of determining which suppliers can do the total job at the lowest overall cost to the company. Therefore, they have to continue to develop relevant measures that will help them determine the lowest total cost across the entire range of packaging requirements.

- IP has placed two of its people inside Tyson to work on product development and explore initiatives for cutting costs. These "in-plants" have added significant value by helping rationalize the number of cartons used and the efficiency with which pallets are built and material handled.

Tyson and IP managers are working together on many ways to reduce the costs of packaging for both companies. Materials account for a substantial portion of the cost of a box or package. Working with Tyson's specific requirements, IP has used performance boards to reduce material costs.

From inviting two IP employees inside Tyson to building more efficient loads and devising cheaper, more durable packaging materials, the strategic partnership of Tyson and IP rests on the bedrock of trust. And a solid part of that foundation is provided by logistics measurement, which both parties agree is critical to the success of their partnering. Only through measurement of total cost of materials and procurement will the relationship withstand the constant scrutiny of both organizations.

Measurement Can Help Change Corporate Culture

Logistics measurement never is and never should be an end in itself. Just as information technology itself is a tool or a means of improving work and the quality of products and services, so, too, are logistics measures tools for taking the pulse of companies, their suppliers, their customers, and their employees. The goal is to diagnose problems—potential or real—and take the appropriate response to keep the company healthy. This prescription, however, requires an open mind and a willingness to learn how to do things better. Often it means accepting entirely new organization structures or creating a new culture to improve business performance—just as companies such as PageNet, Graybar, 3M, and Grainger have done with their logistics measurements.

Logistics measurement can play a key role in how managers manage, how they interact, and also in how they themselves are measured. In the case of Welch's, one sees how measurement can get senior managers working from the same page. Management at Welch's focuses measurement on three key areas—service, cost, and quality. Making use of that framework, the company has set a goal to achieve the lowest overall delivered cost at the desired standard of service and quality. Welch's measures the delivered cost of logistics, inbound and outbound, for all the components that make up the products. Overall product quality is measured several ways, including product safety, impact on the environment, and the degree to which the product satisfies customer specifications. Service is measured by compliance with customer expectations.

But Welch's does not stop at collecting statistics on each area as if it were filling out a checklist. Top executives have worked out a plan to tie the measures to management incentives. Under their plan, the heads of departments that comprise Welch's supply chain processes (including procurement, manufacturing, and distribution) are treated as a unit rather than as individuals responsible for different segments of the corporation. A percentage of their annual variable compensation is based on how well the unit performs. Individually, those executives control only a small segment of the business, but collectively they exert substantial influence.

The appropriate use of measurement can have a tremendous impact on a corporate culture, converting a rock-throwing and finger-pointing culture into one where people are willing to improve performance in areas where measurement has identified root causes of problems. The old turf-war phenomenon becomes a truly outmoded way of conducting business. Measurement allows managers to isolate and work on the root causes of a problem, to "fix the problem rather than affix the blame."

Measurement Helps Companies Define Customer Value

Any business person will allow that all customers must be from Missouri. When companies tell their customers that they have done great jobs for them, the customers, of course, say, "Show me." If the companies are measuring logistics performance, they can. Nothing can help confirm the value and quality of work for customers better than cold, hard facts: 99.5 percent on-time delivery; 98 percent fill rate; 100 percent invoice accuracy; and so on. Furthermore, when a company knows how much various customer services cost, the company can be more responsive to customers and more accurately communicate pricing terms to them.

For instance, surgical supply distributor Owens & Minor has devised a system that allows customers to take control of pricing. Through its CostTrack program, Owens & Minor works with customers to determine which services they need and are willing to pay for. Thus, instead of having to pay a negotiated percentage for distribution, a customer can elect to pay only the cost of fees for selected services. If a customer had been receiving small deliveries six days a week, Owens & Minor might show the company how to reduce its weekly deliveries to two or three days. This cuts Owens & Minor's delivery and handling costs and the customer's internal handling expense, often without increasing the customer's inventory levels. The company can provide that tailored service because it uses activity-based costing (ABC) to determine the actual cost of service. Owens & Minor works with customers to optimize the supply chain by reducing the total logistics cost, with benefits to both trading partners.

Logistics measurement also can help companies deal with customer service issues, often helping customers solve their own problems. Another case study shows how Welch's used logistics measures to improve relationships with customers by helping them solve problems anywhere in the supply chain, even on the loading dock. Welch's collaborated with H. E. Butt (HEB), the largest private company in Texas and the top food retailer in the state. HEB's rapid growth had led to congestion in its distribution centers. Together, the companies addressed that problem by changing the racking and pallet configurations. Yet how Welch's and HEB arrived at that solution was anything but simple. It involved a complex relationship built on an open-door policy and shared information. HEB was willing to open its warehouses to Welch's, and Welch's had to make an initial investment to support the investigation and collect data about the problem. Both companies had to work out a plan for sharing the cost. For Welch's the solution resulted in a slight increase in the cost of pallet "building" and transportation. However, the first year that the plan was in effect, revenue climbed 25 percent. Clearly, that was a plan well worth Welch's investment.

Measurement Is the Only Way to Control Logistics Processes

Many business processes can be optimized with tight controls that allow managers to monitor performance without collecting data. For example, on the manufacturing floor, key activities can be controlled with fixtures, programming, and/or statistical process control. Logistics, unlike many manufacturing activities, is not a controlled process.

A few things can be engineered. Owens & Minor, for example, does not measure on-time delivery. Its customers know that if they place their orders by a specified time, the order will be delivered according to a predetermined schedule. Owens & Minor's trucks run on an engineered schedule, and they arrive at each stop within a narrow time window. Instead, Owens & Minor concentrates on first-time order fill to make sure that the customer's order is on that truck when it arrives. Then, if the order is not filled, it is possible to determine from other measures the reasons for the problem and take steps to prevent or minimize future occurrences.

Because logistics is an open system, with endless cause-and-effect correlations, measurement remains the only way for logistics managers to gain the information they need to understand and manage their key activities and processes effectively.

WHERE DO COMPANIES START?

This chapter has demonstrated how companies of all sizes and in various industries put logistics measurement to work to improve their internal operations as well as the relationships they enjoy with their suppliers and customers. Ask any of them why they go to such lengths to measure in the first place, and they likely will say that measuring logistics performance is critical to their business success and ability to increase their competitive advantage. It also will help them keep an open mind toward what they need to do in the future to stay competitive.

It is not and never has been a rational position that just any measure will do or that any set of measurements can guarantee every company a healthy return on its investments. Nor will the latest management fad enable a company to create a set of well-oiled internal processes or a seamlessly operating supply chain in which all its

suppliers work as if it were the center of their universe. Effective management means looking beyond company boundaries and trying to envision a smoothly functioning, compliant, and effective supply chain.

In the ideal supply chain, there is a high degree of communication. The old maxim about a chain being only as strong as its weakest link is a truism in the world of supply chain and logistics measurement. That is, if a company fails to critically examine the chain from one end to another, it may find itself at the mercy of the weakest member. Any manufacturer that has worked hard to develop a highly integrated, just-in-time manufacturing model is crippled if a key supplier fails to deliver parts at the appointed time—regardless of the health of the company's internal operations.

As will be discussed in the following chapter, getting ready for this next-level efficiency and connectivity requires mobilization and action. New competitors, new markets, new customer demands, and new ways of working with suppliers will continue to challenge old ways of doing business. The order of the day will be partnerships and alliances between members of a supply chain, just as we have seen in the case of TI and Graybar. The essence of these partnerships will be the degree to which members can agree on how to divide resources and responsibilities, share costs as well as information, and measure how well each is doing the job. Arriving at that consensus will, in turn, require that companies jettison their demand

for privacy and independence. Instead, these forward-looking companies will establish a process view of the channel, develop trust, encourage cross-functional relationships internally, and develop cross-organizational alliances across the supply chain.

Where do companies start? Standing in awe before Mount Everest, Edmund Hillary and his Sherpa guide Tenzing Norgay each began by taking one step forward toward the peak. Every marathon runner, who toes the mark, must do the same. Most companies will not get all the necessary logistics measures in place overnight, but they can start with one process or one function—or even with one person. The next chapter begins to lay out the steps that can facilitate this journey.

ENDNOTES

[1] J. T. Mentzer, W. DeWitt, J. S. Keebler, S. Min, N. W. Nix, C. D. Smith, and Z. G. Zacharia, "A Unified Definition of Supply Chain Management," Working Paper, The University of Tennessee, 1999.

[2] M. Hammer and J. Champy, *Reengineering the Corporation: A Manifesto for Business Revolution*, HarperBusiness, 1993, pp. 65-82.

[3] Ibid.

CONNECTING MEASUREMENT WITH STRATEGY

The Punic Wars, which encompass the battles between Rome and Carthage in the third and second centuries B.C., were distinguished from other conflicts of the time primarily by the exploits of one Hannibal. Hannibal was the Carthaginian general who secured his place in history with several stunning victories over Roman forces during the Second Punic War (218-201 B.C.). His feat—incredible as it was given Rome's power and dominance at the time—is even more remarkable because of Hannibal's ability to devise new methods and tools to master complex logistics challenges. Of course, he is most famous for using elephants instead of horses to attack Rome, and he did so by taking an unexpected route—through the treacherous mountains north of Italy.

The march on Rome began in 218 B.C. Hannibal left New Carthage (now Cartagena), Spain, with an army of about 40,000, including cavalry and a considerable number of elephants carrying baggage and later used in battle. He crossed the Pyrenees and the Rhone River and traversed the Alps in 15 days, beset by snowstorms, landslides, and the attacks of hostile mountain tribes. After recruiting additional men among the friendly Insubres, a Gallic people of northern Italy, to compensate for the loss of about 15,000 men during the long march, Hannibal subjugated the Taurini, a tribe hostile to the Insubres. He then forced into an alliance with himself all the Ligurian and Celtic tribes on the upper course of the Po River. Later that same year (218 B.C.), he vanquished the Romans under Scipio Africanus the Elder in the battles of Ticinus (Ticino) and Trebia (Trebbia). In the following year, 217 B.C., Hannibal inflicted a crushing defeat on the Roman consul Gaius Flaminius at Lake Trasimene. After his victory, Hannibal crossed the Apennines and invaded the Roman provinces of Picenum and Apulia, recrossing thence to the fertile Campania, which he ravaged.[1]

Although Hannibal never realized his dream to fell Rome, that was not due to any missteps of his own. Rather, it was because the Carthaginian government failed to provide needed reinforcements (the concept of continuous replenishment had not yet been invented). But his exploits illustrate how even faultless execution can go awry when strategy and logistics are not in synch.

Like Hannibal's march toward Rome, a comprehensive, potent measurement program is no small undertaking. As will be discussed in Chapter 5, an effective logistics measurement initiative actually does not begin or end with measurement. Instead, it begins with companies fully understanding their business strategy and, even more important, the implications that strategy has for their logistics plans. In addition, the initiative "ends" not with formulating the measures themselves, but rather with getting all logistics employees ready to embrace and implement the new measures; tracking the performance of operations, people, and measures; and fine-tuning all three.

Quotes appear around the word "ends" because measurement should not be viewed as a one-time event—an every-five-year "health check." Because, as illustrated in Chapter 2, the bar of performance rises every year, companies must continually revisit the

Exhibit 4.1
MEASUREMENT HELPS CLOSE THE GAP BETWEEN OPERATIONS AND STRATEGY

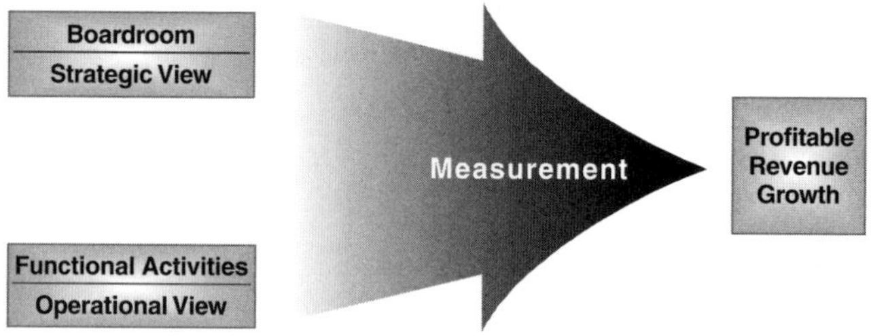

Boardroom
Strategic View

Functional Activities
Operational View

Measurement

Profitable Revenue Growth

measures. If they wait five years to recalibrate them, they could very well find their logistics organizations about to suffer the business equivalent of heart attacks.

THE RULES OF MEASUREMENT

Even before companies embark on measurement programs, it helps greatly to have everyone who will affect, and be affected by, the initiative to assume the right mindset about logistics measurement. *Mindset* means having a common understanding of the essential principles or rules of effective logistics measurement. This chapter not only lays out those principles, but it also illustrates them with examples of companies that have lived by the rules and gone on to make major improvements in logistics performance. Following the rules discussion is a checklist of qualities for individual logistics measures themselves—that is, a checklist for determining what constitutes a good measure.

Rule #1: Start With Strategy

As business performance increasingly relies on a company's logistics capabilities, it becomes critical for logistics to be able to execute the company's chosen strategy. This might seem obvious and simple. In reality, it is anything but. In dozens of large companies, the strategy at the top is not clearly supported by the execution of logistics management. Different business strategies can have profoundly different impacts on a company's logistics strategy. For example, a business strategy to be the low-cost provider requires drum-tight efficiency across an organization—especially in logistics processes, which can account for a significant portion of a product's total cost. To deliver goods at rock-bottom costs, the logistics management of a company might have to consolidate costly warehouses, discourage special orders, and reduce its frequency of deliveries. All fine and good—until the day the company exchanges its strategy for one of, say, excellent customer service. Suddenly, a well-oiled, finely tuned logistics machine built for efficiency becomes a significant barrier to change.

Time and again, research conducted for this book turned up this kind of "misalignment" between the strategies at the top of the company and the strategies and operations of logistics. But in a handful of highly successful companies whose competitive edge comes down to logistics—3M, FedEx, and Wal-Mart, to name a few—business strategy, logistics strategy, logistics operations, and logistics measures are all "flying in formation."

How do they do it? Wal-Mart, for instance, has a group of 11 executives representing different corporate functions who are dedicated full-time to creating "the future of the supply chain." According to Mike Duke, senior vice president of logistics, the group members have "broadened the view of the supply chain, and they support our company strategy and our customers in the total flow of merchandise, from the vendor to the customer."[2]

Similarly, Federated Department Stores has a stated commitment to using logistics to boost growth. Tom Cole, president and CEO of Federated Logistics, which oversees logistics operations for all of Federated's divisions, has noted that his performance is tied closely to that of the stores. He says that his "responsibilities may seem pretty mundane. But at the end of the day, I'm going to judge my success at Federated on how well we are able to grow (comparable)-store sales. Because if what I do doesn't do that, it's not worth a lot."[3]

To create the most effective logistics measures, logistics professionals must begin, not by establishing measures, but by setting their sights at a much higher level: understanding their company's business strategy. They then can derive supply chain strategies from the business strategy, which in turn will define logistics strategy and, ultimately, their logistics measures (Exhibit 4.2).

A corporate strategy, at its most basic, defines the business the company is in, as well as the organization's goals and objectives. The strategy also may identify what the company wants to become within the current confines of its industry, the future state of the industry, or an entirely different industry altogether.

Starbucks, the gourmet coffee roaster and retailer, says its strategy is to "establish Starbucks as the premier purveyor of the finest coffee in the world while maintaining our uncompromising principles as we grow." These principles—which guide decision-making at all levels, from choice of product to where it should be sold—include, "Apply the highest standards of excellence to the purchasing, roasting, and fresh delivery of our coffee"; "Develop enthusiastically satisfied customers all of the time"; and "Recognize that profitability is essential to our future success."[4]

Exhibit 4.2 **STRATEGY ALIGNMENT DRIVES OPTIMUM MEASUREMENT**

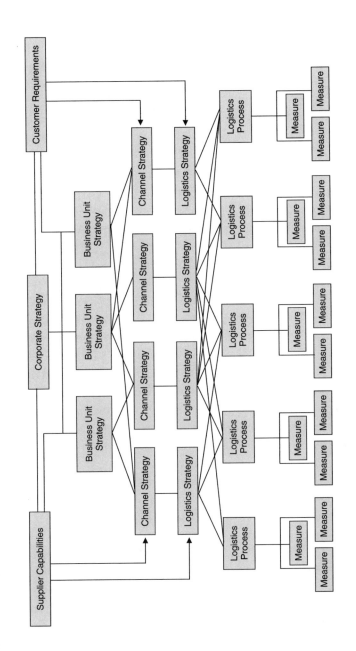

Procter & Gamble's stated purpose is to provide "products of superior quality and value that improve the lives of the world's consumers. As a result, consumers will reward us with leadership sales and profit growth, allowing our people, our shareholders, and the communities in which we live and work to prosper." Procter & Gamble, too, appends a number of principles to its strategy, including "Innovation is the cornerstone of our success" and "We are externally focused."[5]

Nordstrom, the Seattle-based upscale department store, has a much shorter and more succinct mission: "Exceptional service, selection, quality, and value."[6]

On the other hand, 3M has both a mission statement and a set of strategies that guide the company from year to year. Its most recently articulated strategy is to focus on five areas deemed crucial to success: sales growth, customer satisfaction, productivity improvement, employee pride, and protecting and enhancing 3M's reputation.

In their best-selling book, *The Discipline of Market Leaders*, Michael Treacy and Fred Wiersema make a strong case for developing a highly focused strategy and aligning all company operations in support of that strategy. According to the authors, market leaders excel because they have chosen to compete on one of three "value disciplines": operational excellence (delivering an unmatched combination of price, quality, and ease of purchase); product leadership (offering the best, most innovative products); or customer intimacy (providing tailored products and services to meet particular customer needs). When top management selects a value discipline, it also must select an appropriate "operating model"—the operating processes, organizational structure, management systems, and cultures of the business. The foundation of the operating model is a set of core business processes—almost always including logistics—that will generate value for customers, and do so profitably.

For instance, operational excellence relies on highly efficient product supply, customer service, and demand management processes. Product leadership requires excellent invention, product development, and marketing processes. And customer intimacy mandates superior abilities in processes such as customer service and relationship management.[7]

While a multidivisional company may have an overarching corporate strategy, that strategy may or may not be identical to the strategies that guide individual business units or divisions. Differences

The Rules of Effective Logistics Measurement

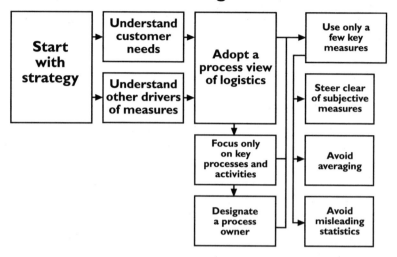

among corporate and various divisional strategies may relate to the type of product being made (one division produces a commodity good that demands a focus on cost and efficiency, while another makes high-value goods that require more "care and feeding" of customers); the type of market being served (industrial versus consumer); the geography into which goods are sold (local, regional, national, or international); or some combination of all three.

Consider the case of 3M. The company is organized to serve 12 very diverse markets: automotive, communication arts, construction/maintenance, consumer products, electronics/electrical, health care, industrial products, office products, pharmaceuticals, safety and security, telecommunications, and transportation. Each market features a distinct type of customer that purchases distinct products and is served in distinct ways. For example, developing, producing, and delivering casting tape to physicians and hospitals is far different from coming up with the next innovation in Post-it notes for the office, which, itself, is far removed from the process of producing materials for the company's semiconductor manufacturing customers.

Two similar companies, Grainger and Graybar, have taken different strategies to reach different markets. Grainger, North America's leading provider of maintenance, repair, and operating (MRO) supplies, services, and related information, has more than 1.3 million customers. To better serve a diverse range of needs and properly allocate their overheads, Grainger has taken an unusual approach to segmentation. Instead of doing a customer segmentation, Grainger has done a business segmentation. The company has divided its business into 11 units, according to the type of products and services provided to customers.

Graybar, another of the world's largest distributors of data communications and electrical equipment, has kept its business on a single profit-and-loss statement but has formed different business units to address different needs. One unit, just discussed, serves the needs of a single customer, literally from within that customer's own organization. That partnership with Texas Instruments serves as a model for Graybar to extend similar programs into other companies, including multiple programs with Lucent Technologies.

Given those wide-ranging divisional differences, it is not enough to understand the corporate strategy. Logistics managers have to connect that to business unit strategies. A business unit strategy of being the low-cost producer for the wholesale club channel would, in turn, require a supply chain strategy that emphasizes flow-through distribution, high inventory turns, and highly efficient processes. On the other hand, a business unit strategy emphasizing customer service would dictate a supply chain that was extremely flexible, able to accommodate custom orders and services, and driven by a large amount of customer data. And a strategy of competing on innovation might focus on the "back-end" of the supply chain—that is, improving the way suppliers work with the company's research and development unit to bring new products to market more quickly.

Of course, in large companies, all three of those channel strategies—and, potentially, numerous permutations of them—conceivably could be present, as shown at the top of the next page.

The challenge for the logistics professional is to ensure that all business unit strategies are supported appropriately so that the high-level corporate strategy can be executed. Once the business unit channel strategies are defined, an appropriate logistics strategy can be developed for each channel. While the channel strategy encompasses larger issues external to the organization—cost/service trade-offs and customer relationships, for example—the logistics strategy focuses primarily on the operations that link the company with its suppliers and customers on a daily basis.

There are, indeed, many instances of tight strategic alignment in companies across industries. One example is Polaroid Corp., which

Alternative Channels of Distribution for Consumer Goods

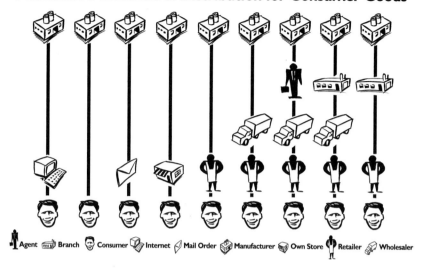

in 1996 embarked upon a logistics strategy development project that would tie the company's logistics activities more tightly to its supply chain and business strategies. As of mid-1998, the company reported making significant progress in its initiative, noting that it already had generated substantial improvements in cost, service, and inventory.[8] Likewise, Koppers Industries, a $500 million manufacturer of bulk commodities, dramatically improved its business performance as the result of its supply chain and logistics strategy initiative, saving millions of dollars in transportation and inventory management costs while making its prices more competitive and boosting profits.[9]

The point is that strategy alignment is a difficult and, at times, seemingly insurmountable challenge. But, as evidenced by an increasing number of companies, it is also achievable.

Rule #2: Understand Customer Needs

A company's successful logistics strategy—one that will drive the creation of the right logistics measures and the right logistics performance—first and foremost requires understanding the company's customers and their needs and then articulating how those needs will be met. That typically happens through an iterative dialogue with customers to determine jointly the company's logistics performance and how that performance will be measured. Modus Media does this by creating a Statement of Work for each major program with each customer. 3M has a Product/Service Agreement for its customers. The two share a common element: Company managers must meet with their customers to determine what they value and whether they are willing to pay to have that value provided.

Companies also must decide whether they will interact with customers via standard practices or tailored services. Standard practices means treating all customers consistently. Tailored services, on the other hand, means doing different things for different customers. Perhaps those are differences in how the company handles orders or how often it delivers. It might mean that the company makes a certain number of proactive customer service calls instead of waiting for customers to phone with problems. Or, it could be building electronic linkages with key customers, enabling them to place orders, check order status, and post payment. Such services could involve the full range of the company's logistics activities or just a few—depending upon the customer and how deeply the service is tailored.

Rule #3: Understand Other Drivers That Influence Measures

While customer needs are critical, they must be balanced against organizational considerations—asset utilization, operational efficiency, and supplier interactions, to name a few. For instance, a company cannot decide to send a truck to a customer every time it needs something. Using an otherwise empty truck to ship one skid clearly does not make good use of physical assets. Similarly, it is highly inefficient to fire up a product line to make 300 snow shovels for a customer that is running low on a snowy winter day or to call suppliers 15 times a day to order small batches of raw materials. There are concerns other than customer needs that are major factors influencing the scope of a company's logistics strategy.

One caution here: It is easy to fall into the sales-surrogate trap—mistaking the desires of the sales force for actual customer requirements. It is fairly common in many firms, and it can result in a bad logistics strategy. In that scenario, salespeople may feel they have no price flexibility or product options in dealings with customers and, therefore, they believe the only way they can differentiate the company from the competition is by changing service parameters. So, they commit to the delivery of all orders by 8:00 a.m. to every customer, or to 100 percent flexibility on order configuration and order size—significantly increasing the company's costs. The problem is that many of those customers do not need or value such services, and if asked directly, they would say so. Therefore, it is critical to confirm exactly how demanding various customers really are before setting their "requirements" in stone.

Rule #4: Adopt a "Process" View of Logistics

One of the biggest mistakes companies make when they dive into logistics measurements is that they begin by putting the stopwatch to narrow activities like driving a trucking route or order-picking at an individual warehouse. Productivity per labor hour can be measured to three significant digits, but that measurement is very unlikely to gain competitive advantage for any company. Such activities exist within a much larger stream of activities, which must be looked at collectively: for example, from customer order to delivered goods, or from the identification of a supplier to the receipt of raw materials. By adopting a process view, a company might discover it can eliminate or streamline a trucking route or warehouse. So why begin by measuring it?

But exactly what is a logistics process? How is a process different from a transportation route or the transportation function? How is it different from the activities that go on in warehouses? To reduce the confusion, consider the following framework and definitions for thinking about logistics processes and activities such as transportation, warehousing, and material handling, as well as the related measurement issues. First, remember the definition of "process."

A *process* is the end-to-end series of linked, continuous, and managed tasks and activities that contribute to an overall desired outcome or result. These activities usually cross the functional boundaries of a company—those of functions such as manufacturing, purchasing, and the like—and culminate with delivery of supplies or goods to another unit, division, or company.

Warehousing, transportation, and material handling are not logistics processes in and of themselves. They are all components of logistics processes, and are more accurately defined as logistics *activities*.

Given those definitions, there are three key logistics processes in a company—whether it is a manufacturer, distributor, or retailer (Exhibit 4.3):

- **Sourcing and Procurement.** Sourcing is the series of activities that results in decisions regarding from whom/where goods, materials, and services should be obtained. Purchasing/procurement is the series of activities that begins with the recognition of demand for supply or replenishment of supply and is completed when the goods, materials, and/or services are received. The procurement process for a manufacturer like Ford involves purchasing components—say, gas tanks, windshields, airbags, and so forth—from its suppliers and having them delivered to its manufacturing sites. The procurement process for a distributor or retailer of finished goods involves the purchase of those finished goods and their delivery to retailers' warehouses or distribution centers.

- **Fulfillment.** The fulfillment process consists of those activities involved from the point of recognizing demand from a customer through delivering the goods or services to the customer, complete with an invoice or similar instrument to facilitate the collection of payment. The fulfillment process of a manufacturer delivers to another manufacturer, a distributor, a retailer, or—in a direct channel model—to an end consumer. A retailer's fulfillment process delivers the goods from a distribution center to the retail store or potentially to an end consumer.

- **Planning, forecasting, and scheduling.** This process consists of those activities involved in the managing and controlling of material requirements, capacity requirements, and the production and distribution of value-added goods and services. Effective planning and forecasting bridges gaps between marketing/sales issues and manufacturing/distribution issues, with major impacts on inventory and customer service levels. The use of expert systems (ES) and artificial intelligence (AI) will result in significant changes to the design and effectiveness of forecasting systems. Increasing the level and detail of information shared with suppliers and customers dramatically increases the effectiveness of this process for all parties.

In Chapter 2, a "supply chain" was defined as *a set of three or more organizations directly linked by one or more of the upstream and downstream flows of products, services, finances, and information from a source to a customer.*[10] Exhibit 4.3, then, illustrates the

Exhibit 4.3 PROCESS VIEW OF LOGISTICS

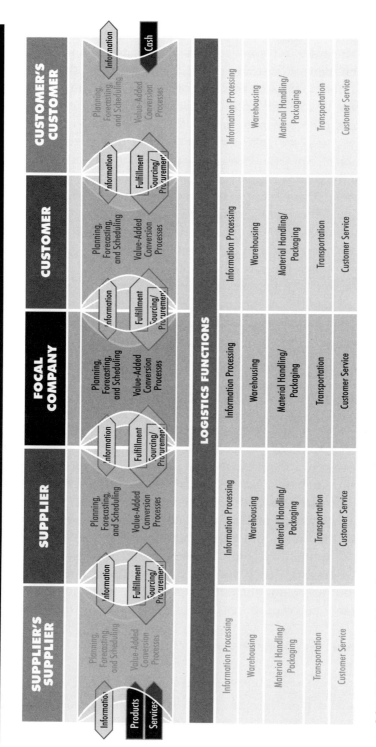

manner in which the three key logistics processes connect sets of three of the parties in a supply chain. Note that very few companies individually manage and control all the activities in the extended supply chain—from extraction of raw materials to delivery of finished goods to the end consumer. Even the biggest companies—auto makers, oil companies, and so forth—do not own all the raw materials required to make their products or deliver them to their final customers. They must work together with their trading partners to manage the overall supply chain for their goods and services.

This terminology is not a game of meaningless semantics. It is important to differentiate a company's logistics processes of sourcing and fulfillment from the supply chain processes that go far beyond one company. Even powerful companies such as Wal-Mart and Dell do not control their industry supply chains; Wal-Mart depends on the performance of suppliers such as Mattel, Procter & Gamble, and Hallmark Cards. Those companies, in turn, depend on the performance of their suppliers. If, for instance, Mattel's supplier of clothing for Barbie dolls does not deliver, then Barbie dolls cannot be shipped in the quantity that Mattel wants to ship them—or that Wal-Mart wants them. In the industry supply chain in which Wal-Mart operates, the performance of a doll-clothing manufacturer in the Far East can affect its performance. That clothing manufacturer's performance may be Mattel's immediate concern; however, its performance is not meaningless to Wal-Mart if the giant retailer experiences a shortage of Barbie dolls. The better Wal-Mart is in projecting demand for Barbie dolls from Mattel, the better Mattel can be in projecting demand from its clothing manufacturer.

It is increasingly incumbent upon all parties in a supply chain to understand the needs and expectations of other parties upstream and downstream in the chain. With modern information technology, it is also far easier for each link in the supply chain to monitor each party's performance and thus do a better job of preparing for bottlenecks or other problems in one end of the chain or another.

Rule #5: Focus Only on Key Processes and Activities

Measurement requires tremendous focus. As mentioned earlier, "Measuring everything that moves" is a recipe for disaster. All logistics processes are not created equal when it comes to satisfying specific customer or supplier requirements. Some customer segments may demand a higher level of service, while others are satisfied by the lowest possible cost, and that, of course, has an array of implications for a company's logistics processes.

Customer requirements are not the only factors dictating which logistics processes and capabilities are most important. Where a logistics process sits in the supply chain also plays a role in determining the extent to which it should be integrated with those of suppliers and customers, and how it should be designed. For example, in the past Nabisco had looked more closely at its fulfillment process, which delivers products to supermarkets and other grocery retailers, than it did sourcing for strategic potential. Today its focus is on both. As one of the pioneers in the Collaborative Planning, Forecasting, and Replenishment (CPFR) initiative in the consumer packaged goods segment, Nabisco strives to be highly integrated with its key retail customers in order to better determine real demand.

At the same time, Nabisco is in the commodities procurement business. As a baker of cookies, cakes, crackers, and other snack foods, the company faces the daily challenge of buying raw materials—flour, wheat, sugar, and so forth—at the best possible price to keep production costs low. So procurement also is a key process in the organization, but it is on a different level. Instead of measurement being highly integrated, procurement at Nabisco is conducted on a fairly simple transaction basis: Give me what I need—today, this week, this month—and deliver it to me at the lowest cost.

American Greetings Corp. provides another example of the need to focus measures on the most important logistics processes and activities. Responding to pressure from large retail customers such as Wal-Mart, Kmart, Eckerd, and other national chains, the greeting card manufacturer has been forced to squeeze production and distribution costs. To satisfy its customers' stringent logistics requirements, American Greetings emphasizes distribution as a key competency, and it implemented an automated picking and packing system that has slashed lead time considerably. The new system also customizes product documentation, which suggests how to merchandise and display the items, to the requirements of each customer.[11]

Rule #6: Designate a "Process Owner"

The ability to improve a logistics process and institute effective measures often benefits greatly by having an individual who controls all the functional activities in that process. Having a single "process owner" can be difficult, especially in a company with a heavily entrenched organizational hierarchy. For some organizations, placing a single person in charge of multiple functions may run counter to "the way we've always done things." A cultural change as radical as this, implemented insensitively or without appropriate communication and training, can backfire quickly.

One alternative to placing a single person in charge is to create a cross-functional team that serves as the process owner. Here, the process is decomposed into individual functions to identify concerns such as specific roles and responsibilities, expectations, and work hand-offs. Then, with appropriate technologies, all players are given access to the same information so the entire process and its activities are visible to everyone connected to it.

Koppers Industries faced such a challenge when it implemented its supply chain initiative. Although the project had early support from top management, those closer to the work initially were skeptical. Plant managers, buyers, and others were unconvinced at the outset that they could perform any better than they already did. It took the creation of cross-functional teams, charged with identifying opportunities for cost savings and developing new strategies, to overcome the resistance to the new model.[12]

Rule #7: Use Only a Few Key Measures

In a large company, the number of potential measures can be mind-boggling. To capture—and act intelligently on—every potential measure within a company would be an exercise in futility. So, recognizing the complexity of the measurement, one must identify the fewer than a dozen measures that have the greatest impact on each of the company's processes.

For instance, Welch's has long been a proponent of the "Perfect Order." But "perfect" can mean many things to many people. Welch's worked with its customers and the Grocery Manufacturers of America (GMA) to reduce the confusion. The GMA defined the Perfect Order to be:

- the right quantity of,
- the right product,
- delivered on time,
- in damage-free condition,
- with an accurate invoice.

Welch's then decomposed each factor into a few component measures to analyze potential problem areas.

Grocery chain H.E. Butt (HEB) has focused its efforts on key functional activities. An estimated 80 percent to 90 percent of its measures are focused on the company's separate functions, including sales, service, inventory, stock-outs, and the like. The company has developed an intranet site known as the "Daily Pulse," which allows people throughout the system to review certain key measures, retrieve current data, and check on any activity in each category occurring within the most recent three months. Thus, for example, managers can determine sales by region, department, or store. If the top-level measures indicate problems, the system allows managers to drill down into each category for a more detailed analysis. By displaying its measures this way, HEB's managers quickly can see key performance indicators and get to the root of problems.

Grainger, the MRO distributor, navigates its complex logistics operations through a "dashboard" or "cockpit" of measures (Exhibit 4.4). The company, headquartered in Lake Forest, Illinois, has operations throughout Central and North America. These operations distribute supplies and components for maintenance and repair to industrial, commercial, and institutional customers. In keeping with its core business—namely, industrial supply—the company's 560,000

Exhibit 4.4 GRAINGER COCKPIT CHART

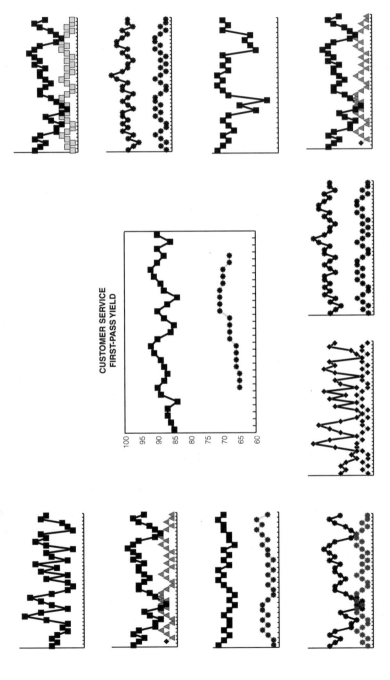

CUSTOMER SERVICE
FIRST-PASS YIELD

Note: Measures and values are proprietary and therefore not identified.

products range from engines and fans to hand tools and testing instruments. The Grainger catalog alone lists more than 80,000 products. The company serves more than 1.3 million customers, making meaningful customer segmentation difficult. As mentioned in Chapter 3, company managers have turned their attention to segmenting the business itself, grouping various services into separate business units. After collecting data and analyzing overhead costs associated with each unit, management structured its costs accordingly.

For each process area, Grainger has developed 10 functional measures, which it displays on a single sheet of paper. Those measures, when combined, add up to a single process measure, positioned in the center of the sheet—similar to the dashboard of a car or an airplane cockpit. The beauty of the dashboard or cockpit model is that it allows decision-makers to identify the key measures of a specific process quickly, and it shows how functional measures relate to each other, revealing the root causes of any deviation in the key measures.

Imagine sitting in the cockpit of a jet airplane, with all the instruments and dials grouped according to function: One set of instruments gives readings on altitude; another set reports fuel consumption and efficiency; yet another provides information on speed; and so forth. Smaller dials in each group report data on factors that affect any of the primary functions. Thus, for instance, a jet pilot has a gauge for wind velocity and direction, knowledge of the total weight of the airplane and its cargo, visibility of other aircraft in the vicinity and their altitudes. All those functions are connected at the highest level (the plane flies), but each can be isolated and analyzed for its contribution to the jet's overall safety and performance.

The Grainger model is not a set of toys for frustrated pilots, however. Senior executives track all key measures, everything that influences—positively or negatively—the primary measure of what Grainger calls "economic earnings" (EE). This is a financial measure based on economic value-added (EVA). It focuses on increasing returns on existing business investments and investing in new projects where the return will exceed the company's cost of capital. More significant for this discussion, however, is that Grainger is organized so that each subsequent level of management keeps watch on a particular set of dials and measures, all the way down to ground zero. For example, in order fulfillment, Grainger tracks a measure called "first pass yield" (FPY). This is shorthand for the number of instances in which a customer's order is filled immediately with an in-stock item, shipped wherever the customer desires from the location most advantageous to Grainger, with the result that the customer is completely satisfied.

The aggregate measure can speak volumes about how Grainger is doing business and achieving its goals. The detailed breakdown and measurement of the tasks that make up that process can help the company identify key areas for improvement.

In the retail industry, Service Merchandise focused on just a few critical measures to improve store replenishment. By partnering with one of its key suppliers, Black & Decker, the retailer uncovered all the steps and time it took to move a product from a supplier's facility to a Service Merchandise store. To get that valuable information, the company asked questions such as:

- How much time does it take for Black & Decker to receive the replenishment order?

- How long does it take the supplier to pick, pack, dock, and ship the order?

- What is the transit time between Black & Decker's dock and the Service Merchandise distribution center (DC) dock?

- How long does it take Service Merchandise to sort the order in the DC?

- What is the DC's response time after receiving the store replenishment order?

- How long does it take to get the order off the truck at the store and onto the shelf?

By decomposing the process measure—shelf-replenishment time—into its component functional measures, both Service Merchandise and Black & Decker clarified the steps in replenishment, who had responsibility, and the expected duration of each step. This is particularly important during breakdowns in the process—when Service Merchandise runs out of stock. Instead of automatically assuming that the supplier is at fault, Service Merchandise can isolate the exact cause of the problem. It may be that the retailer was not clear in communicating its needs to the supplier. Or, perhaps the order was a "rush," which required Black & Decker to change its regular replenishment method. Or, maybe Black & Decker really did drop the ball and just failed to get the order out in time. But the point is not affixing blame; it is creating a set of measures that enable all steps of the process to be visible to everyone involved so that performance glitches can be identified and corrected in the future.

Rule #8: Steer Clear of Subjective Measures

All the measures discussed in the preceding examples are objective, standard, and quantifiable: time, cost, and quantity, for example. In those measures, there is no room for feelings or subjectivity to creep in. Ten minutes, three dollars, or five cases: Those words mean the same thing to all players, regardless of where they are in the process. Problems occur when a company develops what it thinks is a set of objective measures, but has really created metrics that are based on arbitrary or ambiguous definitions—in essence, turning subjective judgments into numbers.

Say a retailer wants to measure its suppliers' on-time performance. But instead of developing, with each supplier, a standard, quantifiable definition of what is meant by "on time," the retailer decides to rate its suppliers on a scale of one to five. At the end of every month, someone assigns a subjective rating to each supplier (depending upon how that person *felt* the supplier performed), and the retailer uses that rating to determine whether or not the supplier delivered its goods on time. The same method is used for several other categories, and the results are totaled for a composite "Supplier Score." Just because it is a number, however, does not necessarily mean that it is an objective measure. Research for this book uncovered a number of companies using subjective measures to rate their suppliers' performance, and most of the companies were not even aware of the inherent problems of their methods.

Rule #9: Avoid Excessive Averaging

Customer satisfaction surveys can support or impede measurement. A company may send out several hundred surveys, asking customers to rate the supplier in various categories on a scale of 1 to 10. When the completed surveys are returned, the ratings for each category are totaled and an average rating emerges: 8.5 on fill rate;

9.5 on on-time delivery; 7 on customer service; and so on. Now, such numbers are interesting and, however relative and subjective they may be, they do communicate some information on performance. But averages are not really useful in pinpointing breakdowns because they obscure the 1s, 2s, and 3s—indications that there are obviously performance problems or at least the perceptions of problems. As a result, the company goes about its merry way believing, because it has a 9 average rating, that it is at the head of the class. In reality, however, there are some customers who may not be at all happy with the supplier. Averages of percentages also should be avoided. They react erratically to changes, effectively becoming "noise" in the system, and they are difficult to tie to economic measures.

Rule #10: Understand the Statistics

Imagine that a company's dock manager is responsible for recording on-time deliveries for all the company's suppliers. He diligently notes the performance of each supplier, every day, without fail. And, at the end of every month, he creates a report for his supervisor that shows the number of times each supplier was on time or late: Supplier A was late once and Supplier B was late 10 times. Now, that is valuable information in its own right. But what is missing is the second half of the ratio: how many times each supplier made a delivery. Supplier A, while late just once, made only 5 deliveries, while Supplier B made 300 deliveries. So the supplier that is late 20 percent of the time is rated more highly than the supplier that was tardy on just 3 percent of its trips. Clearly, only listing the number of late deliveries is a misleading statistic.

THE HALLMARKS OF GOOD MEASURES

The overarching principles of measurement are fairly simple, yet very important. These principles should be on the clipboards of everyone attending the first planning meeting for a logistics measurement program. It also might be helpful if a list of the qualities of good measures were on the clipboard. What makes for a good measurement? Research and experience reveal that good measures share 10 basic characteristics.[13] A good measure:

- Is quantitative

- Is easy to understand

- Encourages appropriate behavior

- Is visible

- Is defined and mutually understood

- Encompasses both outputs and inputs

- Measures only what is important

- Is multidimensional

- Can be collected economically

- Facilitates trust

First, a good measure is *quantitative*. As just illustrated, it cannot be based on feelings or subjective rankings.

Second, a good measure is *easy to understand*. It has to be able to convey, at a glance, what it is measuring and how it was derived.

Third, because of the trade-offs inherent in logistics, a good measure *encourages appropriate behavior*. For instance, if a transportation manager is evaluated and compensated on his ability to minimize transportation costs, he may be inclined to hold orders until they can be combined in one, lower-cost truckload. But, although he has fulfilled his duties based on how his performance is measured, he may have created a satisfaction problem for those customers waiting for deliveries, and that, of course, would be a major problem in a company competing on the basis of superior service. This characteristic is usually best served by two or three measures that balance the tradeoffs.

Fourth, a good measure is *visible*. In other words, everyone involved in the process knows how performance is being measured, and everyone has access to performance measures at all times. Such visibility helps companies pinpoint trouble spots—not to affix blame, but to correct the problem so that it does not recur.

Fifth, a good measure is *defined and mutually understood*. A company cannot arbitrarily decide what is good without getting its internal counterparts and/or external trading partners involved in the decision. Instead, all partners must work together to develop standard definitions: What, for example, is "on time"? What does "order cycle time" mean?

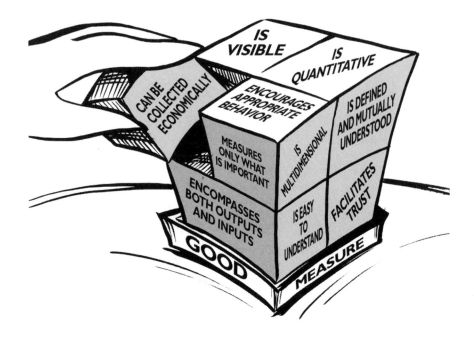

Sixth, a good measure *encompasses both the output and the input* to the process. For instance, the ability of a company to deliver goods to a customer on time is necessarily, to a large extent, dependent upon how well the company's production process is working. A company cannot manage on-time delivery without considering the impacts of order processing, production planning, and production scheduling.

Seventh, a good measure also *measures only what is important.* If it does not play a key role in supporting the company's logistics, supply chain, and/or business strategies, it should not be measured.

Eighth, a good measure is *multidimensional.* Because of the complexity of today's processes, effective process measurements must account for three key dimensions: utilization, productivity, and performance. Utilization is an objective comparison of capacity used versus capacity available—in other words, how much warehouse space has been used in relation to how much is available. Productivity is the result of dividing output by input—the number of pieces produced by a worker, for example. When a company combines figures for utilization and productivity, the result is a measure of its efficiency—how well it is doing things.

Ninth, a good measure *can be collected economically.* The processes and activities being measured are designed for the easy capture of relevant information. The benefits of the measure outweigh the cost of data collection and analysis.

Finally, a good measure *facilitates trust.* To get all parties to believe in the accuracy of the measure, everyone must agree to and see how the information is collected. Relationships with suppliers or customers are strengthened because of the trust engendered by such measurements.

The Pitfalls of Partial Measurement

Many companies fall into the trap of capturing only one measure when they, in fact, may need several to get the true picture on performance. That inevitably leads to trouble. The following is an actual example from a company we will call Acme Manufacturing. Acme has a team of 20 truck drivers who serve one of its key warehouses. Each day, at 8:00 a.m., 19 drivers leave the warehouse with their loads. Most return from their routes shortly after 5:00 p.m., punch out, and go home. But one driver, leaving at the same time, consistently completes his run and returns to the warehouse by 1:00 p.m., proceeding to hang around the warehouse until 5:00 p.m., at which time he punches out and goes home. It is no surprise that the warehouse manager is miffed at having one of his reports standing idle in the warehouse for nearly half the day. Considering this driver to be lazy, the manager prepares his case to terminate him.

Fortunately, somebody told the manager that the driver is not at all lazy. In fact, the driver in question has been the most productive of the 20 drivers, getting his work done in half the time it takes the others, who simply have been expanding their work to fill the defined work day. It is really the manager who is to blame. He has been measuring his drivers strictly on utilization (how many hours a day they are busy) instead of also considering productivity (how much they get done in a certain amount of time). If he had done the latter, he would have realized that instead of firing the productive driver, he really should be using him to teach the other 19 drivers how to be more productive, and he should pay him more to do it.

MOVING AHEAD

As discussed in this chapter, companies must do a significant amount of work before they can launch measurement programs. The time to begin educating senior executives, logistics managers, and logistics professionals about logistics measurement programs is before the programs begin. Everyone must understand the rules of the road before the logistics organization turns the key on its measurement program.

The next chapter explains how to conduct the program itself, step by step. It also discusses the challenges that companies should expect along the way, and, so that they do not derail companies' plans, how they should address those challenges. Before any company tries even to launch a program, however, it can gain a great deal of momentum if key personnel understand the rules of logistics measurement that have been explained in this chapter.

ENDNOTES

[1] Excerpt taken from *Funk and Wagnalls Encyclopedia* online at http://www.funkandwagnalls.com/encyclopedia/low/articles/p/p020001416f.html, February 2, 1999.

[2] "Logistics Grows Up," *RT Magazine*, September 1998, p. 45. This article provides a summary of remarks made during a panel discussion at VICS 98, the Retail Supply Chain Business Conference, in New Orleans.

[3] Ibid.

[4] Taken from the Starbucks Web site at http://www.starbucks.com/company/mission.asp, February 2, 1999.

[5] Taken from the Procter & Gamble Web site at http://www.pg.com/about/overview/english/pvp.html, February 2, 1999.

[6] Taken from the Nordstrom Web site at http://www.nordstrom.com/aboutus/company-hist/nordstrom_today.html, February 2, 1999.

[7] M. Treacy and F. Wiersema, *The Discipline of Market Leaders*, Addison-Wesley Publishing Company, 1995.

[8] F. Quinn, "Building a World-Class Supply Chain," *Logistics Management & Distribution Report*, June 1998, as published on the Web site http://www.manufacturing.net/magazine/logistic/archives/1998/log0601.98/06suply.htm.

[9] T. Minahan, "Supply Chain Key to Growth at Koppers," *Purchasing*, April 17, 1997, as published on the Web site http://www.manufacturing.net/magazine/purchasing/archives/1997/pur0417.97/042trans.htm.

[10] J. T. Mentzer, W. DeWitt, J. S. Keebler, S. Min, N. W. Nix, C. D. Smith, and Z. G. Zacharia, "A Unified Definition of Supply Chain Management," Working Paper, The University of Tennessee, 1999.

[11] B. Keenan, "Selling's New Breed," *IndustryWeek*, September 21, 1998, p. 41.

[12] Ibid., 9.

[13] Adapted, synthesized, and expanded from the following two references

- J. T. Mentzer and B. P. Konrad, "An Efficiency/Effectiveness Approach to Logistics Performance Analysis," *Journal of Business Logistics*, Vol. 12, No. 1 (1991), pp.33-62.

- C. Caplice and Y. Sheffi, "A Review and Evaluation of Logistics Metrics," *International Journal of Logistics Management*, Vol. 5, No. 2 (1994), pp.11-28.

5

IMPLEMENTING AN EFFECTIVE MEASUREMENT PROGRAM

Until now, this book has been creating the rationale for measuring logistics. The authors do not take lightly the challenges to managers who embark on this path, and they are well aware of the tension between the twins of "possibility" and "challenge." It is hoped that thus far, it has been demonstrated that the struggle will be worth the effort. This chapter discusses an approach to make the measurement struggle successful.

In architecture, form follows function. In logistics, measurement follows strategy. It is a firm's strategy that serves to differentiate it in the marketplace. For the purpose of simplification, the three dominant strategies described in *The Discipline of Market Leaders* by Treacy and Wiersema—operational excellence, customer intimacy, and product leadership—will continue to be used as the basis for illustration. A company's management systems, which include how and what is tracked to improve performance, must be consistent with the overall business strategy—whether it is to provide the best customer service, products at the lowest cost, products that are the most innovative, or some combination of those factors.

When logistics measures are not aligned with a company's business strategy, a logistics measurement program actually can degrade its marketplace performance. Suppose, for a moment, that a hospital supply company appoints a new CEO, who establishes the firm's strategy as one of excellent customer service—placing priority on getting the goods to customers anytime, anywhere, accurately, and in the form they need them. Logistics managers, following prior strategy, designed their processes for low cost, and evaluate route delivery drivers and warehouse workers primarily on efficiency.

Because routes were engineered and standardized to be efficient, there is little flexibility in the logistics system to deliver goods when customers really need them. Unless the company changes both its logistics operating model and measures from efficiency-driven to customer-driven, it will have a difficult time providing non-standard, premium service. They will reduce the effectiveness of marketing, customer service, and other investments meant to promote and make real the company's new marketplace promise of excellent service. If the old logistics model and measures continue, they will undermine the company's new strategy.

> **Measurement is a key factor in management control systems, and its careful use and application are essential to the success of the enterprise.**

This chapter will explore how to implement effective logistics measures. It will look at measures of logistics processes and activities, as differentiated from the functional measures often used in the past. It will detail a seven-step approach to get an effective measurement program in place or expand existing measurement activities:

1. Record the existing measures

2. Determine potential future measures

3. Evaluate and prioritize the desired measures

4. Develop a prototype of the new measures

5. Implement and test the prototype

6. Refine and reiterate (loop to step 1)

7. Train the organization and roll out the new measures.

This approach begins with an assumption that little or no measurement is taking place. If your company has a logistics measurement program, it is still recommended that you follow these steps—even if your starting point is a little farther down the trail.

LOGISTICS MEASUREMENT IMPLEMENTATION APPROACH

One of the barriers to implementing a measurement program is its perceived complexity. The scope of the effort appears enormous—

somewhat analogous to the old question, "How can you eat a whole elephant?" The answer is the same as the punch line: "One bite at a time!" You start by selecting three to five key measures from your list of desired measures, develop a prototype for gathering, recording, and presenting the information, and begin "keeping score." When that first iteration is complete, repeat the process (Exhibit 5.1). Each time you will be evaluating the desired measures, comparing them to the list of measures that you now have in place, and setting priorities for the next round of prototyping and implementation. The initial iteration (steps 1-5) should be completed as rapidly as possible—preferably within four weeks, certainly no more than eight weeks. At that point, you begin to get real measurement data that can help identify and prioritize the key areas in the next iteration. Throughout this process, you should maintain a spirit of experimentation and discovery. Time and cost expenditures should be minimal. To quote Nike's famous commercial message, "Just Do It!"

Exhibit 5.1 IMPLEMENTATION APPROACH

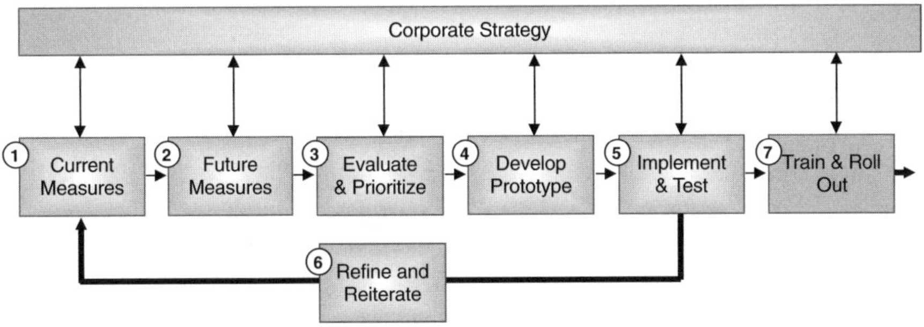

At some point during your iterations, you will reach a "critical mass" and be in a position to roll out the measurements to other parts of the organization. At the same time, you should have definitive information on how well your processes are performing. This will help you determine whether process improvements or redesigns are needed. You can address that issue at the same time that you are formally instituting your measures (Exhibit 5.2).

Change of any kind, even incremental change, requires leadership, coordinated action, and shifts in behavior. Simply following the steps outlined will prove insufficient. Implementing effective logistics measures involves three activities: developing agreement in the

Exhibit 5.2 ITERATIVE IMPLEMENTATION APPROACH

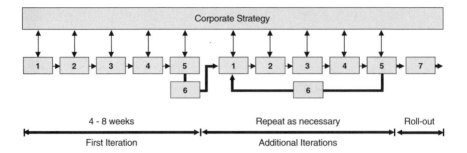

executive team on the changes that must be made (or "executive alignment"); getting middle managers to support the program ("incorporating middle managers"); and getting the buy-in of lower-level employees (or "mobilization"). These will be illustrated throughout the chapter.

Step 1: Record Existing Measures

Step 1 in an effective logistics measurement program involves understanding the measures that currently are driving the logistics operations and determining whether they can be used (if they are not already) in building the core process measures essential to excellent logistics performance. The chart in Exhibit 5.3 can help you document and understand your current measures. Although this may seem like a trivial exercise, it is a very effective way to understand your current measurement environment. As you gather this information, you may be surprised by the number of measurements, often redundant, in your organization, and by the use, or lack of use, of the resulting data.

Measures generally can be divided into three groups: time, cost, and quality. There are other measures that do not fit neatly into these groups, such as *Approved Exceptions to Standards* and *Availability of Information.* For that reason, an "other" group is provided. You may find that some measures (especially quality-related) will fit into more than one group. Do not waste time trying to decide where the measure belongs; just choose the group most appropriate for your circumstances. For best results, managers should create these charts of *current* measures by process.

Exhibit 5.3 CHART FOR RECORDING CURRENT MEASURES

	Measure					Performance		
	Name/ Description of Measure	Data Required for Calculation	Frequency of Measure	Responsibility for Measuring	Purpose of the Measure	Current Goal	Current Performance	Future Goal
Time								
Cost								
Quality								
Other								

- *Name/Description of Measure*—Record a descriptive name and a short explanation of what is being measured.

- *Data Required for Calculation*—List the data elements that will be required as numerators and denominators to calculate the value of the measure.

- *Frequency of the Measure*—List the minimum time frame for which the data will be accumulated and the calculation made. It is easy to add time periods together. However, resist gathering data too frequently, which increases costs.

- *Responsibility for Measuring*—List the individual (by position) responsible for recording the data, making the calculation, and either publishing or forwarding the results.

- *Purpose of the Measure*—This is a concept, not a value. It should express why the information has been collected, in a way that leads to action and can be measured. For example: "to improve on-time delivery performance," or "to determine overall cost of freight." If that question cannot be answered for a particular measure, it is a good sign the measure may not be needed. For example, a company was measuring loaded miles for its private fleet, and counted all miles with any quantity of goods on the vehicle as a "loaded mile." Upon investigation, logistics managers found that the purpose of the measure was to compare the company's performance against industry benchmarks for private fleet utilization. However, those benchmarks were based on capacity utilized per mile. The information they captured was misleading.

- *Current Goal*—List the current performance goal for the measure (e.g., 98 percent on-time shipment).

- *Current Performance*—List the current performance for the measure (e.g., 92.7 percent average for last time period—list time period).

- *Future Goal*—If a future goal has been established, list it. If the current goal is the only identified goal, leave this blank for now.

The focus of this assessment should be on the measures themselves. However, managers will find it difficult not to assess the performance of their processes at the same time. It will be useful (but not mandatory) to your company's current performance levels as measured by current methods, so columns are provided to record in the chart. The assessments of measures and the values of those measures (i.e., their performance) must be segregated carefully. The assessment of measures should be done at a detailed level, and the performance assessment at a higher, more generalized level. The place to begin evaluating performance really is after the first iteration. Subsequently, the focus can shift from the measures themselves to the values of the measures, what they indicate about your logistics performance, and which processes you should improve first. To accelerate the measurement implementation process, focus on the measures first.

Fill in charts like this for each logistics process and function (refer to Chapter 4, page 107, *Process View of Logistics*, for processes and functions). These documents, and the ones you will create in Step 3, become your method for managing your inventory of measures. They should be updated as you add new measures or drop old ones. This information should be collected as quickly and painlessly as possible. It is not necessary to analyze every measure you are using. It is more important to know *which* measures exist, and to understand *where* the data for the new measures may be located. The result of this exercise may be surprising. In some instances, the measure may have been based on suspect data. One retailer, for instance, based its merchandisers' performance and bonuses in part on a measure it called "lost sales revenue due to out-of-stocks." However, customers who find empty shelves rarely tell store clerks, "I would have bought it if it were in stock." An investigation of the measure revealed that nobody really knew how the measure was computed. The employee who programmed the report had left years earlier.

In gathering data, you should survey managers of other functions who are part of, or directly affected by, the three key logistics processes of sourcing/procurement, fulfillment, and planning/forecasting/scheduling to ensure that you have collected all current measures. Taking the time to document and understand the current measures is a good investment in your measurement initiative. Not only will you learn a lot about the motivators in your work environment, you also will have a solid foundation for developing your new measures.

Step 2: Determine Potential Future Measures

The goal of this step is to determine the measures that should be driving your key logistics processes. This means identifying the measures that tell you how you are performing for customers, and how your suppliers are performing for you. The idea is to identify the key measures, and then wait until after the measurement program gets rolling to identify and collect data on a wider set of measures.

While there are hundreds of measures logistics managers could use, research has shown that less than two dozen process measures are critical to evaluating and improving the performance of the logistics processes (Exhibit 5.4).

Furthermore, these basic measures are fundamental to any company—manufacturer, retailer, or distributor. They are important regardless of which business or logistics strategy drives the organization, whether it is to be the low-cost producer, the product innovator, or customer-service leader. A company ultimately should have in place measures in *all* of these basic categories to keep its logistics

Exhibit 5.4 PROCESS MEASURE CATEGORIES

Time	Cost
On-time Delivery/Receipt	Finished Goods Inventory Turns
Order Cycle Time	Days Sales Outstanding
Order Cycle Time Variability	Cost to Serve
Response Time	Cash-to-Cash Cycle Time
Forecasting/Planning Cycle Time	Total Delivered Cost
Planning Cycle Time Variability	* Cost of Goods
	* Transportation Costs
Quality	* Inventory Carrying Costs
Overall Customer Satisfaction	* Material Handling Costs
Processing Accuracy	* All Other Costs
Perfect Order Fulfillment **	* Information Systems
* On-time Delivery	* Administrative
* Complete Order	Cost of Excess Capacity
* Accurate Product Selection	Cost of Capacity Shortfall
* Damage-free	
* Accurate Invoice	**Other/Supporting**
Forecast Accuracy	Approval Exceptions to Standard
Planning Accuracy	* Minimum Order Quantity
* Budgets and Operating Plans	* Change Order Timing
Schedule Adherence	Availability of Information

** Contains a time component
* Indicates a component of a process measure – shown as explanation

operations performing well. Recognize that the emphasis on each process measure (and on the related activity and task measures) will vary from company to company, and will depend on the company's overall business strategy.

At the same time, you should determine the measures that are important to your customers, and to your company as a customer of your suppliers. Customers must be asked how *they* measure your performance. Suppliers must be asked what measures they use to quantify the logistics performance they deliver to your company.

To get a measurement program off the ground, logistics managers should begin with a limited number of key customers and suppliers. Working with too many customers and suppliers at first may create confusion and lead to unachievable expectations that slow progress. Select the one or two customers and suppliers that are important to the company, generally receptive to discussions on improving their performance, and knowledgeable about the business and competition. (In the next chapter, the section on *Choosing the Right Partners* discusses expanding the measurement program to a larger sample.)

Recognize that each customer may have unique requirements in the kinds of measures they use and how they define those measures. One customer might place high value on receiving only one shipment per purchase order, so order fill (at the case fill and line fill level) and backorders would be key measures. Another may value quick response, and accept multiple shipments to complete the order. At first glance, these would seem to be contradictory, but they are not. Both require essentially the same data. By capturing the customer information for each order along with the shipment information, you can compare performance against both requirements.

As important as understanding customers' unique requirements is understanding how those requirements create value for those customers. What customers actually value may not be readily apparent in the measures they request. In some cases, you can add value by collecting and supplying the information to your customer, as many third-party providers do for their customers. Try to gain agreement with customers on the roles and responsibilities of each party in the gathering and communication of measurement data to prevent duplication of efforts. On the first iteration, focus on the three to five basic measures that are most important to each customer and to yourself as a customer of your supplier—the ones used to manage the business.

When dealing with suppliers on issues of logistics measurement, one goal is to understand how to become a good customer. Have you communicated with your suppliers what you value? As their customer, you need to be specific about the basic data elements—e.g., case fill, line fill, the product numbers, and sequence of orders—and the definitions and corresponding performance goals. Again, as with customers, each party's roles and responsibilities must be mapped out clearly.

Step 3: Evaluate and Prioritize the Desired Measures

At this point, the analytical phase of the project begins. In the first two steps, the questions for each category of measures were:

- Where are we?

- Where do we want to be?

In this step, the questions for each category of measures are:

- Which measures are missing or incomplete?

- Which of those measures are most critical to managing the business and thus should receive priority for development.

This is a good time to check the validity of the measures in use. Some companies have the right measures in place but calculate them incorrectly or base them on flawed data. One consumer products manufacturer discovered this to its chagrin. Thinking its on-time delivery performance was 95 percent, the company analyzed its measure and found that orders going through sales brokers were dated incorrectly. Brokers changed the order date to the time when they shipped it—even though the "clock" already had been ticking for a couple of days. When it investigated further, the manufacturer found its on-time performance was closer to 25 percent.

Once logistics managers are sure their measures are valid, they can prioritize the new measures that must be developed. A word about priority: In logistics measurement, every measure cannot be a top priority. Logistics managers must decide which measures to develop first, second, third, and so on. In setting priorities, consider *importance* and *urgency* as primary criteria and weight them equally. The most important measures are those that track your key basis of market differentiation. Urgency is identified through customer or management requirements to manage performance. In some cases, your customers will measure you in areas in which you are not collecting information. In other cases, two trading partners may be using similar but different measures: The customer measures order fill one way, while the supplier measures it another way. These areas should receive priority.

As stated throughout the book and again at the beginning of this chapter, it is very important to align a logistics measurement program with business strategy. Based on the three basic business strategies discussed in Chapter 4, the following guidelines should help you determine your initial focus.

In companies whose business strategy is primarily one of **operational excellence**, measures should emphasize the following:

<u>Fulfillment Process</u>

- total delivered cost

- order cycle time variance

- accurate product selection

- accurate invoice

- availability of information (timely and accurate)

<u>Sourcing/Procurement Process</u>

- on-time delivery/receipt

- order cycle time variance

- total delivered cost

- complete order (fill rate)

- damage-free product

- accurate invoice

- availability of information (accurate)

Companies that compete on **innovation** (product leadership)—being first to market with a new product—should focus on the following:

<u>Fulfillment Process</u>

- order cycle time

- damage-free product

Sourcing/Procurement Process

- order cycle time (the time it takes them to order and receive material from suppliers)
- complete order (fill rate)
- approved exceptions to standard practices (minimum order quantities, change order timing, etc.)

Companies with a primary strategy of total **customer service** (customer intimate) generally will value these metrics:

Fulfillment Process

- on-time delivery
- order cycle time variability
- transportation costs
- complete order (fill rate)
- approved exceptions to standard practices (minimum order quantities, change order timing, etc.)
- availability of information

Sourcing/Procurement Process

- response time
- damage-free product
- approved exceptions to standard practices—especially the timing of change orders

It is interesting to note that customer-intimate companies do not place as much emphasis on cycle time as product leadership companies. Customer-intimate firms are much more interested in cycle time variance. Discussions with these companies have revealed that their customers value having goods consistently arrive at the time they were promised more than they value having them arrive in the shortest period of time.

Of course, most companies are not aligned with a single strategy. In most cases, they tend to follow a primary strategy for each of their

main channels, and have some combination of elements that make up their overall logistics strategy. Using the same format as in Step 1, Exhibits 5.5 and 5.6 illustrate this scenario with two examples:

Exhibit 5.5—Sourcing/procurement for a company with an operational excellence strategy

Exhibit 5.6—Fulfillment for a company with a customer intimate strategy

Blank spaces have been left to indicate measures you feel are critical to your particular processes. These examples are intended as a guide—a method for you to organize your priorities—not as a directive. You should create a similar chart for each logistics process and function in your company.

In Step 1, it was recommended that you use the column "Purpose of the Measure" to express why you collected the information in the past. In Step 3, you should use this column to establish a goal for the measure, and express it in a way that you can do something with the information. This will serve as the criteria against which you will test the result in Step 5.

It is strongly recommended that logistics measures on the fulfillment side (i.e., the performance customers will get) be supported by the logistics measures on the sourcing side (what suppliers must deliver). Essentially, you cannot give what you cannot get—or at least without incurring additional expense. For example, a customer-

		Measure				Performance		
	Name/ Description of Measure	Data Required for Calculation	Frequency of Measure	Responsibility for Measuring	Purpose of the Measure	Current Goal	Current Performance	Future Goal
Time	On-time delivery							
Time	Order cycle variance							
Time								
Cost	Total delivered cost							
Cost								
Cost								
Quality	Complete order receipt							
Quality	Damage-free product							
Quality	Accurate Information							
Other	Availability of information							
Other								

Exhibit 5.6 **FULFILLMENT MEASUREMENT CHART: CUSTOMER INTIMATE**

		Measure				Performance		
	Name/ Description of Measure	Data Required for Calculation	Frequency of Measure	Responsibility for Measuring	Purpose of the Measure	Current Goal	Current Performance	Future Goal
Time	On-time delivery							
Time	Order cycle time variance							
Time								
Cost	Transportation cost							
Cost								
Cost								
Quality	Complete order							
Quality								
Quality								
Other	Approved exceptions to standard							
Other	Availability of information							
Other								

intimate company that emphasizes complete order in its fulfillment process should be supported by suppliers that score high in response time. Otherwise, in order to provide high levels of service, the company will be carrying too much inventory. Research suggests that the synchronization of measures between inbound and outbound logistics performance is not commonplace. Overcoming this will require communicating clearly to suppliers what the company is trying to achieve with customers, and then crystallizing these goals into concrete measures. As Michael Dell says, "Your supplier can't be a partner if it doesn't know what you're trying to achieve."[1]

Keeping score on sourcing/procurement and fulfillment is critical to improving performance. However, it is not enough. Simply knowing that a particular month's order fill rate was 98.7 percent and the order delivery cycle time was an average 3.5 days will not give logistics managers all the data they need to improve logistics performance. They must also know how much these performance metrics deviate from what was desired—that is, reality versus plan. Comparing what happened to what was expected to happen requires measuring the third key logistics process—*planning/forecasting/scheduling*.

Forecasting involves both anticipating future conditions and events, and analyzing the relevant, available data to minimize uncertainty in predicting those future conditions or events. Planning means setting goals, creating designs, and establishing procedures. It involves formulating a program of action—more generalized at the strategic level and more detailed at the operational level—based upon forecasts or predictions. The more accurate the prediction, the more informed the planning; the more developed the measurement and control system, the more likely goals will be achieved. Forecasting and planning are continuous and interactive. Decisions made last week might have to be changed based on new predictions today. Scheduling assigns a timetable to actions.

Normally, predictions about the future drive the logistics planning process, which in turn drives decisions about capacities, materials, and resources required to accomplish the plan, based upon constraints faced by the firm. There are different types of logistics planning, such as capacity planning, materials planning, and production planning based on demand forecasts; network designs based on anticipated stocks, flows, and related costs; and transportation equipment planning, load planning, and route planning. In most cases, there will be a few key process measures, as illustrated in Exhibit 5.7.

Exhibit 5.7 PLANNING/FORECASTING/SCHEDULING MEASUREMENT CHART

		Measure				Performance		
	Name/ Description of Measure	Data Required for Calculation	Frequency of Measure	Responsibility for Measuring	Purpose of the Measure	Current Goal	Current Performance	Future Goal
Time	Forecasting planning cycle time							
	Planning cycle variance							
Cost	Cost of excess capacity							
	Cost of capacity shortfall							
Quality	Forecast accuracy							
	Planning accuracy							
	Schedule adherence							
Other	Availability of information							

Comparing the logistics plan to actual performance is especially important because planning activities commit significant corporate resources—people, transportation equipment, warehouses, technology, and so on. Logistics is a resource-intensive process. It is also a resource-constrained activity: All customers on the same route cannot have an 8 a.m. delivery from the same truck. So that they do not waste valuable resources, logistics managers must "keep score" of their planning effectiveness—i.e., their forecasts, schedules, and budgets. A point that must be emphasized is that planning—at least set-

ting goals or predicting outcomes—must precede measurement. By focusing on the three key logistics processes and on the appropriate measures, companies can improve the value of logistics for their customers and themselves.

Step 4: Develop a Prototype of the New Measures

In this step, the goal is to develop more specific measures from the basic process measures you selected in Step 3—i.e., measures that will drive logistics activities such as warehousing and transportation, and tasks within those activities—and then put those measures together in a working prototype. The reason to build the prototype is to work out the bugs before any major efforts are committed to a full-scale measurement program. Refining this prototype, iteration by iteration:

- Minimizes initial cost and efforts

- Begins data collection as soon as possible

- Gathers input from affected parties (customers, suppliers, and internal functions) before the measure is refined and standardized

- Uses data collected in the next iteration to evaluate the process itself, and to develop a cost/benefit analysis for further efforts

- Generates momentum by demonstrating wins and improvements

Logistics managers must not rush into automating data collection, because in their haste they may spend great time and money automating the wrong things or the right things the wrong way. This also can delay initial implementation and stall momentum.

Eventually, information systems—the role of which will be discussed in Chapter 6—will be important. At this point, however, you should collect the data already available from existing sources and systems. For example, if your carriers are not providing notifications of delivery, request that they begin to do so. Then, start collecting them in a format that makes it easy to enter and analyze. Your accounting systems can provide many of the "counts" needed for calculations. Use spreadsheets or similar tools to begin to turn that data into useful information.

In many companies, existing measures are more task- or functionally oriented than they are process-oriented. For example, warehouses may be evaluated on efficiency, inventory accuracy, and cost against budget. However, the movement of goods through those warehouses and transportation equipment—from factory to the customer's dock—may not be measured. It is appropriate at this time to consider a hierarchy of measures.

Exhibit 5.8 PROCESS MEASURE COMPOSITION

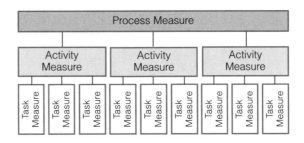

Process measures can be decomposed into activity measures, and then into task measures (the latter two often are called functional measures). It is important to understand how these measures fit together and affect and balance each other. The reason is to determine what is going wrong in a large, complex business process when process measures fall below target. By measuring the smaller components of a logistics process, managers can analyze process failures, an activity known as "root-cause analysis."

Consider the following two scenarios, in which a CEO is meeting with his senior staff, as outlined by John Mariotti in *IndustryWeek* magazine:

In scenario A, the CEO declares, "Our on-time delivery is awful and we must improve it—fast. Now let's get out there and make it happen."

In scenario B, however, the CEO asserts, "We must increase our on-time deliveries from 65 percent to 95 percent or better. During the last month, the following reasons contributed to late deliveries: engineering changes—35 percent, late receipt of customer specs—29 percent, equipment downtime—20 percent, internal quality problems—12 percent, and other reasons—4 percent.

"You all have copies of a report providing additional detail about the nature of the problems. What I need from each of you is a plan of action showing how your department can help to substantially reduce the problems affecting on-time deliveries."[2]

The answer to the rhetorical question "Which will be more effective?" is obvious. By understanding the components of the process, managers can construct process measures that allow more detailed analysis. (For more information on the task-level measures that can serve as components of the activity- and process-level measures, please refer to the book *Improving Quality and Productivity in the Logistics Process*, published by the CLM.)

Exhibit 5.9 provides a simple illustration of the hierarchy of measures for the fulfillment cycle time in a "make-to-stock" company. As you can see from this example, the careful selection of a few measures allows managers to evaluate what the company needs, what the customer values, and how employees are performing against goals. The prototype should focus on a limited base to minimize the

Exhibit 5.9 PROCESS MEASURE COMPOSITION EXAMPLE

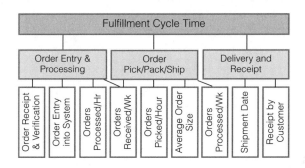

amount of data to be collected manually. The idea is to get it up and running so that customers, suppliers, and internal managers can visualize it and add their input.

A key point to consider is that the measures be balanced. This means that they consider trade-offs in performance in time, cost, and quality. Measures that are properly balanced motivate the proper behaviors. For example, special packaging will reduce pick/pack/ship efficiency and, therefore, must be captured and noted in the overall productivity measure. Careful attention to the variables and the drivers of those variables will produce measurement systems that are fair and reflect good performance for good effort.

Minimum, target, and exceptional values for the measures also should be established and subject to frequent review. These would be recorded in the three far right-hand columns of the charts you have created for each process (see Exhibit 5.10).

Merely adjusting the targets until they can be achieved is not recommended. At the same time, you should not set goals that cannot be attained. The former is delusional and the latter is dysfunctional. Involve the key customers and owners of the process in setting the target values. Having everyone understand the rationale for the goals will greatly improve the chances that the measures are accepted.

Exhibit 5.10 RECORDING CHART – PERFORMANCE

	Measure					Performance		
	Name/ Description of Measure	Data Required for Calculation	Frequency of Measure	Responsibility for Measuring	Purpose of the Measure	Current Goal	Current Performance	Future Goal
Time								
Cost								
Quality								
Other								

As a checklist, refer once again to the 10 characteristics of good measures (Exhibit 5.11), repeated from Chapter 4.

Exhibit 5.11 CHARACTERISTICS OF GOOD MEASURES

A good measure:	Description:
• Is quantitative	• The measure can be expressed as an objective value
• Is easy to understand	• The measure conveys at a glance what it is measuring, and how it is derived
• Encourages appropriate behavior	• The measure is balanced to reward productive behavior and discourage "game playing"
• Is visible	• The effects of the measure are readily apparent to all involved in the process being measured
• Is defined and mutually understood	• The measure has been defined by and/or agreed to by all key process participants (internally and externally)
• Encompasses both outputs and inputs	• The measure integrates factors from all aspects of the process measured
• Measures only what is important	• The measure focuses on a key performance indicator that is of real value to managing the process
• Is multidimensional	• The measure is properly balanced between utilization, productivity, and performance, and shows the trade-offs
• Uses economies of effort	• The benefits of the measure outweigh the costs of collection and analysis
• Facilitates trust	• The measure validates the participation among the various parties

Step 5: Implement and Test the Prototype

This step involves implementing and testing the new logistics measurement prototypes, and collecting data and information. Based on your circumstances and your organization, you will need to decide how many prototype measures to implement simultaneously. It may make sense to work process by process, with one measure for one process and one small group of people at a time. Or, you may decide that it is more effective to implement several measures but with only one customer or supplier. Again, limit the scope to what you can handle successfully, and get it under way. Set up methods to collect, test, and evaluate the data and information to answer the following questions:

- Is the frequency of data collection and reporting appropriate?
- Is it clear who is responsible for collecting the data?
- Does the measure provide managers with the right information to evaluate the performance of the process, and does the data appear to be reliable?
- Will the measure encourage appropriate behavior?
- Is the value of the information worth the cost (time and/or actual dollar cost) of collection?

At this point, you are ready to perform a simple validation check. The evaluation of the measure requires revisiting the goals that you established in Step 3 for frequency, responsibility, and purpose of the measures, and comparing the information you are receiving against those goals. If the information is sufficient to fulfill the purpose, you can move ahead to the next priority, develop that prototype, and continue. If it is not what you wanted, refine this prototype before moving forward. After one or two iterations, logistics managers also can begin to look at the performance of the process, and at the gap between current and desired performance.

- How does the value of the process measure compare with the "future goal"?
- Do the values of the component measures that make up the process measure reveal potential causes for performance compliance or shortfalls?

A note: The simple act of measurement will improve the performance of a logistics activity to some extent, a "Hawthorne effect"[3] if you will. Lasting process improvement, however, likely will require change to the process—and you will need to collect this performance information to know what to change. This will be discussed in more detail in Chapter 6 in the section on *Creating a Case For Action*.

It is also appropriate at this point to begin communicating your results with your management, the people in the operations being measured, and your customers or suppliers (if applicable). Demonstrate the success and share the credit.

Step 6: Refine and Reiterate

Effective measurement can be a large undertaking. In a new program, going too broad and too deep—especially too soon—can spell disaster. The adage of "Ready, Fire, Aim"[4] applies to logistics measurement; rather than developing a long-range plan to roll out a measurement program over several years, it is better to gain organizational momentum by demonstrating a series of small successes. This does not mean to begin your initiative by looking at measurements of narrow logistics functions. Rather, it means first linking together a few key functional measures to establish one or two process measures in the critical areas you identified in your assessment. In other words, demonstrate success in intervals and build momentum.

For instance, referring to Exhibit 5.12, you may decide to focus on Order Entry and Processing in the first iteration. When those measures are in place, your next priority may be Delivery and Receipt. On the third iteration, you might decide to pick up Order Pick/Pack/Ship, and then tie everything together for the complete process measure.

As you return to Step 1, you will have new measures to add to your "existing measures" chart. You may have decided to discontinue measuring something else. The key is to re-evaluate the steps of each iteration in light of the new information and knowledge you acquire.

Small successes will build on each other, improving relationships within the company and between it and its trading partners. As the relationships with trading partners expand, you can expand the

Exhibit 5.12 **PROCESS MEASURE COMPOSITION EXAMPLE**

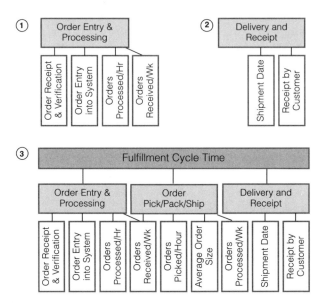

number of contacts between the companies, which will solidify the foundation of measurement.

As you repeat the steps in the measurement development approach, you should consider other areas in which greater analysis will pay additional dividends. Many of these will require analysis unique to your organization, but some areas are common for everyone. Several of these areas will be explored later in this chapter in a section on *Continuous Review and Improvement*, and in the next chapter in *Increasing the Odds for Success*. Before that, however, is the discussion of the final phase.

Step 7: Train and Roll Out

When you have completed several iterations and your measures are defined, tested, and refined, you are ready to prepare your organization to use them. Getting personnel to embrace the measures will be far easier in companies that are culturally predisposed to measurement than in companies in which measurement is not a prevailing practice. Before new logistics measures can be rolled out, logistics managers must communicate the importance of the new measures to all critical constituencies; educate and train the managers and workers about how to utilize the new measures (e.g., how

Linking Measures to Incentives

In 1997, GTE Supply, a major distributor of telecommunications equipment and a unit of GTE Corp., installed an incentive system that linked pay to the performance of work teams and the entire business unit. The new measures and incentives have helped boost team performance significantly.

GTE Supply supplies telecommunications gear to telephone companies, telecommunications manufacturers, and other GTE units. As part of a larger program to measure and improve logistics, the company changed the performance measures and incentives of employees operating in nine U.S. regions and four major warehouses. Today, every employee—hourly or salary, from stock handler to warehouse manager—has 15 percent of his or her annual compensation at risk. Work units are organized by team and measured as a team. The measures for a typical team are as follows:

Supply Core	Quality (Q) or Financial (F) Measure	Threshold	Target	Maximum
Customer Satisfaction Survey (GTE Supply composite)	Q			
Training (hours)	Q			
Return on Investment (total)	F			
Cash Flows - Total Company	F			
Days of Supply - Consolidated	F			
Commercial Net Income	F			
Team Objectives (Logistics)				
Customer Satisfaction Survey (regional/warehouse composite)	Q			
Days of Supply (region/warehouse)	F			
Incurred Cost vs. Budget	F			
Line Item Availability (total and regional)	Q			
Shipping Accuracy	Q			
Inventory Accuracy	Q			
Safety	Q			
Shrink as % of Throughput	F			
Freight as % of Purchases	F			
Overall Regional Performance	Q			

Most of the measures are captured automatically by the company's logistics computer systems; the customer satisfaction survey is conducted by an independent research organization. To ensure the integrity of the measures, the company allows any measure to be subject to an appeals process and/or audit.

Executive management establishes performance goals in each category. The members of a team receive the same rating. If the team is rated at the "threshold" level, team members receive 4.5 percent of their base pay. Achieving a "target" rating means that the team's base pay and bonus are at parity with other workers performing a similar function. To get the full 15 percent bonus, the team must achieve the "maximum" ratings.

Team members hold monthly meetings to discuss progress. They post their results and review them at quarterly breakfasts. Teams get their bonuses annually and, if they meet their goals, celebrate their successes at special luncheons. For those clearing the "threshold" hurdle, it might be pizza. For achieving the top rating of any geographic region, it is a full sit-down-and-be-served, catered affair. In every case, managers review team performance annually and set the next year's goals before they hand out the bonus checks. All employees understand why the team did well, or not so well, and how they contributed to the performance.

In the first year, many employees had a "wait-and-see" attitude. However, when they received the first bonus check, they began to believe. The second year brought good improvements in both operational performance and in their bonuses, and the third year looks even better. Now, employees police themselves and quickly integrate new members into their team. No one wants to let the team down. This makes supervisors' jobs much easier and gives them more time to focus on making further operational improvements. Incentives linked to logistics measures are working at GTE Supply.

to collect the data, how to interpret it into information, and how to make decisions based on that information); and revisit incentive systems to ensure that the behavior required by the new measures will not be impeded by the compensation and other reward systems of the past.

The ability to institute new logistics measures or place more emphasis on measures already in use demands that logistics executives understand how existing measures are reinforced by the company's incentive systems. What are the current incentives and how do they support the performance improvements with customers or with manufacturing that the company must achieve? To get their employees to operate according to the new measures, logistics managers must understand how the current reward system may affect the new measures, and how incentives may have to change.

of computing cost to serve and customer profitability far more achievable than in the past.

YOU CAN DO IT . . . OTHERS HAVE

Companies wishing to realize lasting business change must consider measurement, process, and technology simultaneously. The right process, enabled by the right technology, with that technology capturing the right data as an integral part of the work, will enable logistics managers to work with their trading partners on the entire supply chain and derive benefits for all parties.

The approach and hurdles to logistics measurement that have been discussed may sound like they are too high to traverse. However, research and experience show that they are not. The next chapter profiles three companies with success stories in logistics measurement: Motorola, Modus Media, and 3M. Their experiences provide strong lessons on how to get past the barriers to effective measurement—and the rewards for companies that do.

ENDNOTES

[1] D. Lambert, M. Emmelhainz, and J. Gardner, "Developing and Implementing Supply Chain Partnerships," *The International Journal of Logistics Management*, Vol. 7, No. 2, 1996, pp. 1-17.

[2] A. D. Chandler, *Strategy and Structure - Chapters in the History of the Industrial Enterprise*, The M.I.T. Press, 1962.

7

THREE WINNERS IN ACTION

Looking for a window of opportunity, you may not notice when the door of decision opens. In walks a new CEO or a new manager who is ready to send your corporate culture to the dry cleaners. Or maybe it is a stalker, a competitor with dollars in hand, who wants to acquire your company despite all the unfilled orders that still sit in that database you keep in the basement. Perhaps the person walking through the door is a customer who is dissatisfied with your on-time delivery rate or a supplier who wants to suggest to your employees how they can help save him money through better management of the supply chain.

In this allegory of opportunity, the shadow darkening the doorway may not be a person at all. It may be the specter of reengineering, promising to infuse new levels of efficiency in your operations. Alternatively, it could be the prospect of business failure due to the buckets of red ink spilling forth from your balance sheets. The figure may take any number of shapes, each disguised as a unique opportunity that knocks but once and then disappears unless you open that door, however tentatively, and coax him inside.

In many cases, a number of these visitors come knocking at the same time. Whether your company measures everything possible, or whether it has a history of measuring almost nothing, how wide you open that door of decision will depend on how well you understand the allegory and how prepared your company is to face the issues arising in any of these situations. As stated throughout this book, the companies that are responding successfully to the new challenges are using logistics measurement to help them better understand those forces of change and seize the opportunity when it knocks.

This chapter examines, in detail, three companies from three different industries that have adapted their measurement programs to new demands and opportunities. All three have track records for measuring their logistics processes, although each has conducted the measurement for very different purposes and with somewhat different results. And all three have encountered one or more compelling events—sometimes from internal sources, sometimes from external forces—that have inspired them to measure or to use measurement more effectively.

Motorola Inc., which has a long-standing practice of measuring, seized an opportunity when it hired a new director of distribution for the pager group. In part through his efforts, the division began looking outside its four walls to determine how measurement could improve the supplier and customer relationships it had worked so hard to establish. In the software management and publishing industry, Modus Media International represents a relatively new company on the scene, having been formed in 1981 and spun off in 1997. Like Motorola, Modus Media concentrated primarily on measuring its internal operations, but soon discovered many external opportunities for building better relations with large customers by managing the supply chain for software and software manuals of companies such as Sun Microsystems, IBM, and Microsoft. Finally, 3M is an extremely large and diverse concern with a long history of measurement. It continues to innovate to seize new opportunities from integrating its databases, making information accessible to its customers and suppliers, and presenting "one face" to the outside world. No matter what or how much your company measures, there are important lessons to be learned from these three case studies. Their solutions, of course, may be quite different from the ones you discover, but the steps they have taken can prove instructive for anyone—those just starting out on the journey, as well as well-seasoned travelers. Here, then, are their stories.

MOTOROLA PERSONAL COMMUNICATIONS SECTOR
NORTH AMERICAN PAGING SUBSCRIBER DIVISION

The electronics giant Motorola has a well-deserved reputation for its insistence on logistics measures as a key business activity. After all, the frequently cited measurement Six Sigma—which allows for only a very small number of defects, measured in parts per million—was literally invented here and has been adopted by scores of companies worldwide. From cellular phones to computers to communications satellites, Motorola has operations in some 60 countries and in 1998 had almost $29.4 billion in sales. Despite the size and power of the company, however, one division of Motorola—its North American Pager Subscription Division headquartered in Boynton Beach, Florida—has faced particularly tough challenges from competitors, challenges it is overcoming through better logistics measurement and management.

Problems and Challenges

As noted in Chapter 3, the pager division responded to these market challenges in part by seeking to solidify its relationships with customers such as PageNet, the world's largest wireless messaging company. For the pager division, this effort is affected by several conditions that make this case study exceptional.

First, the division deals with a relatively small number of customers that generally place orders for mixed lots at frequent intervals. Like most companies, a few large customers account for approximately 85 percent of the division's sales. While Motorola manufacturing had a reputation for high standards of quality, some of these customers were finding the company to be inwardly focused, and not as responsive to customers as those customers would prefer. Managers of the division had to find workable solutions that would improve customer satisfaction if they hoped to keep customers loyal. If the division failed to make this case to its customers, Motorola would have to depend completely on product innovations to deter customer flight.

Second, the pager division is completely a make-to-order operation. It rarely manufactures units without firm orders and keeps almost no finished goods inventory. Each pager is individually configured by a unique identification number and carrier frequency signal. Customers also can instruct Motorola to add labels (identifying logos, etc.), load pagers in retail packaging, or put 100 pagers in a single carton for business use. While this aspect of the Motorola pager division distinguishes it from many other companies or manufacturing operations, the principles of logistics measurement, as will be illustrated shortly, remain virtually the same and are universally applicable.

Third, the market for pagers was in transition. Volumes for the low-end items were declining, and the new high-end market was still being defined. Manufacturing was under pressure to do more with less—to increase utilization of equipment, raise productivity, and release manufacturing capacity to other Motorola products. Cross-functional teams were working to design items that were more suitable to postponement (the process of delaying final configuration during production, to customize the final product at the last possible stage). All of these efforts had to be balanced for optimization and lowest total cost.

At one time the division required a 120-day lead time between the receipt of orders and the delivery of products to the customer, but allowed changes in those orders up to the last 30 days before shipment. What resulted is a practice commonly called "booking orders"—customers basically reserved capacity by placing an order, and then changed it as demand became more apparent. Change orders were choking the system and creating havoc in manufacturing. Motorola offered multiple lines of pagers, and it was not unusual for a customer to place an order for several of each style or type. After the manufacturing process began, however, that customer might switch styles, change quantities or even cancel the order altogether, thus increasing Motorola's costs considerably.

Earlier, managers of the pager division measured delivery performance with a measure known internally as Scheduled Ship Dates (SSDs), which measured compliance with the internal committed delivery date. All told, the process, as the division measured it, scored a nearly 93 percent on-time completion rate. When Motorola's salespeople told customers about this achievement, however, the customers had a different story to tell: In fact, shipments did not arrive when customers requested. Instead, it was more a case of "We'll tell you what we can ship, and when we will ship it." In Chapter 4, it was stated that a good measure is *defined and mutually agreed upon*. Motorola's measures were internal measures, and lacked the customer's perspective on measuring the critical components of the business.

Solutions and Implementation

Distribution logistics at Motorola includes all parts of the fulfillment process that occur after a unit is manufactured, up until the time that it arrives in the customer's hands. Thus, at the pager division, distribution is in charge of the value-adding steps that included applying bar codes and labels, packaging, and shipping. Three years ago, customer service was a separate function, and did not speak directly to the customer; all communications passed from the factory through customer service to the sales department, and then on to the customer. This practice is common with many manufacturers. Materials was also a separate function, and was linked with manufacturing.

The problems outlined earlier were threatening Motorola's dominant position in a rapidly changing marketplace. To overcome the problems, several new mid-level managers recognized an opportunity to build cross-functional teams of employees to cooperate, share information, and create alliances with customers.

One of their first steps was to balance the measure of SSD (scheduled shipping date) with CRSD (customer requested ship date). Although a subtle difference in naming, the shift in focus was enlightening and extremely difficult to instill. Any shift from an internal perspective to an external one—this one emphasizing the customer—is difficult to achieve when employees are used to seeing things the other way. The objective in this case was to track the dates on which customers wished to receive shipment, and then close the gap between that date and the ship date committed and actually achieved.

Second, it became clear that there had to be a single point of accountability within the division to become customer-focused. A solution here would require much more subtle and far-reaching changes, because the field sales force could not be expected to manage internal manufacturing processes. In what gradually evolved from a case-by-case, customer-by-customer trial, sales gained confidence in the internal customer service function, and willingly shifted the responsibility for customer communications to them. Now, from the time that orders are placed completely through the fulfillment process, customer service is the single point of contact for the customer.

Third, the internal teams began working more closely with key customers, forming what Motorola called "customer alliance teams." Team members would work on site with a key customer to fully understand its processes, and to determine how each company could minimize costs and maximize value. In some cases, the teams have been able to reduce customer handling costs by 20 percent to

30 percent. The 120-day interval that allowed changes at any time until 30 days before shipment was practically useless: Not only was it rarely adhered to, but it also increased the amount of paperwork in both Motorola's and the customer's systems. For every order, Motorola had 1.5 change orders. While the solution seems obvious now, this change to 30-day order cycles required a major shift in planning cycles and manufacturing philosophy. Capacity was constrained more by materials than by machine capacity. Motorola sources approximately 60 percent of the material content from outside of the region. To make the changes, the company had to closely coordinate sales, materials planning, and plant scheduling. The customer alliance teams are achieving success, being expanded to more customers, and adjusting their make-up by adding members from engineering.

After more than a year of small, step-by-step changes, a new organization had evolved at Motorola Paging Products Group. A group of formerly separate functional areas was now under a common management and responsible for each step of the fulfillment process from demand recognition to customer delivery and follow up. This includes order capture and management, packaging and fulfillment, and post-sale customer service. This new organizational model now is being studied for implementation across other divisions at Motorola.

Scheduling at Motorola follows a process of "entitlements." Each step in the fulfillment process is "entitled" to a certain time frame— as little as two hours, sometimes as much as 48 or 72 hours or more, depending on the product and the activity. The main point is that each step is "time boxed" within its own time frame. The fulfillment process is divided into six groupings of activities, as illustrated in Exhibit 7.1.

If orders move through the process according to schedule, no additional efforts are required. If an order exceeds its entitlement, the entire process becomes subject to team review during short meetings held twice a day. This variation on activity-based management has proven very successful to Motorola. It has allowed a reduction in equipment capacity by 30 percent while increasing equipment utilization by more than 33 percent. Higher targets since have been set. The company clearly is doing more with less.

The changes also have proven beneficial to employees of the pager division. By giving them access to information, they have been

Exhibit 7.1 MOTOROLA FULFILLMENT ENTITLEMENTS

Write to Book 1	**Book to Order Release to Scheduling** 2
Credit Holds	**(ORL)**
Change Orders	Material Issues
Customer Report Card Feedback	Credit Issues
	Customer-Specific Requirements
	Waiting on Queue for Production

OTL to Order Vendor Material (VEND) 3	**Vend to Fabricate (FAB)** 4
Factory Run Rates	Manufacturing
Pull System	Quality Fall-out
Pick Materials	FIFI Order Management
Material Shortages	

FAB to Inbound Audit (IL) 5	**IL to Manifest** 6
Customer Quality Audit (CQA)	Custom Packaging Requirements

empowered to create better customers relationships. Improved capability in information technology has helped streamline the order process and reduce bottlenecks. Process teams now "own" an order from start to finish. As mentioned earlier, if an order falls behind schedule, the team must determine a solution, whether it is clearing up a credit hold or expediting critical materials. In their daily meetings, team members discuss only exceptions and delays, working out ways to bring orders back on schedule, or at worst, to communicate with the customer at the earliest possible stage to discuss alternatives.

Because acquiring available materials is one of the most critical issues in a make-to-order process, Motorola officials also have learned how important it is to work closely and productively with suppliers. This area historically has been one of strength within Motorola. The company has a scorecard for evaluating key suppliers and shares data that allows those suppliers to forecast customer demand. The same scorecard is used across all divisions, as many suppliers work with multiple divisions. With monthly reports and quarterly reviews, suppliers know how they stack up in terms of quality, costs, lead times, inventory turns, and the like. Included in that report is an index showing Motorola's cost of doing business with that supplier, based on the areas just listed. If that index is 1.05, that means that it costs Motorola an extra five cents on the dollar to receive, inspect, and correct materials received from that supplier. Suppliers also are given a chart that compares their performance to that of other suppliers. The message for under-performers becomes very clear.

Furthermore, teams now have the authority to stop a part of the manufacturing process whenever they see that a line is consuming materials that are critical to another order currently on hold. Although each type of pager is unique, they all share a number of components, which are subject to shortages at any time. But now the various division teams have a sharper vision, because they are allowed to see which orders are on stand-by for the arrival of certain parts and the impact that a decision to proceed with one order will have on other orders.

There is a customer quality audit (CQA) performed in the factory, based on criteria that were jointly developed with customers. Essentially, a member of the quality staff assumes the role of the customer and inspects the finished product "through the eyes" of the customer. The key criteria are "fit, feel, finish, and function," combined with customer-specified options and configurations. The pager division also distributes a customer response card with each shipment to track this degree of satisfaction and identify places where the CQA or fulfillment process has broken down. An example of this card is shown in Exhibit 7.2.

If the customer response card indicates a problem that is not part of the CQA, a check for that problem is added immediately to the CQA until it can be determined if the problem is a fluke or has been corrected and controlled. Once again, measurement is used to ensure process control, but not used to measure processes known to be in control.

Results and Benefits

The results of these logistics measures are very encouraging. For one thing, the factory can work around shortages, now that it knows what it can build, what it is waiting for, and how to tightly coordinate the procurement, scheduling, and fulfillment processes. As mentioned earlier, Motorola has reduced manufacturing capacity 30 percent, while production levels are at an all-time high. It has cut factory order batch size and increased order flexibility. Motorola continues to work with suppliers to ensure that they keep a requisite number of components in stock. The division measures those inventory levels to keep the necessary parts coming in, and yet be sure that the suppliers are not carrying too much inventory. The latter would eventually lead to higher total costs in the supply chain as

Exhibit 7.2 MOTOROLA CUSTOMER RESPONSE CARD

01/23/1998   14:58

HELP!

IN OUR CONTINUING EFFORT TO ACHIEVE BETTER CUSTOMER SATISFACTION, WE NEED YOUR

INITIAL PRODUCT PERFORMANCE REPORT

FOR IMMEDIATE HELP PLEASE FAX THIS SHEET TO 1-561-739-3072 OR
CALL 1-800-553-7592 FROM 8:00AM TO 4:30PM E.S.T.

Please return this sheet **immediately** after testing or installation of your unit.

F.O./ITEM/PAGE 2715892127884/001/001

SKU / MODEL   A05UYB5861AA

FREQUENCY   929.212500   QTY   000100

FIRST SERIAL   12AUXS6BN7

FIRST CAP CODE   A075073411111111

FIRST CODE_A   A0750734

COMPANY NAME _____   YOUR NAME _____

PHONE NO. _____   FAX NO. _____

ADDRESS _____

CITY _____ STATE _____ ZIP_____ COUNTRY _____

Tape Here - Fold Here First   Tape Here

NO POSTAGE
NECESSARY
IF MAILED
IN THE
UNITED STATES

BUSINESS REPLY MAIL

FIRST-CLASS MAIL   PERMIT NO 276   BOYNTON BEACH, FL

POSTAGE WILL BE PAID BY ADDRESSEE

(M) MOTOROLA

PAGING PRODUCTS GROUP
PO BOX 3736
BOYNTON BEACH FL 33424-9950

Fold Here Second

PAGER ISSUES   **CONDITION**(Circle one) **QTY**   **DESCRIPTION** (Circle all that apply and explain)

COSMETICS   GOOD / FAIR / DAMAGED _____   BUTTONS / DISPLAY / FEATURES / OTHER _____

OPERATION   GOOD / FAIR / DAMAGED _____   BUTTONS / DISPLAY / FEATURES / OTHER _____

PROBLEM DESCRIPTION _____

UNIT SERIAL NUMBERS _____ / _____ / _____

If more than 4 units are affected, please fax a copy of the packing list or call the number listed above.

ORDER ISSUES: DATE RECEIVED_____   CARRIER: FedEx / UPS / RPS / Other SERVICE TYPE: NEXT DAY / 2NDDAY / Other

	WRONG	MISSING	DAMAGED	QTY	DESCRIPTION
PACKING LIST	☐	☐	☐		
USER GUIDE	☐	☐	☐		
UNIT PACKAGE	☐	☐	☐		
WARRANTY CARD	☐	☐	☐		
ACCESSORIES	☐	☐	☐		
LABELING	☐	☐	☐		
PRODUCT	☐	☐	☐		

SHIPPING CARTON CONDITION: GOOD / FAIR / DAMAGED   DESCRIPTION _____

COMMENTS_____

well as excess inventories due to product obsolescence. This is not
seen as excessive meddling or bureaucracy run amok, for suppliers
stand to gain huge benefits from these logistics measurements. As a

result, not only do these companies remain high on Motorola's list of preferred suppliers, they also minimize their own costs.

It is difficult, if not impossible, to assign strict cause-and-effect relationships between logistics measurements and improvements in productivity and customer satisfaction. That is, one cannot say that having measured the customer complaint rate and instituted various changes in the order fulfillment process, Motorola managers have once and for all solved the problem of customer flight to competitors or found the magic formula that keeps the wheels of production turning without friction. That said, the numbers are suggestive of major improvements across the board. One of Motorola's customers, under the old way of doing business, was getting 30 inventory turns, but had experienced as many as 40 stock-outs per month. Using the new ordering processes, inventory turns were reduced to 14 (as measured in a two-month period), but stock-outs were eliminated. The net result was greater revenue realization and, ultimately, greater profits.

At the same time, Motorola has managed to help customers control their order process better, with the result that the division now receives individual orders for fewer products, but does so on a more frequent and predictable basis, helping to take the lumps out of the demand cycle.

Motorola's own key distribution cycle time—that is, the time from the completion of a product's fabrication until the time it is shipped to a customer—has been reduced from several days to merely a few hours. Ultimately, all of these improvements mean fewer change orders, fewer interruptions to the manufacturing process, and faster distribution, which translates into higher revenues and more satisfied customers.

One word perhaps best sums up the Motorola pager division's accomplishments: discipline. While maintaining the desired casual environment at the division, management has instilled a disciplined approach to securing, processing, and fulfilling orders so that customers remain satisfied and loyal. To be truly disciplined, however, requires an across-the-board acceptance of certain principles: both suppliers and customers have to assume a level of responsibility and be willing to work with each other in what Motorola prefers to call "alliances"—a meeting of equals joined together for their common good. (A "partnership" suggests for the pager division, as it did for Theodore Roosevelt, that someone is probably carrying a big stick.)

Likewise, people within Motorola's pager division have to practice discipline and make hard decisions about ranking orders for production and using components when shortages threaten. However, their decisions can be based on measurements rather than subjective criteria. The process teams now have to be concerned about manufacturing capacity, production levels, machine utilization, and customer responses. The people at Motorola know what it means to win the prestigious Baldrige Award, having done so in 1988. With logistics measures proving to have extraordinary benefits to the pager division, another win may not be far away.

MODUS MEDIA INTERNATIONAL

Modus Media International, a $700 million privately held company headquartered in Westwood, Massachusetts, once exemplified the companies alluded to in Chapter 3 that are data-rich but information-poor. Formerly a division of the publishing company R. R. Donnelley & Sons Company, Modus Media was bred in a culture that demanded data and made decisions based on facts. In its early days, after separation from the parent company, this culture continued. But while systems were in place to measure many things, they lacked the cohesive structure necessary to turn that data into usable information.

Modus Media had its origin as the Documentation Services Group of R. R. Donnelley. Through a variety of mergers, acquisitions, and restructurings, Modus Media became a company in its own right in November 1997. The company provides outsourced supply chain management activities to the high-technology industry, such as hardware assembly, licensing, channel management programs, and, above all, software manufacturing. The latter consists primarily of order management, manufacturing, and order fulfillment for software manuals and compact discs for more than 200 customers such as Microsoft, Sun Microsystems, Hewlett-Packard, IBM, and Intuit. For example, the user manual accompanying shrink-wrapped software or a new computer equipped with Sun's operating system Solaris is almost certain to have been printed and bound at Modus Media. In addition, the company operates call centers and Web sites for software orders for its customers (the technical support sites are separate operations). Modus Media also prints and assembles the manuals and the CDs used in Microsoft training classes, prints and binds the teaching manuals that accompany those discs, and ships the items to any class site in the world.

Problems and Challenges

In 1996, the single biggest problem facing Modus Media (then part of Stream International) was quite simple: It was not as profitable as it wanted to be. Modus Media had invested in information technology and had developed from a culture in which practically everything was measured. The data was available in the organization, but various measures—of finances, business processes, customer satisfaction, and so forth—often were not brought together in ways that could help direct corporate strategy and improve performance.

As often occurs in companies with a high percentage of temporary labor, employees blamed each other for improperly filled or delayed orders, for mistakes in dealing with customers, and for errors that crept into the system. Indeed, the culture was described as "rock-throwing and finger-pointing." Morale ran at a very low level, a sure sign of danger in the quick-paced high-tech industry where people change jobs almost as frequently as they change lanes on the morning commute. Modus Media was not a fun place to work. Many employees simply had no idea of what value they actually brought to the products or the processes they worked on.

One of Modus Media's key customers, Sun Microsystems, had a supplier scorecard with measures for on-time delivery, order fulfillment, quality of products received, and so on. Sun complained to Modus Media managers that Modus Media was not performing at the level Sun expected. In fact, due to its positioning in the supply chain and the use of certain manual systems, Sun was not able to capture actual data on some of the measures, and relied on the manual record-keeping for its purposes. Modus Media believed that it was performing at a higher level than the one Sun was recording, but knew that more information was needed.

In addition, the company was engaged in what had become a commodity business driven by price-sensitive customers. Contracts went to the lowest bidder, and low margins were the order of the day. Clearly, Modus Media needed to reinvent its business. The company needed to leverage its manufacturing flexibility to create a demand-based, "pull" fulfillment process. In addition, it had to use its core competency in measurement to prove to Microsoft, Sun, and other key customers that better management of the supply chain would produce benefits for both trading partners.

Solutions and Implementation

That call was trumpeted throughout the organization: Modus Media had to reorganize itself in order to present a single face to the customer. The company would have to make additional efforts to convert data into useful and accessible information, and place more attention to aligning its measures with those of key customers. Modus Media also would have to implement information systems needed to support the new fulfillment process. In short, it was necessary to create a "culture of measurement" to replace the old culture of "measures for their own sake."

Starting in 1996, the company undertook a number of initiatives, including the following:

- A concerted effort to exit the long-run offset printing business in favor of an on-demand manufacturing platform to fulfill a need for reduced inventory models and highly customized end products

- Selective investments in CD-ROM technology

- Heavy investments in the integration of Web technology with the company's transactional management systems, the upgrading of its MRP systems, and in improved reporting systems, enabling the company to upgrade and tailor these improvements for each customer/program

- Major investments in project and process management training and development

These efforts were guided by the goals set at the corporate level. The leaders of Modus Media identified five key objectives and developed strategies to achieve those objectives throughout the organization. They refer to these objectives as the five "Sine Qua Nons" (Latin—literally translated, "Without Which There Is Nothing"). The goals were:

- Improve profitability of software manufacturing to * percent

- Increase demand manufacturing revenues by * percent

- Increase programs to * percent of total revenue

- Stabilize the I/T infrastructure

- Move to a regional organization structure
  (* indicates quantifiable but confidential information)

The last two objectives are management-oriented and difficult to quantify at the highest levels. These were broken down at departmental levels with measurable goals. The first three objectives were quantifiable and operationally oriented. These were the ones that needed the support and alignment of the entire organization.

One of the first changes the company made was creating a business management structure focused on the key processes. The business unit manager would have responsibility for presenting the company's single "face" to the customer and would, in effect, become the fulfillment process owner. An individual business unit manager was assigned to each major client. Measurements had to be gathered and directed to useful purposes. They were spelled out in "work statements" that specified the services Modus Media offered customers, the cost of those services, and the reports and logistics measures that would provide empirical evidence of a job well done. This statement of work is not a simple document. It contains nine sections, with multiple topics in each section (Exhibit 7.3). It outlines the basic framework for each agreement, but is tailored for each customer, detailing every major segment or channel—sometimes as many as three or four for each customer—as well as the cost of each.

Next, Modus Media managers developed a set of evaluation criteria that were aligned to those used by major customers, especially Sun Microsystems. The principle here is a simple one: Know what your customers expect, give it to them, and keep records that show you have given them exactly what they asked for. Key to keeping Modus Media's measures in line with customers' measures is a negotiated agreement that sets criteria for evaluation and specifies the steps to be taken to *show* that the criteria have been met. Logistics measurement thus takes much (but not all) of the subjectivity out of the equation and gives both the customer and the supplier a set of data on which it is hoped some agreement can be reached.

Exhibit 7.3 **SECTIONS IN MODUS MEDIA STATEMENT OF WORK**

❑ Program Scope and Overview
❑ Financial Management
❑ Information and File Management
❑ Sales and Order Management Operations
❑ Planning, Scheduling, and Manufacturing Operations
❑ Transaction Processes
❑ Key Customer Interfaces
❑ Additional Services
❑ Reports and Metrics

The breakthrough came in the creation of a program that is now called VVA, short for Validating the Value Add. The goal of this program was to link the business strategy directly to the shop floor—to link the performance of each functional unit to the company's performance. Each unit was asked to provide three responses to the simple question, "How do you add value for the customer?" The responses were based on service, productivity, and quality (a variation on the standard theme of time, cost, and quality). Modus Media is a service company. As such, everything it does should add value for the customer. Examples of these statements are as follows:

- In the call center, "I add value by answering 80 percent of all calls within 20 seconds."

- In receiving, "I add value by processing all incoming orders into the MRP system within 4 hours of receipt."

Management then went a key step further by creating a mechanism to track the reasons employees were unable to meet their goals, and then training and empowering them to determine how to resolve the problems (i.e., "root-cause analysis"). Injecting a bit of humor into an otherwise serious effort, managers created a company slogan encapsulated in the abbreviation "MUI" (pronounced "moo-ee"), which stands for "Measure it, Understand it, Improve it." In each work area, a VVA Center was created to display charts that were updated daily and evaluated in weekly meetings. The root-cause charts were posted as well and helped focus the teams to resolve key issues and get benefits quickly. Teams were required to submit success stories on a monthly basis, and to judge each other's submissions, with prizes awarded to the winning teams.

The real change in the Modus Media corporate culture did not come directly from logistics measurement. Rather, it came from employees' realization that someone was actually doing something about a number of long-standing problems. As managers found, the trick is to help everyone see that their work performance does make a difference. Although there was initial resistance throughout the organization, especially from employees who thought that the measures would be turned against them in evaluating job performance and quotas, many soon realized that the new procedures were designed as part of the company's strategy to stay competitive. A shop floor team, for instance, might select three measures, such as the percent of time that the presses were in use, the number of hours a press setup takes, and the number of errors that occur in a press run of, say, 50,000 manuals. The team then would track the results of these measures each week, chart the improvements, and post the results for everyone in the company to see. The three measures became something of a badge of accomplishment for each function. This was not an easy transition, and it did not happen overnight. It involved much more than putting up some signs and standing back to watch. But according to the managers at Modus Media, it has been one of the most rewarding experiences in their careers.

Results and Benefits

Sun's scorecard had the positive result of forcing managers at Modus Media to trap the data already being collected and turn it into useful information. By doing this, Modus Media was able to demonstrate to Sun that its performance was better in some ways than shown by Sun's scorecard. There was also a side benefit to this initiative.

In 1996, a number of companies, including Microsoft, Novell, Dell, Compaq, American Express, and L.L. Bean, had become concerned with the level of service quality provided by outsourcing organizations. The companies developed a set of service levels, called the COPC-2000 Standard, specifying minimum operational requirements in 32 critical function areas. Achieving status as a COPC-certified supplier requires a company to run its business on measures and data, both comparative and absolute, based on how buyers and end users rate their services and products. In addition, current and potential customers are assured that the supplier has systems and methodologies that have been assessed by an independent firm. The programs of linked measurement that Modus Media had put in place allowed its facilities to achieve certification levels on accelerated schedules.

Even more significant, the company began instituting its scorecard with some of its suppliers, thereby extending the logistics measures further upstream and working to align all elements of the supply chain. Rolling out a supplier scorecard program takes time and effort from the customer, and needs an equal commitment on the part of the supplier for it to be successful. In drafting its supplier partnership program, Modus Media was careful to use objective measures to quantify the performance expected from suppliers. An example of the report card is shown in Exhibit 7.4.

To support this report card, Modus Media also gives its suppliers a manual that specifies the criteria and scoring levels for all defects (examples shown in Exhibit 7.5), and it provides suppliers with a Global Metrics Guide that specifies definitions and expectations for all report card measures. These were first developed for internal quality control and assurance, and then combined into the supplier partnership program to ensure uniform quality definitions and levels from supplier to customer.

On the other end of the supply chain, Microsoft (for one) has adopted the measures developed by Modus Media and now uses them in evaluating and managing other suppliers. This is one of the most exciting benefits of logistics measurement, for it has the widest-ranging effects and offers one of the most compelling reasons why such measurement is critical. In effect, it means that Modus Media now sets the standard for its industry and stands ahead of competitors that are struggling to meet the more stringent evaluations. Ultimately, such uniformity serves to strengthen the entire supply chain as each link is forged in the same values and expectations. When the same measures are used up and down the chain, there is less possibility for misinterpretations and frustration. For example, everyone knows what "on-time" delivery means.

Within Modus Media, the reorganization into the business unit structure has led to numerous benefits in productivity and profitability. As noted, one of the compelling events for the company was the realization that it was not sufficiently profitable, and that its long-term survival was threatened if it could not find a way of satisfying its biggest customers. The new focus on measurement with a purpose, however, helped the company achieve a major turnaround. It

Exhibit 7.4 **MODUS MEDIA SUPPLIERS REPORT CARD**

Suppliers Report Card

Supplier:	Quarter:
Number of Receipts:	Date of Review:

Product Quality	Score	Points Available	Points Given	Comments
Incoming Lot Acceptance		20		
MMI Major DPPM<200		10		
MMI Minor DPPM<6,000		10		
Total		40	0	

Receiving

	Score	Points Available	Points Given	Comments
R01 - Damaged		2		
R02 - Documentation		4		
R03 - Incorrect Part		8		
R04 - Incorrect Quantity		4		
R06 - Pkg, Pallet & Skidding		2		
Total		20	0	

Late/Early Delivery

	Points Available	Points Given
Total	30	0

Service

	Points Available	Points Given	Comments
Invoice Inaccuracy	5		
Non-Conforming Material Response	5		
Total	10	0	
Grand Total	100	0	

Critical Deductions:		
Critical Additions:		

Report Card Score	
Status	

Q1/98 =	Q2/98 =	Q3/98 =	Q4/98 =

Improvement Recommendations:

Purchasing Manager:	Quality Manager:

Exhibit 7.5 EXAMPLES OF SCORING CRITERIA

4   Late/Early Delivery

   4.1   <u>On-Time Delivery</u> – 30 points will be awarded for 100% of all deliveries arriving on time based on the agreed delivery date as stated on the P.O. or as amended by the buyer, or up to two working days prior to the agreed delivery date. 1 point will be deducted for each percentage point below 100% on-time delivery.

5   Service

   5.1   <u>Invoice Accuracy</u> – 5 points will be awarded for 100% of invoices received accurate to the final fulfillment of issued purchase orders. 1 point will be deducted for each 1% less.

   5.2   <u>Non-Conforming Material Response</u> – Up to 5 points will be rewarded for timely response to non-conforming material issues as recorded by the buyers and the Quality Control Department. Two points will be deducted for every response taking longer than two working days.

also enabled Modus Media managers to perform an elementary analysis of cost-to-serve and customer profitability. Using this information, the company approached its unprofitable customers to either renegotiate cost and/or service levels, or failing that, to regretfully decline further business.

As expected, a few customers walked, but the company returned to profitability in the first year of the program. In the following year, 1997, revenues were down, but earning before interest and taxes (or EBIT, the company's key financial measure) increased more than 22 percent. In 1998, revenues were up, though still 5 percent below 1996 levels, but EBIT was up almost 77 percent from 1997, and a total of 116 percent over 1996 levels. As a side note, in late 1998, two key competitors announced that they were ceasing operations altogether, or at least in the area with which they competed with Modus Media.

Overall, Modus Media's insistence on measurement with a purpose has proven extremely beneficial. It has enabled managers to tell current and potential customers, "Here's what we have done for Microsoft, for example. And here's what we can do for you. And we've got the data to prove it." To get to this point, however, the company had to undergo major changes in corporate culture and move from a blame-finding mindset to one of cooperation and teamwork. In multiple locations around the United States and around the world, Modus Media has become a much more enjoyable and affirmative place to work.

These improvements have enabled Modus Media to reverse its decline and become a more profitable company by focusing not on the mere collection of data, but on using logistics measures to drive its reorganization and improved relationships with major customers. It is a winner in its industry because it successfully has aligned its corporate strategy from boardroom to shop floor, and because that strategy is based on measures that are meaningful and practical. And it is a winner for the people who make up the company. Measurement has helped Modus Media become a great place to work, because people know what is expected of them, how they can contribute to its success, and how they are doing continually in light of their individual goals.

3M (MINNESOTA MINING AND MANUFACTURING COMPANY) 3M LOGISTICS

St. Paul, Minnesota-based 3M has a well-deserved reputation for doing things by the book of measurement. True, there are stories about the company's sometimes unconventional ways of innovating, such as the serendipitous discovery of a use for an adhesive practically everyone thought was worthless. After all, it would hardly stick to paper, and who would want it? What nobody wanted, however, turned out to be the adhesive that made Post-it notes a household name and an office staple. And that is just one of 3M's 50,000 products, most of which are leaders within their categories. In their drive to be the most innovative enterprise and preferred supplier to their customers, 3M managers have identified three key initiatives for growth:

- Supply chain excellence

- Earning customer loyalty

- "Pacing Plus" (developing significant new products that change the basis of competition)

Innovation is required at 3M. The company's goal is that 30 percent of each year's sales come from products that are less than four years old. This case study is less concerned with product innovation *per se* than with how 3M managers in the company's logistics division are applying that same innovation to supply chain measurement, data warehousing, and customer service—and making fact-based decisions on a worldwide basis.

As an essential business activity, measurement long has been ingrained in the 3M culture. Today, measurement and management tools such as activity-based costing are well established. It is as easy for the company to segment its products by customer as it is to segment customers by products. Among the companies surveyed for this book, 3M ranked at the top of the class in terms of having access to information and being able to analyze, dissect, and manipulate it to discover what the company does best and what it needs to do better.

Problems and Challenges

One of the most obvious problems 3M faces is also one of its claims to fame: namely, its size. It is a $15 billion company, characterized by a diversity of products and customers and more than 40 different business units. From its original interest in manufacturing sandpaper, the company has branched out widely into products ranging from reflective material for license plates to orthopedic pumps, and from Scotch™ brand tapes to electrical connectors. In fact, the company is so diverse that it is unlikely that any single customer—even an industrial supplier or distributor—would deal with all of 3M's business units. While the company is world-renown for its product innovation, it continually searches for innovative ways of managing this diversity and setting corporate strategies that rest on the solid ground of logistics measures.

Nearly all large companies have an ongoing problem with trying to present one face to their customers—one person whom they can contact to answer any question about a purchase order, shipping date, an error in order fulfillment, or damage in transit. Although 3M frequently is cited as an exemplar of customer intimacy, the company believes there is always room for improvement. To quote from a presentation given at the CLM 1998 Annual Conference, "The fact that 3M is a multi-national, multi-division, multi-product company is not our customer's problem." In the past, a large customer might encounter problems in dealing with a number of business units within 3M, each of which had its own profits and losses to contend with. Receiving a single shipment, and a single invoice, from a single order, was nearly impossible.

3M conducted a survey across a sample of its global customer base, asking customers to rank the factors that were of highest importance to them. The results, ranked in order of importance as shown in Exhibit 7.6, were fairly predictable, and at the same time, enlightening.

Exhibit 7.6 3M CUSTOMER SURVEY RESPONSES

- ❑ On-time delivery
- ■ Product performance
- ❑ Response to emergency needs/rush orders
- ❑ Condition of product on delivery (damage to product/packaging)
- ❑ Accuracy of shipment as specified
- ❑ Consistency of delivery (dependable delivery cycle)
- ❑ Capability to deal with emergencies
- ❑ Order status and delivery information
- ❑ Complaint and problem handling
- ❑ Completeness/accuracy of documentation
- ❑ Conformance to customer delivery requirements
- ■ Products manufactured to specific quality standards
- ❑ Orders shipped complete/order completeness
- ❑ In-stock service levels (back-orders/stock availability)
- ❑ Responsive office staff

While 3M is best known as a product innovator, only two of the 15 items selected focused on product (those noted with a black box on the figure). Perhaps customers viewed product as a given, or in some cases as a commodity. In any case, the message was clear—customers obviously value high-quality logistics processes and good customer service.

Solutions and Implementation

Supply chain management recently has become a separate entity and function, serving multiple business units within 3M. Whereas in the past the company had relied on numerous people to coordinate its logistics activities, each with responsibility for a single business function, today one person heads the cross-functional team that coordinates and supports the complex internal logistics processes. That person coordinates the efforts of scores of business units.

3M continually looks for meaningful ways to quantify the relationship between products, services, costs, and customers. Thanks to information technology, the integration of this extensive collection of data that 3M has amassed now allows managers to retrieve information in practically any conceivable format. A number of other logistics innovations help bring the customer focus deeper into 3M's treasure trove of information. To illustrate three of the many, the following will be discussed:

- Customer profitability analysis
- Product/Service Agreements
- InfoMyWay™

Customer profitability analysis presents data to 3M managers on individual customer sales and the costs incurred in manufacturing, distributing, and servicing products. An extensive data warehouse, coupled with activity-based costing and management, has enabled 3M managers to quantify relationships with customers. This allows them to evaluate customer profitability and track the costs incurred in servicing the customer.

Product/Service Agreements (PSAs) pinpoint unique features established for any customer, and specify the services the customer requests and which ones 3M will provide. The goal of the PSAs is to enable 3M business managers to tailor each offering to the particular needs of the customer, estimate the costs of fulfilling special requests, and measure performance against expectations. Key steps in the establishment of a PSA are:

- Understand customer requirements and expectations
- Match the customer's needs with 3M product and services capabilities
- Make commitments based on 3M capabilities and profitability (team-based negotiations)
- Document and communicate the agreement throughout the 3M supply chain
- Measure performance against the agreement

Product/Service Agreements vary in complexity based on customer requirements and 3M capabilities. The agreement can range from a general marketing plan to a formalized, legally binding contract. If 3M could not quantify the cost of providing tailored service, and if it could not measure its performance against its commitment, the PSA would be an empty promise. Measurement is the key to this service.

InfoMyWay™ is a special Internet-based service provided to 3M's customers. After logging in their user names and passwords, customers can place an order and/or check order status, including shipping and billing information. It is available 24 hours a day, seven days a week at https://infomyway.mmm.com.

- *InfoMyWay*™ Order Entry enables customers to send orders to their 3M customer service representatives quickly and securely over the Internet. It is designed to allow fast data entry and smooth navigation.

- *InfoMyWay*™ Order Status enables customers to track the progress of their 3M orders on the Internet. It gives the customer direct, immediate access to information on the status of orders, including estimated ship dates, quantities shipped, carrier name, and reference numbers.

Allowing the day or night access to place and track orders has proven to be very popular with customers, and has the side benefit of cost containment for 3M. This additional service was offered without increasing staff.

Accurate information is obviously a requirement to make all three initiatives work. 3M tracks not only the transactions themselves, but also the number of completed transactions. For example, the system requires a notification of delivery from the carrier to complete the measurement of on-time delivery. Two lines appear on the graph for on-time delivery—the first line indicates the performance against the measurement, and the second shows the percentage of the total transactions tracked. 3M will not estimate or manually enter the delivery date, as this might corrupt its data or damage the credibility of the information. Both measures have performance goals. When the company started tracking this in 1993, it could track only about 30 percent of the transactions. The figure is now more than 90 percent on average.

In early 1999, 3M was receiving more than 35 percent of its orders through electronic data interchange (EDI). It has a target to increase that to 50 percent in the near future, although *InfoMyWay*™ may have an impact in that area. On an EDI order, if the price is incorrect, if a field is not filled in, or if the delivery date is inside the allowed window, the system flags the omission, pushes the order out of the queue, and notifies the customer service representative. This enables the company to more quickly process "clean" orders, and to get incomplete or incorrect orders corrected quickly.

Results and Benefits

These initiatives and others like them support a key strategic focus on logistics excellence. Logistics plays a very large part in supply chain excellence, one of the three areas of 3M's business strategy focus mentioned earlier. Logistics obviously has the support of top management, without which none of these programs would get off the ground. What benefits has this logistics emphasis brought to 3M? For one thing, as mentioned in the opening chapter, it has significantly reduced the cost of logistics as a percent of sales during a five-year period.

3M customers have the opportunity to specify what services they value and discuss how to measure performance. Accordingly, those customers become loyal partners of 3M, which gains a competitive advantage over others in its industry that are unable to keep up the pace.

At the same time, when information is shared with 3M employees, the company has found that people do a better job. Warehouse personnel, for example, monitor the same figures for on-time delivery and order fulfillment that top 3M managers see. With advanced warning about heavy shipment schedules, people can adjust their work schedules, with the result that on-time shipments at regional distribution centers have increased from 85 percent to 98 percent, with no additional employees.

Significant service improvements are another benefit of measurement. 3M instituted its Supply Chain Excellence program in 1995. Using that year as a base, and measuring through the end of 1998, the company has improved domestic on-time delivery by 32 percent. Tracking the last two years of that period, it has improved its intercompany cycle time (a measure of the total cycle time required to replenish non-U.S. companies from U.S. company stock and/or production) by 25 percent.

Making these kinds of improvements requires cross-functional teams using the data to analyze problems and identify areas for continuous improvement. Often it is a problem that can be corrected with the proper application of the data that already has been collected. For instance, as mentioned earlier, EDI transactions now are paired with an automated service that verifies the price of an item before it is billed and shipped. The technology has significantly improved accuracy and reduced discrepancies, which boosts customer satisfaction.

LESSONS FROM LOGISTICS

Stepping back from the details of these three case studies, one sees that the primary theme running through each account is the idea that logistics measurements have many critical uses within the company, that in no case should that data ever be hoarded and guarded as if it were some mythical treasure trove. The culture at 3M is and always has been data-rich and data-based. If anything, it is more so than in the past. Logistics, as noted in Chapter 1, is in the limelight, and nowhere does that light shine brighter than at 3M.

In addition, all three cases show the importance of having someone at or near the top of the organization who champions the effort to include logistics measurement in the big picture of setting strategy. Identifying the compelling events that sound the alarm for change, this champion outlines the reasons why measurement either must be started or how it can be improved and incorporated into the decision-making process. In some cases, that leader will become the owner of the processes that ensure measurement is accessible and accurate. In other cases, especially at very large organizations such as Motorola and 3M, there may be many process owners or teams that oversee the creation and maintenance of a Web site, for instance, or an order-fulfillment process, or product/service agreements such as the ones 3M offers its customers.

Employees, suppliers, and customers—indeed, all stakeholders—have to see that the emphasis on logistics measurement is not just a fad or the project for the day. They must understand that it is an essential part of the company's culture. It is how work is done here and now. As illustrated in the case of Modus Media, employees did not believe that change was possible until they saw the company leaders were behind the effort and that someone took seriously the value that each employee could bring.

The final key to success lies in the ability to demonstrate a quick win, a success story that has relevance to all stakeholders, evidence that there are tangible benefits that employees, suppliers, and customers can enjoy. Money saved is an extremely persuasive argument to those downstream as well as upstream, but the rewards can be felt in other ways as well. Managers at Modus Media, for example, turned the company culture into a much more inviting environment in which to work, thus attracting people in the high-tech industry where salaries and blood pressures tend to run very high.

As will be discussed in the final chapter, the future success of most organizations today will depend on such factors as efficiency of logistics, manufacturing, and order fulfillment processes; customer intimacy, which includes access to databases and information; high-quality products and services; and employees' satisfaction with their workplaces. All of these factors are subject to logistics measurement, as companies such as Motorola, Modus Media, and 3M have discovered and used to their advantage. And there is no shortcut to it. As managers at Motorola might say, it takes *discipline.*

8

PREPARING FOR THE FUTURE

The three case studies presented in Chapter 7—Modus Media, 3M, and Motorola—detail many of the advantages that well-designed logistics measurements can have on bottom lines, revenues, relationships with customers, and employees' work life. Your company may not be as large as Motorola, have as many products in its innovation hopper as 3M, or be as sensitive to customer demands as Modus Media. However, you most likely have just as deep a concern for your company's or business unit's efficiency and profitability as the logistics managers and executives at these three models of supply chain innovation. And it is a sure bet that you are just as concerned about reducing costs while keeping your company on a growth pattern that spells better service and products for customers. In the current business environment, the level of customer satisfaction seems to know no direction but up. Meeting those customers' expectations, however, can take a heavy toll on both your company's personnel and its revenues, at the very time that shareholders demand to see increases in profits and shareholder returns.

One of the main themes of this book is that the *proper* implementation of the logistics measurements that are *right* for your company can help you better manage logistics processes and balance service, cost, and revenue growth. Through achieving this balance, you can *add value* to the way your company delivers its goods. Those italicized terms hold the key to the book's central argument: that measurement is not a panacea, a "one size fits all" program to cure all ills. The book does not suggest that what works for 3M, Modus Media, and Motorola will necessarily work for your company. Each company is unique in that the forces of competition, regulation or deregulation, customer demands, supplier relationships, and corporate goals affect different companies differently. The book does argue, however, that understanding those forces will help you determine which measurements are best for your company.

Whether your company competes on offering the best price, on innovating, on customizing products and services, or on some combination of these objectives, the areas and activities you measure should be commensurate with your corporate strategy, and with how you create value for the customer. If you decide to differentiate customer service by offering features such as a fee-per-call technical support, free upgrades, and discounts on other products or services, this strategy has to mesh with your overall corporate objectives and truly match your customers' demands.

Research for this book has included detailed studies of both large and small companies in a variety of industries and in a number of different kinds of supply chains. It suggests that those executives and managers who understand where their companies stand within their industry and where their industry is heading are the ones who will keep their companies in leadership positions. There is, of course, no crystal ball that will guarantee the forecast of things to come. The business world is too complex, too intertwined with political, economic, cultural, and historical conditions to permit such certainty or arrogance.

The watchword of the revitalized culture built around logistics measurement will be *value*. If a company is keen on competing in the area of product leadership, its leaders must ask how they can reduce time to market in both in-bound and out-bound logistics. If operational excellence is the goal, logistics measurements must drive the company to new heights of efficiency. If the company decides to compete on customer intimacy, it will have to evaluate how much it is willing (and able) to devote to satisfying customers' needs, especially in light of its physical, and fiscal, constraints. None of these options, as has been argued in this book, should be decided by mere intuition.

Logistics measurement must supply the hard data to support executive decisions as momentous as these about how to bring goods to market, and how to create customer value. Only logistics measurement—if relevant, reliable, and replicable—will enable you to show results that are verifiable and can satisfy employees, suppliers, customers, and Wall Street all at the same time. There is a com-

ponent of persuasion that has to occur in any company that elects to go the route of logistics measurement: People must be convinced that the measurements themselves are accurate, purposeful, constructive, and vital to the health of the company. To collect data and use it secretively will only heighten the level of distrust and discontent within the organization. In contrast, by making the information and the results visible in a public format, you can contribute to a culture of openness and honesty.

It does not take a psychologist to point out that customer satisfaction is short-lived. The levels of performance you have defined this year as "on-time" delivery, the "perfect" order, or the "error-free" product can change overnight. Only you and the other members of your supply chain can determine what new levels are acceptable. Once trained or socialized to expect the very best, customers will keep raising the bar on what constitutes the best. For this reason, many companies will have to aim for perfectibility. This is not the same thing as perfection, of course; rather, it is the progress toward perfection.

The history of business has shown that competitive forces and market demands, not to mention the human desire for perfection, have driven companies constantly to improve the quality of their products and services. True, there are many companies where "good

enough" has been the watchword for decades, and no doubt will continue to be for years to come. But fewer leaders today are willing to take this risk, and they recognize that performance records, like the marks of athletic superstars, are only temporary.

Now imagine that you have installed an effective measurement system like the one prescribed in this book. Where previously you had incomplete information that often forced you to make suppositions, you finally have valuable, up-to-the-minute information on your sourcing/procurement and fulfillment processes. You have verified your hypotheses about the strengths and weaknesses of the company's logistics operations. Your hunch about the company's warehouses was correct—that they are too inefficient and too many. But you may not have appreciated the vitality of your transportation activities. In either case, you have the data to understand your company's strengths and weaknesses.

With the right measurements in place, you have clear performance targets in sight, and you know where your operational bottlenecks are. In fact, you know how your operations are performing by the day. Your logistics measures alert you to potential problems before they become real—the inventory buildup in the St. Louis warehouse, the eroding on-time delivery performance of the Atlanta trucking operations. Because you have data on the big picture (your end-to-end process performance) and the small picture (the performance of the activities and tasks that make up those processes), you can get to the bottom of logistics problems. You have gone from looking at the symptoms of your logistics problems to understanding their root cause.

Furthermore, your employees are one step ahead of you. Access to operational information gives them the chance to see what is coming. Drivers know before they leave their warehouse if the priority on their load is urgent or standard. Like 3M's warehouse employees, who get the same measurement data that senior executives get

(such as early alerts to heavy shipping conditions), your people change their work schedules to balance the ebbs and flows of their jobs. Because they know the objectives of their business unit, the team, and themselves, they frequently reorganize their work to boost their performance. Like the employees of Modus Media who turned from skeptics to adherents when they saw how the MUI guideline ("Measure it, Understand it, Improve it") improved the company's logistics performance, they embrace the new measures.

LIFE AFTER MEASUREMENT

After you know how logistics are performing at your company every day, now what? How are your logistics operations likely to change now that their performance is clear at both a high and low level? And how is *your* role likely to change now that you and your team spend far less time gathering information and putting out daily fires? Research and experience shows that a comprehensive logistics measurement program will have at least three major consequences:

1. It uncovers many process problems and becomes the catalyst for continual, and sometimes radical, operational improvement.

2. It frees logistics management from focusing on daily operational problems to concentrate on longer-term strategic issues.

3. It drives those managers to aggressively use information technology to link with supply chain partners and reduce the inefficiencies of their business relationships.

The following pages will explore the profound changes of logistics measurement for companies and their logistics managers. Understanding and preparing for these changes are essential to managing with logistics measures and getting the most out of those measures.

Change #1: The Spotlight Will Shine on Operational Flaws

With tremendous information about how well your logistics processes are meeting the performance goals you have mutually defined with several key customers, and how well several key suppliers are meeting the performance goals you mutually defined with them, your organization's blemishes and warts will become evident. Internal debates about how well the logistics organization was performing and what changes were necessary to improve that performance will subside. The data your measures are generating will end those arguments and point the way to better performance. If that performance is lacking, then managers must determine what it will take to improve, and whether the investment in people, equipment, and time is justified by the expected return.

In other words, logistics managers will be able to take a more surgical approach to process improvement. If their measures suggest

that incremental improvement is all that is necessary—just a matter, for example, of boosting the efficiency of a single warehouse—then the organization will not invest unwisely in a radical process improvement initiative. However, if managers determine that their logistics performance is seriously behind what is necessary for continued market growth, they will know that making operational tweaks is not likely to get them what they need. Used in this manner, logistics measurement becomes the due diligence necessary before anyone launches a logistics operational improvement program. Measurement becomes the case for action—or the case for maintenance, if the vital signs point to robust logistics health.

Given the pace of rapid change in nearly every industry these days, it is more likely that your logistics measures will highlight the need for improvement. But you will have much in your favor at this point: a much better idea about where to begin. Which activities and tasks are the sources of your logistics problems? Which customers are worth improving for (and by how much), given that you now know the gap between their demands and your performance, and (through activity-based costing) what closing that gap will cost and what the return is likely to be? Which customers can you work with jointly to eliminate duplication of effort, unnecessary costs, and other vestiges of an era of arm's-length relationships? Where do you have potential to share assets, rather than just shifting the cost of the asset from one place in the supply chain to another?

When it comes down to choosing customers or suppliers for true supply chain partnerships, there is a simple rule: Work with trading partners that you can trust, that have an equal incentive to improve, and that are in a position to create value in the supply chain. It is impossible to overstate the importance of trust between two companies that want to work together to improve logistics through measurement. The programs between companies like Texas Instruments and Graybar exist only because of a high level of trust between the firms, and a mutual desire for continuous improvement. Discussing operational inefficiencies and measuring performance is bound to expose both companies' flaws. Without trust, companies will not be willing to admit to their inefficiencies; they will worry about being punished by customers if their delivery inadequacies are documented. If one of the purposes of measurement is to eliminate waste from each company's logistics processes—non-value added work, duplication of effort, and so on—both parties must open themselves to each other and look objectively at both operations. Trust is the foundation of a solid logistics measurement program between organizations.

Change #2: From Fire-Fighting to Opportunity-Sighting

With operational improvements identified and made, logistics managers will have helped their companies play catch up to customer demands and competitors' capabilities. Now they will be in a position to make a significant leap forward: taking their supply chain initiatives to the next level (getting more customers and suppliers involved, customers of those customers, and suppliers of those suppliers); deciding whether to outsource logistics activities that others can do better and less expensively; and participating in the increasingly popular senior management activity of "reinventing the business model." That means designing the future logistics model that enhances business performance.

After getting a few customers and suppliers on board, the company will have hard-to-dispute evidence of the benefits that await other customers and suppliers that come to the measurement table. Supply chain partnership or not, the long and often acrimonious arguments over definitions such as what "on-time performance"

really means will have ended. The measures and the systems will be in place to bring on other customers and suppliers. The supply chain initiative can be taken to the next level. Your suppliers' suppliers can understand what their customers are being measured on. In other words, companies in the entire supply chain—from "dirt to dirt"—can see the measures that are driving everyone's performance. Often for the first time, they can see how to erase the duplication of effort, the monumental paperwork, and the unnecessary checks and balances that are hallmarks of companies focused internally rather than externally.

In the next decade, an increasing number of organizations will remove the barriers that slow the flow of information, data, materials, and products up and down the supply chains in which they function. Several barriers were discussed in Chapter 4: the distrust for logistics measurement, the lack of support at the top of the organization, the resistance from employees who feel threatened by the punitive use of performance measures, the absence of clear definitions that everyone in the supply chain understands, and the like. These barriers will fall as companies grow more dependent on their logistics processes and more sophisticated in measuring them.

By understanding the cost and performance of their warehouses, transportation, material-handling, and other activities, logistics managers will have a much greater vantage point for deciding whether to farm out those activities to third parties. Outsourcing of logistics activities—already a pronounced trend—will increase rapidly as logistics managers focus their attention less on commodity logistics functions and more on those functions in which they can add great value. Graybar effectively has staffed Texas Instruments' manufacturing, facilities, and communications stockrooms; Modus Media operates Microsoft's call center; Ingram-Micro configures Compaq computers for the government, educational, and medical markets. These companies operate so closely that it is difficult to determine where one stops and the other starts.

In all cases, logistics measures play a significant part in the governance of the relationship. In choosing an outsourcing partner, measurement is a key criterion. Third-party logistics providers must have the measurement systems of a Caliber Logistics in the automotive business or a Modus Media in the computer industry. (By the way, these companies are not entirely unique; other third-party providers such as Schneider National, Menlo Logistics, and Exel Logistics have demonstrated excellence in measurement systems with their customers.) Managing third-party logistics providers will become a major responsibility for corporate logistics managers. But with measures in place, this task, too, will become far easier to manage.

When they are not talking to trading partners or third-party logistics providers, logistics managers will have more time to spend discussing with senior managers in their organizations about ways to "reinvent the business." With the rapid growth of electronic commerce, many top executives have been asking questions that get to the fundamental premises on which their businesses are based: What value do we really offer our customers? Could someone else offer that value without all the assets (logistics and others) that we have in place? These kinds of discussions are happening with increasing frequency in companies ranging from the mightiest manufacturers (e.g., Procter & Gamble) to the strongest retailers (The Home Depot). It is clear that logistics must be represented at the table when companies consider who has the core competence.

Change #3: IT Will Revolutionize Measurement

The final change in logistics and the logistics profession involves information technology. It is no exaggeration to say that IT—from the Internet and supply chain optimization software to ERP systems and global satellite communications tools—will revolutionize measurement.

The impact of such technologies will unfold in several waves. The first wave, occurring during the next five years or so, will include the standardization of data, dramatically reduced costs of data collection and communication among trading partners, rising frequency of measurement, higher quality logistics, and an increase in the number of companies that are measuring.

- *Standardization of data.* EDI, ERP, and supply chain software packages are forcing companies to adopt common practices for invoicing, bills of material, shipping, and accounting for other key business practices. As more logistics transactions become standardized, measuring performance across the supply chain will become easier.

- *Reducing the cost of data collection and communication.* The high-speed electronic pathways within an organization or between that organization and its trading partners have yielded enormous benefits in the past. These systems have enabled companies to share information in ways that are practically foolproof and secure. Across these lines pass information related to purchase orders, credit approvals, distribution instructions, inventory status, trends in sales, and the like. Furthermore, this network ensures rapid and relevant interchange among trading partners, thus improving the flow of products, services, and information essential to business.

Among the drawbacks of EDI, however, are its high costs and limitation to only those business partners who are part of the network. Because every company that is part of the network must be "wired" to the system and use proprietary software, the initial cost of installation can be staggering. Maintaining the system, building firewalls, and preventing hackers from infiltrating the network requires a constant outflow of money. However, the Internet is in the process of lowering the cost of entry to electronic commerce to a point at which virtually any company can afford it. In fact, a survey of retailers and their suppliers, conducted in December 1998 by CSC and *Retail Info Systems News*, indicates that almost one-fourth of the respondents plan to adopt Web-based EDI within the next year, whereas another 25 percent said that they planned to implement

such a system within two years.[1] The results suggest that many in the retail industry see the value that this electronic capability can bring to supply chain transactions.

Retail giant Dayton Hudson Corp., for example, has signed up to use General Electric's InterBusiness Partner program to communicate online with its employees, customers, and 12,000 vendors via the World Wide Web.[2] By using the Internet to replace or augment EDI, Dayton Hudson is changing the way it communicates with vendors—from labor-intensive, paper-based communication to real-time, online sharing of information. As a result, Dayton Hudson can offer a quick and accurate means for vendors to access time-sensitive procedures and confidential information such as the company's vendor partnership manuals and newsletter. Manufacturing and inventory barriers are broken down and become distant reminders of how business used to be conducted.

- *Accessibility of data:* Whereas Hewlett-Packard and others post performance records daily, imagine the benefits of having up-to-the-minute information on deliveries, inventories, distribution, and supply chain capacity. Although some employees might at first look upon such reporting as excessive, logistics managers can show them the benefits of continuously monitoring performance, in much the same way that the vital signs of a patient in an intensive care unit are monitored every second of the day and night.

Software is becoming available that will act as an activity hub to interrogate trading partners' legacy, ERP, and SCM systems for order and supply data, consolidate it onto servers, and redistribute it to partners along the supply chain. Much more than middleware, this is a Web-based and -hosted service that will act as an integration layer to the supply chain, adding value to the data by building in event tracking and alert capability that track specific orders and shipments through their entire life cycle. As late orders, back orders, short ships, other transactions that affect product supply, and customer shipments are posted to internal systems, the software will collect the information and, in real-time, notify appropriate personnel via browser, e-mail, or fax.[3]

- *Higher-quality logistics processes:* Through increasing use of logistics measurement and growing electronic links between trading partners in a supply chain, reliability and flexibility problems in logistics processes—inconsistent cycle times, incomplete orders, etc.—will decrease dramatically. Increasing measurement by all parties in the chain will mean that everyone identifies its quality problems earlier. Company-to-company communication of orders, invoices, schedules, and plans through EDI and the Internet will reduce the amount of error introduced by manual intervention.

- *Greater reach to trading partners:* According to a 1998 survey of 1,025 plant managers by the National Association of Manufacturers, the number of business-to-business transactions that have been automated has increased to 42 percent, while the number of electronic transactions between product designers and suppliers is 33 percent.[4] Various industry-related sites have sprung up recently, promising to become major virtual centers for order processing, routing, and distribution. Milacron Inc. (www.milpro.com), for example, sells machine tools and products on the Internet to contract manufacturers. Most of the products it sells are in the low-price category (the most expensive costs about $1,000) and can be handled as a regular credit card sale.

If the Internet can provide greater reach, it also can help ensure that the alliances and partnerships are truly collaborative. In the well-oiled network of the future, participants in a supply chain will be able to synchronize their inventories, shipments, replenishments, and forecasts of future demands. The first indications of how powerful such a system can be already are on view at Wal-Mart, which allows selected suppliers to peer behind the curtain and keep tabs on merchandise in every Wal-Mart store. Not a wrench is taken from the shelf and passed through the checkout scanner that an Argus-eyed supplier does not see, record, and order a replacement for. Imagine a supply chain so flawlessly automated that it can detect not only what items in an inventory are sold and when, but can search through a list of specified suppliers, find the one that has the lowest cost, and replenish that inventory—all *without* human intervention.

That is the wave of the future, and riding its crest are companies such as Procter & Gamble, Wal-Mart, and Dell. The success of these

companies reside, in part, in getting the lowest possible costs for the latest products that customers want. Dell manages to do it by reducing its inventory of disk drives, processors, and other components to a minimum, such that it is not left standing with near-obsolete items when the technology changes. Who would want a large supply of 300 MHz processors on hand when Intel is promoting its current version that packs even more power into its punch?

Those will be among the first order of impacts from technology. A second order of impacts could follow. One may very well be that a company's planning/scheduling/forecasting systems automatically drive those of its suppliers. This is Michael Dell's vision for the computer industry:

"Today the whole process of forecasting and resupplying requires human interaction both on our side and on the supplier's side. Given that our factories run on a continuous-flow manufacturing model, we'd like our suppliers to be even more seamlessly linked to us. Our goal is to get to a point where when we use a power supply or disk drive, another one immediately shows up and the supply just keeps replenishing itself, automatically, as we need it."[5]

Nabisco Foods' view of the grocery industry is similar. The company wants to replace forecasting measures with information on actual demand. To react to customer demand and fulfill without stock, the company believes it must replace its forecast with its customers' forecasts. Having more accurate data on real demand, companies will be able to have less inventory in their distribution chan-

Exhibit 8.1 ABSORPTION RATES OF NEW INFORMATION TECHNOLOGIES ARE ACCELERATING

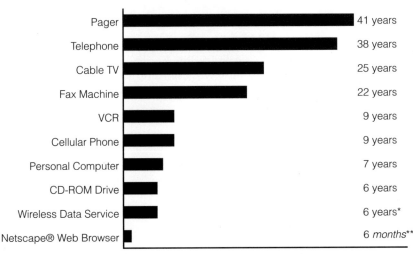

The following is the time it took (or is taking) for these technologies to reach the 10 million customer mark after being introduced to the mass market:

Pager	41 years
Telephone	38 years
Cable TV	25 years
Fax Machine	22 years
VCR	9 years
Cellular Phone	9 years
Personal Computer	7 years
CD-ROM Drive	6 years
Wireless Data Service	6 years*
Netscape® Web Browser	6 *months***

Source: USA Today, Info Tech, Pac Tel Cellular, and Netscape Communications

* Based on a forecast through 1999
** 38 million in 18 months

nels—or at least less inventory collecting dust in warehouses and more inventory in transit. Federal Express's massive investments in package tracking technology is vital to its vision to have its airplanes become "flying warehouses" for companies that want to keep less stock in their own supply lines.

How soon might such a future arrive? The answer to that question, to a great extent, depends on the adoption rates of various new technologies. If history is the gauge, the answer will be sooner than anyone ever thought possible (Exhibit 8.1). While enterprise resource planning (ERP) systems have a way to go before they are ubiquitous—if indeed they ever will be—sales of other, more specialized packages such as warehouse management systems (WMS), transportation management systems (TMS), and advanced planning systems (APS) have been increasing annually. Of the respondents participating in research for this book, for example, more than 78 percent had implemented or were in process of implementing EDI capabilities.

If such a technology future does come to pass, the effect from having so many powerful technologies in place—ERP and supply chain management software, the Internet, global satellite communications systems, barcoding tracking equipment, and so on—will be cumulative. It will mean that corporate logistics operations have the built-in monitors and control systems that factories have enjoyed for some years. A company will be able to control its far-flung logistics processes much the way the manager of a large factory can control his or her factors of production today. However, managers must not assume that any technology will deliver lasting competitive advantage. As the absorption rates continue to drop, the time between early adopters and general usage will continue to shrink.

The point here is to stress the need to stay atop advances in information technology. In logistics, it is so easy for managers to become overwhelmed with the daily details of their work and lose sight of revolutionary forces that are over the horizon. As logistics managers use measurement to get on top, and get ahead, of their operational issues, they will have more time to look up at the big-picture trends. In a business world in which an "Internet year" is a few months, the future will not be one of the big eating the little; it will be one of the fast eating the slow.

In 1996-1997, Apple Computer Inc. lost more than $1.8 billion. In 1997-1998, a 40 percent smaller version of the company made $309

> **"The best way to manage the future is to create it."**
>
> **– Peter Drucker**

million. Analysts and Apple management have placed a significant amount of credit on changes the company made to its logistics processes, and in particular to the focus on inventory brought by a new senior vice president for worldwide operations, Timothy D. Cook. "We've gone from 10 turns to 180 turns... In a year or two, I'd prefer to be able to talk inventory in terms of hours, not days."[6] Whether Apple can sustain growth and profitability likely will continue to depend on the company's historical strength in product innovation. However, the company's resurgence is due in large part to streamlining its logistics to fulfill demand for the iMac in 1998.

This does not mean a company has to be the market share leader to survive, only that it must have the basics in place to keep from falling on its face. One of those basics, as set forth in this book, is a viable logistics measurement system.

A VISION OF THE FUTURE

Imagine a future in which a consumer sits down before her personal computer and, with the wave of a hand or by activating the system with her voice, orders a new car. Using sophisticated technology, she places an order with an automobile manufacturer, chooses a bright red from among hundreds of colors on the palette (or even creates her own version of red) and selects an engine by specifying the number of cylinders and horsepower she wants. She touches her computer screen to feel the eight or ten fabrics (virtual, of course) that might serve for upholstery. Another option lets her hear the actual sound reproduction of six different options for a stereo and CD player.

The choices are innumerable, but this consumer can try out any set of combinations and even get to test-drive her virtual vehicle, without getting up from her computer, before she makes a final decision. Another click away is a lending institution that is willing to record the financial data she submits and instantaneously complete a credit check to guarantee the loan. A final click and the deal is sealed (without the consumer's ever speaking directly to an auto

salesperson). The happy consumer can even arrange to have the new vehicle delivered to her house at the hour of any day she specifies. Now that is one-stop shopping!

Receiving this wealth of data, the auto dealer of the past would have hemmed and hawed, checked inventories, perhaps looked in other states for a vehicle that somewhat matched the customer's request, and promised a similar car in . . . well, three months. That is the auto dealer of the past. In this future scenario, the Internet-empowered dealer would not even have to contact the manufacturer (because all this information would have been forwarded automatically). The auto company would be able to decide almost instantly whether to make or buy a component, whether a supplier in Tokyo or one in Tacoma can construct the stereo system the customer wants at the lowest price, when the special paint job can be scheduled, and what carrier will truck the vehicle to the customer's address. It will be able to offer the buyer a firm idea when her dream car is "available to promise." If the car cannot be delivered on the day the buyer needs it, the car manufacturer will immediately be able to tell her what could be changed on the order to meet her delivery date (e.g., a stereo cassette instead of a CD player), or what the delivery date will be for her current order.

This futuristic supply chain, so well coordinated and collaborative, will be able to keep costs at a minimum while producing a vehicle completely customized to the consumer's specifications. No matter where its trading partners are located, the manufacturer will access data on inventories and distribution so that it can communicate with the consumer and promise delivery on a date that it actually can meet. Since each link in the chain adds value, the resulting product represents a successful collaborative effort in harnessing the forces of change that will have the greatest impact on the supply chain. This entire scenario would be enabled by a set of finely tuned and appropriately measured logistics processes.

The implications of this futuristic scenario have enormous potential for rewriting the book of business and its chapters on logistics and supply chain management. If your company decides to open its databases (at least some of them) to trading partners, to what extent will you allow them to control the workflows that your company now manages? Can that degree of control be rendered mutually beneficial and streamlined up and down the supply chain so that your company, for example, controls suppliers' inventory levels, shipments, and product customization? If you are a supplier, how does this potentially powerful technology affect your strategies and corporate goals, your core competencies, and your ability to compete in the market? Will Internet-based transactions establish an industry-wide standard for certain measures, as opposed to current EDI standards, which may vary widely from business to business or across industries?

In a customer-driven world of e-commerce, which will allow highly customized products and deliveries, manufacturers may well find that they have to deal with fewer returns and reshipments of orders. Able to plan with suppliers, these companies are likely to experience fewer stockouts and higher sales, particularly with the expanded market space available through the Internet. It is within reach to imagine a future in which a product comes with an embedded chip that identifies it and allows one to follow it—much as marine biologists today track the paths of sonar-equipped dolphins, the police trace a stolen vehicle equipped with an anti-theft device, or a veterinarian implants an identifying computer chip in the ear of an animal. Such a product could be tracked at every step of the delivery process, enabling the customer to know its precise time of arrival. Left embedded, the chip might function throughout the product's useful life, enabling a manufacturer to identify exactly who owns the product and where it is located in case there is a need for an upgrade.

Although the most cynical will warn of a world gone mad with embedding chips and measuring activities to the extent that privacy is compromised and confidential material is opened to public scrutiny, this is an area best left to business ethics. As has been argued throughout this book, logistics measurement is only a tool to be used to improve processes and performance. The book's intention is to demonstrate how appropriate uses of logistics measurement can elevate people and companies, enabling them to deliver products in less time, with less effort, and with greater accuracy.

A CALL TO ACTION

Walter Curd, IT vice president at San Jose-based Fujitsu Semiconductors Inc., noted that his company's new Internet site will bring together customers and suppliers in ways never before possible, even down to the customer's ability to see the details of Fujitsu's inventory (a controversial move). Although current customers have not begun clamoring for the new service, Curd observed that "if we wait, it will be too late, because other companies are already doing this. This is the way the world is moving."[7]

For too long, it seems, companies and their suppliers have been heading in the other direction. They have been trying to function productively together, even while they operate at very different levels of technology and logistics measurement. In fact, they have operated at a significant mismatch of capabilities and levels of sophistication. You promise your customers a better order fill rate, but can you be sure your suppliers can get the needed materials to you to complete the order? And what your suppliers actually send you may be far removed from what you have promised to send to your customers. Even worse, you and your suppliers may be using different measures altogether—not unlike an auto mechanic trying to use a set of metric wrenches to repair a vehicle in which all the nuts and bolts are calibrated in inches.

This mismatch between suppliers and customers often has enabled a strong player in an industry to take control and set the standards to which other players in this industry must adhere if they wish to compete. It is particularly evident in the high-tech and telecommunications industries, where the stakes are at astronomical levels, but also can be seen in relatively quiet industries such as steel manufacturing, groceries, and publishing. And pity the technology-challenged supplier that furnishes materials or products to customers in various industries or to many partners in a single supply chain. In situations like this, it seems that measurement standards are written in different alphabets and often require entirely different protocols.

It is a logistics manager's worst nightmare. But it need not disturb your sleep at all, not when a well-designed logistics measurement program can benefit your company by reducing costs significantly, improving customer service, and allowing you to pursue opportunities for new growth. Coupled with Internet-based activity, such a program can help lead to a consensus as to what the standards should be for the industry in which you operate. The discussion may be rancorous at times, and some members of the supply chain (including you) may chafe at the prospect of having to alter their logistics measurements to accommodate the group. But can anyone possibly envision a world free of e-commerce and the Internet? The rule of technology—from the invention of the wheel to the creation of high-definition television—has always been this: Once it empowers people, it is impossible to live without it. And nowhere is that rule more evident than it is in the Internet-based business world, where logistics measurements are used to streamline the work of the supply chain, improve products and services, and enable people to perform at their best.

As Internet-based companies are proving, nearly all supply chains are beset by tremendous amounts of embedded infrastructure, uneven cost profiles, shifted versus shared assets, and general waste—from the supply chains of personal computers and consumer electronics to those of cereal and office furniture. With many products now commodities, dramatically improving the services offered, while controlling and reducing the costs to your company and your customers, is the new competitive differentiator. This is the future of logistics.

This book was written with the hope of greatly accelerating improvement initiatives across supply chains and the logistics activities of companies that make up those chains. To that end, the book has defined a set of measures by which companies can evaluate their and their suppliers' performance to meet customers' ever-rising demands. As important, the book also sought to explain how to implement those measures.

But getting these measurements in place is only the first critical step. Creating logistics operations that improve business performance, and that delight shareholders, customers, suppliers, and employees, requires acting on the report card those measures bring—good or bad. But with the right measures in place, the quest for continual improvement in logistics performance will become far more attainable. These measures will provide companies, their customers, and their suppliers with the roadmap they need to chart their way to supply chain excellence.

ENDNOTES

[1] Computer Sciences Corporation and *Retail Info Systems News*, "Driving Retail Strategy in the 21st Century," supplement to *RIS News*, June 1999.

[2] C. Dion, "They're Webbifying," *Consumer Goods*, March/April 1999.

[3] *The AMR Research Alert on Supply Chain Management*, April 5, 1999.

[4] C. Wilder, "E-commerce: Old Line Movers Online," *Information Week*, January 28, 1999.

[5] M. Dell, (with Catherine Fredman), *Direct from Dell*, HarperBusiness, 1999.

[6] D. Bartholomew, "What's Really Driving Apple's Recovery?" *Industry Week*, March 15, 1999, p. 36.

[7] Ibid., 4.

APPENDICES

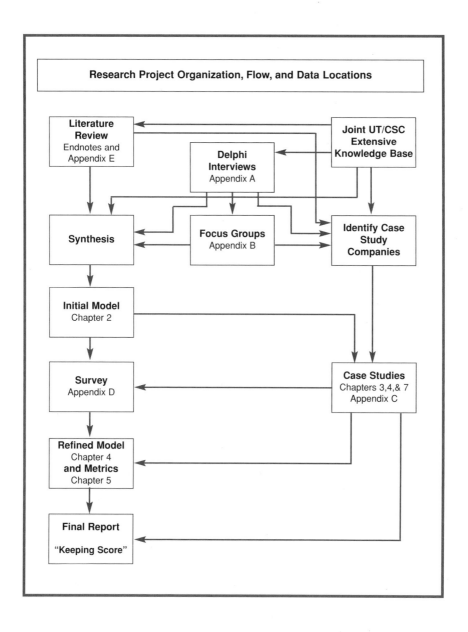

Research Project Organization, Flow, and Data Locations

APPENDIX A
DELPHI STUDY

METHODOLOGY

The Delphi interview methodology allows for the full explication of a topic in a short period of time. This method is helpful in understanding a research area and setting goals and priorities. Surveys are held with subject-matter experts, practitioners, and other professionals. The questions are open-ended, allowing respondents to fully discuss the area without significant parameters. Results are summarized, and areas of consensus and disagreement are provided to the group. A second survey, building on the knowledge gained during the first iteration, typically is developed, administered, evaluated, and summarized.

The Delphi methodology helped ensure that the research team did not overlook key areas for future discussion. The learnings from our inquiry of thought and practice leaders helped guide our case studies and survey questionnaire construction.

We conducted two Delphi surveys. The first was mailed in mid-July 1998 to 103 industry professionals, consultants, and educators. Responses were received in late July and early August. We sent the results of the first survey with the second survey to 101 individuals on August 10, 1998, and received responses in late August. For the first survey, telephone calls were made to people who did not respond by the requested date. For the second round, we sent a fax to each person who had not responded by the requested date. In addition, the offer of complete results to the first survey was made, but that offer could only be accepted by checking a box on the second survey, and returing the response form. In total, we received 25 responses to the first survey, and 27 responses to the second. Of the 27 people who responded to the second survey, 14 had responded to the first round, 11 were new participants, and two responded with letters and comments but not directly to the questions we asked. Sixteen of the 25 respondents to the first survey requested the complete results of the survey. In the first survey, 15 respondents were from industry, eight were consultants, and two were academics. In the second survey, 12 respondents were from industry, two were from government and military, seven were consultants, and four were academics.

		Responses	New Responses	Responded to Previous Survey	Requested Results from 1st Survey	Industry	Government/ Military	Consultants	Academics
Survey	1st	25	25	NA	NA	15	0	8	2
	2nd	27	11	14	16	12	2	7	4

KEY FINDINGS

In the second survey, we asked the participants to define the differences between supply chain management and logistics management, and to identify the key processes within each. Despite all of the literature on the subject and the definitions offered by key organizations (including the Council of Logistics Management), there was a wide disparity in definitions. Some individuals offered narrow definitions of logistics processes, defining them as a sub-set of supply chain processes. Others included many more processes as logistics processes, but maintained the sub-set relationship. One individual indicated no difference between the two. This individual also felt that the term "supply chain" was misleading, as it implies sequential processes, when in reality the supply chain is closer to a complex integrated network of processes.

Measurement initiatives across companies were very much the exception rather than the rule. Among the 12 company respondents to the second survey, only two indicated that their firm had relationships with key customers or suppliers that included shared measurements and initiatives to improve those measurements. Several comments were made with regard to "pockets of excellence," "relatively few but very effective relationships," etc. These are from individuals and companies thought to be among the leaders in supply chain measurement. The barriers to effective intercompany measures and initiatives may be higher than their perceived benefits. We concluded that this area would be a focus of our case studies and broader survey.

The first and second surveys indicated that a key barrier to intercompany and intracompany (cross-functional) measures may be a perceived lack of alignment around key measures, multiple definitions and interpretations of those measures, and the difficulty of comparing measurements of different companies (or even different departments or divisions of a single company). This confirmed the CLM research committee's belief that this research would be critical to the logistics profession. One respondent also offered that "there is too much emphasis on 'measuring' vs. 'doing'..." and that "measuring is important, but we are doing some (things) that we don't yet have good measures for."

One or two people in both surveys recommended that we conduct focus groups in addition to the case studies (and in place of the Delphi surveys). In response to these requests, the research team worked with the CLM Roundtables and conducted focus groups in Cleveland and Dallas in early December 1998. A summary of the methodology and results is in Appendix B.

SUMMARIZED FINDINGS FROM THE FIRST DELPHI STUDY

Please note that comments made in the second survey about the findings of the first survey have been incorporated into the following. In general, response was generally positive, with most people in agreement with the summary. The survey questions are in bold type. The responses are in the general order of frequency.

1. **What business and market factors are stimulating companies to move toward a supply chain process orientation and away from functional silos?**

   – Lower margins and competitive pressures to reduce costs

   – Customer service, customer focus

- Cycle time pressures/demands
- Seeking competitive advantage/regain competitive position
- Continued consolidation of the supplier and customer base
- Increasing complexity of the supply chain due to globalization, slower growth in developed markets, and increased expansion to developing markets.

- **What are the barriers companies face in moving toward a supply chain process orientation?**
- Organizational structure and related issues, such as: resistance to change, lack of infrastructure, lack of leadership commitment, and the lack of trust among partners
- Information technology (I/T) infrastructure: outdated/obsolete, lacking, no funding, Y2K/ERP priorities
- Lack of metrics to measure improvement
- Performance metrics that reward functional/geographical behaviors
- Retaining cost savings within individual corporations
- Absence of new performance measures and objectives that are process spanning rather than functional
- Lack of data

2. **What are the key activity or process measures being used inside companies today?**
- Specific functional measurements (case fill, inventory turns, cycle time, inventory levels, days sales outstanding, costs vs. budget)
- Performance to expectation/requirement (on-time delivery, over/short/damaged)
- Broader measures/process measures are discussed but not being widely used (cash to cash, economic value added, or EVA)

3. **What are the supply chain measures being used between companies today?**

- **Are there generic performance measurements that transcend different industries? What are they?**
- **Are there generic performance measurements that transcend different linkages in the supply chain? What are they?**

(These are grouped, as most responses were similar across the three questions)

- Quantitative measures:
    - On-time delivery, fill rate, "perfect order," order cycle time
- Qualitative measures:
    - Customer satisfaction surveys
    - Process improvement opportunities
- Respondents indicated they were generally dissatisfied with what they are measuring, how well they are measuring, how frequently they are measuring, and the impact of that. Some of this stems from the confusion over definitions and lack of standardization of measures.
    - Example – on-time delivery. As measured against customer's original request, the initial commitment date, or the last revised commitment date?

- **What are the key business-to-business linkages that should be measured (if not referenced above)?**
- Forecast accuracy
- Performance against collaborative planning and goals
- Customer service/satisfaction
- Total supply chain costs (including total channel inventory)/impact on EVA or shareholder value/other economic measures

4. **Please comment on the evolution of the process of measuring activities across firms. What is the current stage? How fast is it evolving? How much progress will occur in the next five years?**

- The current stage is an awareness that it is necessary, but there is a lack of knowledge about how to implement it

- Many organizations, even today, do not have cross-functional performance measures in place
- Evolution will be based on collaboration among firms
- Expect dramatic changes over next five years; logistics measurement likely to become cost of doing business with Tier 1, maybe Tier 2 companies

5. **What will be the effect of electronic commerce on business-to-business performance measurement?**

- Major enabling tool; real-time information availability, common language for data exchange, facilitate standardized measurements, provider of infrastructure to support measurement
- Not a panacea! Will not change anything in and of itself – managers must initiate the changes, and use e-commerce as a tool to facilitate

SUMMARIZED FINDINGS FROM THE SECOND DELPHI STUDY

1. **Much has been written regarding the definition of a supply chain. One such definition states that: "Supply chain management is the integration of business processes from end user through original suppliers that provides products, services, and information that add value for customers." How would you define the difference(s) between Logistics Management and Supply Chain Management?**

- Supply chain management is broader in scope, and encompasses logistics management activities
- Logistics management is functionally oriented, and within a company, where supply chain management focuses on the processes and linkages up and down the channels
- Logistics management is tactical and execution-oriented. It focuses on the physical handling and flow of goods, and on the associated information flows. Supply chain management is more strategic in nature, and involves collaboration among companies. It is focused more on the "conversion processes," and on customer and supplier relationships.

- **What key processes or activities are included in "logistics"?**
  - General consensus as logistics activities
    - Transportation and warehousing (flow and storage of goods and services)
    - Order fulfillment/order entry/order processing
    - Inventory control and management
  - Approximately 75% defined as logistics/25% as supply chain
    - Customer service (except direct customer management activities)
  - Approximately 50% defined as logistics/50% as supply chain
    - Sourcing/procurement/purchasing
    - Planning and scheduling
    - Forecasting
    - Information flows directly related to all of the above processes

- **What key processes or activities are included in "Supply Chain" that are not included in "Logistics"?**
  - General consensus
    - Manufacturing/production
    - Demand management/customer management/sales
    - Product development and commercialization

2. **For discussion purposes, we have hypothesized that many companies are following a path of development from functional measures and benchmarks through process measures to intercompany measures, as further defined below. Please agree or disagree with our premise, comment if you wish, and indicate where you feel your company is on this continuum. Consultants and academics should skip the rating, but please comment on the premises.**

   - *Stage I* – **Awareness of logistics functions and the benefits of supply chain management.**

- *Stage II* – Measuring functional activities within logistics or transportation, and comparing to average and/or best-in-class benchmarks.
- *Stage III* – Identifying underlying factors for performance against Stage II measures, estimating costs and benefits to improve performance, and implementing initiatives.
- *Stage IV* – Measuring intracompany cross-functional processes using measures that are both functional and financial in nature. Estimating costs/benefits and implementing initiatives.
- *Stage V* – Measuring intercompany logistics activities with a customer or supplier.
- *Stage VI* – Structuring a formal or informal relationship with a customer or supplier to measure intercompany activities, how these activities impact intracompany activities and costs, and estimating costs/benefits and implementing initiatives.
- *Stage VII* – Extending Stage VI through more than one link of the supply chain (to customer's customer, supplier's supplier, or supplier to customer).

Based on the above criteria, I estimate that my company is now predominantly in Stage:

I   II   III   IV   V   VI   VII

Based on the same criteria, I estimate that my department/division is now in Stage:

I   II   III   IV   V   VI   VII

- General comments on the ratings and criteria
  - Of 13 respondents, two rated their companies in Stage II, one in Stage III, eight in Stage IV, and two in Stage VI
  - Of 12 respondents, one rated their departments or divisions in Stage II, one in Stage III, seven in Stage IV, and three in Stage VI

- Two of the 14 practitioners had specific com-
  ments on the rating criteria, and urged additional
  emphasis on using the
  information gained vs.
  just measuring
- Four of the seven con-
  sultants objected to the
  ratings criteria in one
  way or another

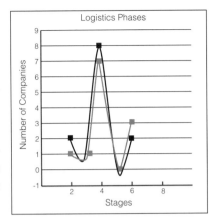

- It was very difficult to rate an entire company, or even a
  department or division, because different functions or
  processes were at different stages. In many cases, the ratings
  reflect "pockets of excellence" rather than overall performance.

COMMENTS

Additional information and guidance in helping managers integrate their initiatives with those of their customers and suppliers, and
in helping them identify the costs and benefits of the initiatives to
which they are applying the measurements, would be of value.

"There is too much emphasis on 'measuring' vs. 'doing.' I agree
that measuring is important, but we are doing some (things) that we
don't yet have good measures for."

APPENDIX B
FOCUS GROUP STUDY

In addition to the two Delphi surveys, we conducted two focus group tests in early December 1998. The CLM Roundtable groups in Cleveland and North Texas (Dallas) agreed separately to use this event for their December meeting. The purpose of these focus groups for the research team was to assure that the scope of the study was appropriate, that all relevant variables were being considered, and that the research was moving in the proper direction.

METHODOLOGY

The attendees were divided into groups (four in Cleveland, three in Dallas), and rotated through a series of rooms. A team of two or three moderators was in each room. The moderators were from CSC and the University of Tennessee. Moderators asked questions and recorded the group's responses on wall charts. The same questions were asked in each room during this time period.

FINDINGS

More than 60 professionals participated in this exercise. The overall findings and discussion with the CLM members validated the findings and the direction of the research team.

SAMPLE QUESTIONS

Time Period 1 – Issues

- What are the critical logistics issues facing your company today?

- Of the list in Question 1, select the three most important issues.

- What is the most critical process in your organization?

- For each of the four processes (defined by the researchers as order fulfillment, customer service, sourcing and procurement, and planning, forecasting, and scheduling), what company would you consider to be "best-in-class" overall?

Time Period 2 – Current State

- What do you measure?

- Which of these are the most important (top 3)?

- For each grouping, are the definitions of these measures consistent among the users?

- Optional – if time permits
    - How often do you evaluate the use of your measures?
    - What is the process for adding or eliminating measures?

Time Period 3 – Impact of the Measures

- Here are the top three measures identified by previous team
    - Agree/Disagree
    - For your organization, why are they the most important?

- Who uses these measures outside of this function (function of the room)?

- Are any of these measures tied to compensation/annual evaluation – if so, which ones, and who (title) do they affect?

- What would you like to measure, but are not currently measuring?
    - What would you need to be able to measure it?

Session 4 – Implementation

- Have you changed what you measure in this process during the past two years?

- What/who are the barriers and/or enablers to the change?

- How does technology impact what you measure?

APPENDIX C
CASE STUDIES

METHODOLOGY

We selected companies for case studies based on the literature review; our perception that they were among the leaders in measuring logistics in their industry; that they were willing to share their measures, barriers, and successes for the study; and that they would allow their company names to be used. We solicited nominations from a variety of sources, including:

- CLM Research Committee members
- CSC and UT team members
- The CSC Supply Chain practice
- Participants in the Delphi surveys and the focus groups

Based on the research direction agreed to by the CLM Research Committee, we targeted the following industries:

- High technology
- Health care
- Automotive
- Consumer package goods

Initially, the intention of the CLM Research Committee and the CSC/UT research team was to locate and interview groupings of three companies that represented a complete local supply chain (supplier, focal firm, and customer), and that were measuring and sharing information on measurements across all three companies. Efforts to locate such companies were unsuccessful. We then focused on identifying companies that were jointly measuring with at least one trading partner.

When we contacted companies, we gave them an introductory background on the study and explained the case study process. The discussion went as follows:

The purpose of the case studies is threefold:

- *to identify process measures being used between companies, and potentially across the supply chain*

- *to understand barriers and benefits associated with developing and implementing these measures*

- *to provide industry with a series of activities that companies can undertake to assess and improve process based performance*

We are focusing on the interaction between a firm and a significant supplier and customer, and look forward to interviewing individuals who can further our understanding. These individuals should have some understanding of how the firms interact, probably at a functional level. We would like to interview individuals knowledgeable in purchasing, order fulfillment, logistics, supply chain management, information technology (as it relates to logistics) and finance. We would like to spend about one to one and one half hours with each person.

In all but three cases, the interview team consisted of at least one participant from CSC and one from the University of Tennessee. The actual format of the interviews varied widely, according to the time and availability of the people to be interviewed. The ideal session lasted a full day, began with a kick-off meeting for all participants, and then proceeded to interviews with individuals from the various functional areas noted above. In some cases, the primary contact from logistics or supply chain management was able to stay with the team the entire day, and provide continuity across sessions. Due to time constraints, four case studies were conducted through telephone interviews.

We distributed an interview guide (see Exhibit A) to all participants, usually in advance, to help them prepare and/or gather support materials, if available. We solicited charts, graphs, and lists of measures, with the strict agreement that only the measures would be used, not their numerical values. When possible, we taped the interviews. If they requested, we sent copies of the transcripts to the key contact in the company. These transcripts were for reference only, and will not be published or released. In all cases, it was agreed with the participating company that we would have their permission for what was published in the book.

RESULTS

In all, we conducted more than 55 in-depth interviews with 22 companies. Initial telephone interviews with several other companies did not result in complete interviews. The companies that declined did so due to time availability of key staff, or a belief that they were not leaders in the area of measurement. Key findings from the case study interviews were used throughout the book. Participating companies included:

3M	Modus Media International
Avery Dennison Corporation	Motorola Inc.
Caliber Logistics Inc.	Nabisco Foods
Compaq Computer Corp.	Owens & Minor Inc.
Defense Logistics Agency	Paging Network Inc.
Graybar Electric Company Inc.	Service Merchandise Company Inc.
H. E. Butt	Sun Microsystems Inc.
Ingram Micro Inc.	Texas Instruments Incorporated
International Paper Company	Tyson Foods Inc.
Loblaw Companies Limited	W. W. Grainger Inc.
The Martin-Brower Company	Welch Foods Inc.

EXHIBIT A
Measuring Logistics Activities in the Supply Chain
Case Study Interview Guide
CLM Process Measurement Project

I. Introductions

II. Purpose of the study

    A. Two major goals of the research project:

        1. Identify the set of high-level logistics performance measures in common use across the supply chain

        2. Understand, synthesize, and present the various ways in which those measures (and the lower-level measures from which they are constructed) are being used throughout the supply chain

    B. Purpose of the case studies

        1. Determine what companies are measuring internally—specifically, what measures are they using to manage their business (not the ones that end up in a thick quarterly report, but the Key Performance Indicators)

        2. Determine the measures that trading partners are using to measure their own performance with the partner, and the partner's performance with them

        3. Determine if incentives are being tied to these measures, and the nature of the incentives

        4. Examine the barriers that companies have to overcome to establish the measures/partnerships, and the benefits that they are achieving from them (in general terms, or percentages—not in real dollars, days, etc; this is not a benchmarking project, although we hope it will facilitate such projects in the future)

        5. Provide the industry with a set of activities that companies can use to assess their own performance measurement level, understand the levels of other companies in their industry, and initiate improvements in their process-based performance and measurement.

III. General questions on I/T implementations and on business and logistics strategy

IV. Interactions with your best supplier (or customer)

    A. What criteria do you use to think of them as "best"?

    B. Can you describe the chronological steps that were taken to move forward together?

    C. What processes do you feel are most important in linking you with this particular supplier (customer)?

        1. Please see generic processes listed in Table 1.

    D. For the most important processes, how would you rank them:

        1. Please see Measurement/Integration Matrix

        2. What are the most important measurements used for the most important processes?

V. In an ideal world, how would you change what or how you measure?

VI. Organizational structure—Enabler? Barrier? Both? Neither?

VII. Summary

    A. What should we have asked that we did not ask?

Table 1
• Order Fulfillment
• Customer Service
• Transportation/Distribution
• Warehousing/Storage
• Planning, Forecasting, and Scheduling
• Information Capability

APPENDIX D
SURVEY

METHODOLOGY

We mailed the survey to 3,185 logistics professionals in the United States and 179 abroad. The mailing list was derived primarily from the membership list of the Council of Logistics Management. The list was edited so that each company received only one survey, which was addressed to the senior logistics or supply chain practitioner. CLM members identified as consultants, academics, and recruiters were also deleted.

The list then was merged with the current Fortune 500® listing, and with the top 150 companies listed in the article "America's Greatest Wealth Creators" from the November 9, 1998, issue of *Fortune*. We added 83 companies from the latter two lists that were not on the CLM list, and that were likely to have significant logistics functions.

To gain a more comprehensive view of the role of logistics and logistics measurement, we surveyed other executives in these companies in addition to logistics professionals—chief information officers, chief financial officers, managers of purchasing and/or sourcing, and managers of customer service. Each mailing to a logistics professional contained an additional survey for one of those four other executives. Logistics managers were then asked to distribute the survey to the proper individual.

The surveys were mailed from December 1-3, 1998, with a requested return date of December 18. A follow-up postcard was mailed December 8. In all, 355 logistics surveys were returned by January 29, 1999. Returned forms were carefully screened to remove duplicates. Of the 3,185 surveys sent to U.S. addresses, notification of bad addresses and recipients who were no longer with the company totaled 28, for a total effective response rate of just over 11%. The respondents approximate the industry sectors of the CLM membership.

Findings

Key findings from the survey can be found primarily in Chapter 2. Additional findings of interest can be found below.

I. ORGANIZATION

The first six slides are from the Organization section of the Survey. This graph shows by percent of respondents how supply chain/logistics management is viewed in their organizations. Respondents stated cost center was the most commonly held view; this clearly demonstrates the continued focus on cost.

This was further evidenced by Exhibit D.2. When respondents were asked to identify the top three issues facing their organization in the coming year, cost control won a clear majority.

Information technology also received a high percent of responses; it is thought that part of the appeal of technology is its ability to reduce or minimize logistics costs.

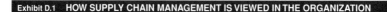

Exhibit D.1   HOW SUPPLY CHAIN MANAGEMENT IS VIEWED IN THE ORGANIZATION

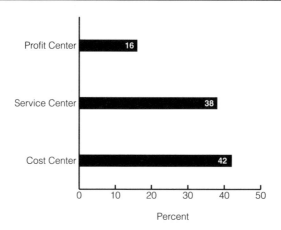

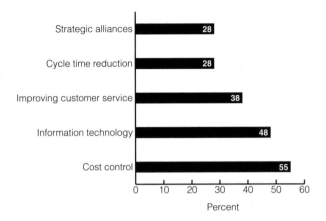

Yet, how will that be accomplished? While we expected the vast majority of companies to have implemented or be implementing an enterprise resource planning (ERP) system, in fact, only 52% had started or completed an ERP solution; a full 33% have no plans to implement an ERP solution in the future. *This is mirrored by the split view regarding transportation management solutions, like Manugistics, i2 Technologies, and Optum.*

Exhibit D.3   USE OF TECHNOLOGY BY RESPONDENTS

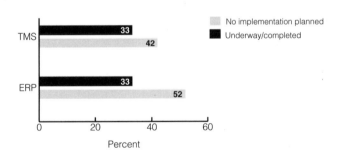

Interestingly, given the focus on cost control, some tools were not well represented in the responses. Specifically, 56% of the respondents were not planning to utilize Advanced Planning & Scheduling (APS) in their organization; the same percentage did not plan to use Activity-Based Costing/Activity-Based Management tools to manage costs. These tools can help minimize logistics and transportation costs.

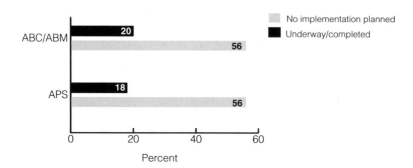

Exhibit D.4 USE OF TECHNOLOGY AND BUSINESS PRACTICES

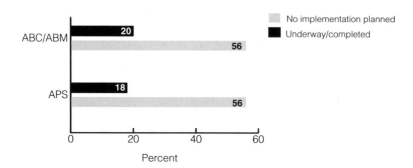

Much as been written about the importance of partnering with customers and suppliers. Partnerships were defined as "Companies have formed *partnerships*, and share significant level of operational integration, each viewing the other as an extension of themselves; no end date planned." Integration was defined as "*Integration* of activities; longer-term focus, but not indefinite; may have multiple divisions and functions within both companies involved." Coordination is exemplified by those firms who, on a limited basis, *coordinate* activities and planning, and are primarily short-term focused.

Exhibit D.5 AVERAGE NUMBER OF RELATIONSHIPS BY A TYPICAL RESPONDENT

	Customers	Suppliers
Partnership	5	5
Integration	10	9
Coordination	28	23
Transactional	713	298

A coordinated relationship may have only one division or functional area from each company involved in the relationship. Finally, transactional relationships are arms-length in nature, and do not require joint commitment or joint operations beyond some limited shared information.

As was expected, the number of partnerships is rather rare— given the other types of relationships a firm can have with customers and suppliers.

II. LOGISTICS MEASURES AND STRATEGIES

The following exhibits further explore how specific logistics measures are used by respondents, and their importance to the organization.

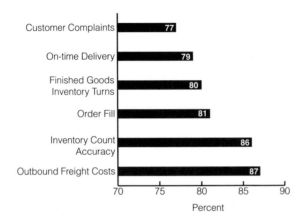

Once again, the respondents highlight the critical importance of cost in the service equation. Exhibit D.7 below highlights some of the least-used logistics measures. Interestingly, but not unexpectedly, these least-used measures are more boundary-spanning in nature, increasing the difficulty in gathering the appropriate level of data.

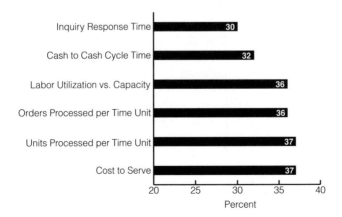

It was also instructive to determine the number of companies that did not calculate or utilize some of the more popular measures in the logistics discipline. A full 21% did not capture on-time delivery on a regular basis in their company; this highlights the need for some firms to focus on the basics before attempting significant change.

Exhibit D.8 PERCENT OF RESPONDENTS NOT UTILIZING POPULAR MEASURES

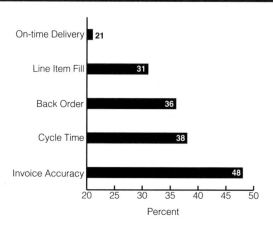

Respondents were then asked to indicate the importance of each measure to the logistics function and to the company overall. The importance of several logistics measures and the extent to which they are used can be found below.

Exhibit D.9 MOST IMPORTANT MEASURES FOR THE LOGISTICS FUNCTION

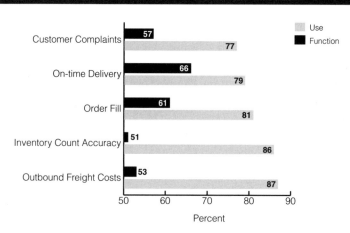

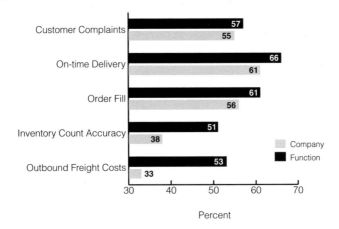

Exhibit D.10 MOST IMPORTANT LOGISTICS MEASURES TO THE COMPANY

Customer Complaints — Function 57, Company 55

On-time Delivery — Function 66, Company 61

Order Fill — Function 61, Company 56

Inventory Count Accuracy — Function 51, Company 38

Outbound Freight Costs — Function 53, Company 33

Company / Function

Percent

In four cases measures were thought to be more important to the company than to the logistics professional. These measures were overall customer satisfaction, cost to serve, days sales outstanding, and invoice accuracy.

Exhibits D.11-D.16 represent an analysis of the data based on how respondents viewed specific processes in relationship to their competitors. Respondents were asked to indicate if they had a major advantage, advantage, parity, disadvantage, or major disadvantage in such processes as customer service, order fulfillment, sourcing, and transportation.

Next, respondents were divided into two groups based on their responses on each process. One group consisted of those who claimed a major advantage or advantage in the process. The second group consisted of those who professed a disadvantage or major disadvantage in the process. Our analysis is based on the significant differences between the two groups.

The following exhibits indicate those measures for which the between-group responses were statistically significantly different at the .05 significance level. Unless otherwise indicated, each response was more important to those that had an advantage in the process than those that did not. It would be beneficial for firms desiring to attain an advantage in these areas to consider the use of the measures, and better understand the importance placed on them.

SIGNIFICANT MEASURES FOR RESPONDENTS HAVING AN ADVANTAGE IN CUSTOMER SERVICE

- **Measures Used**
  - Customer complaints
  - Overall customer satisfaction
  - Cost to serve
  - Inquiry response time
  - Inventory count accuracy
  - Labor utilization vs. capacity
  - Outbound freight costs
  - Cash to cash cycle time
- **Important to the Function/Department**
  - Customer complaints
  - Processing accuracy
- **Important to the Division/Company**
  - Overall customer satisfaction
  - Processing accuracy

SIGNIFICANT MEASURES FOR RESPONDENTS HAVING AN ADVANTAGE IN ORDER FULFILLMENT

- **Measures Used**
  - Overall customer satisfaction
  - Cost to serve
  - Inventory obsolescence
  - Labor utilization vs. capacity
  - Equipment downtime
  - Back orders
  - On-time delivery
  - Perfect order fulfillment
- **Important to the Function/Department**
  - Customer complaints
  - Overall customer satisfaction
  - Back orders
  - On-time delivery
- **Important to the Division/Company**
  - Overall customer satisfaction
  - Units processed per time unit
  - Out of stock
  - On-time delivery
  - Perfect order fulfillment

- **Measures Used**
  - Overall customer satisfaction
  - Cost to serve
  - Inquiry response time
  - Invoice accuracy
  - Processing accuracy
  - Out of stock
- **Important to the Function/Department**
  - Labor utilization vs. capacity
- **Important to the Division/Company**
  - Inbound freight cost

- **Measures Used**
  - Inquiry response time
  - Space utilization vs. capacity
  - Cash to cash cycle time
- **Important to the Function/Department**
  - Product units processed per transportation unit
- **Important to the Division/Company**
  - Case fill
  - Forecast accuracy

- **Measures Used**
  - Inventory carrying costs
  - Equipment utilization vs. capacity
- **Important to the Function/Department**
  - Customer complaints
  - Line item fill
- **Important to the Division/Company**
  - Customer complaints

Exhibit D.16 SIGNIFICANT MEASURES FOR RESPONDENTS HAVING AN ADVANTAGE IN INFORMATION CAPABILITY

- **Measures Used**
  - Customer complaints
  - Overall customer satisfaction
  - Cost to serve
  - Inquiry response time
  - Invoice accuracy
  - Third party storage costs
  - Processing accuracy
  - Labor utilization vs. capacity
- **Important to the Function/Department**
  - On-time delivery
- **Important to the Division/Company**
  - Customer complaints
  - Equipment downtime
  - Out of stock
  - On-time delivery

Exhibit D.17 SIGNIFICANT MEASURES FOR RESPONDENTS HAVING AN ADVANTAGE IN PLANNING/SCHEDULING/FORECASTING

- **Measures Used**
  - Overall customer satisfaction
  - Cost to serve
  - Inquiry response time
  - Invoice accuracy
  - Forecast accuracy
  - Logistics cost per unit vs. budget
  - Product units processed per warehouse labor unit
  - Product units processed per transportation labor unit
  - Labor utilization vs. capacity
  - Equipment utilization vs. capacity
  - Equipment downtime
- **Important to the Function/Department**
  - Product units processed per transportation labor unit
  - Labor utilization vs. capacity
  - Equipment utilization vs. capacity
- **Important to the Division/Company**
  - Over/short/damage
  - Outbound freight
  - Equipment downtime

Respondents were also asked to identify a smaller set of measures that were used by their customers/suppliers to measure their performance. On-time delivery and order fill were the most frequent responses to this question. The importance of these measures can be found in the following exhibit.

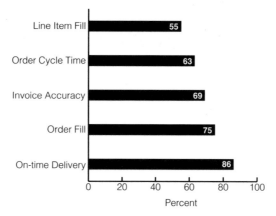

These have consistently been the same measures (and rankings) for several years. The percentage of respondents not measuring some of what is considered "basic logistics measures" is somewhat surprising. Before significant improvement in logistics or supply chain management occurs, we will have to focus on the basics.

As anticipated, on-time delivery was considered to be very important by a large percentage of survey respondents. This is followed by the ability of the respondents to fill orders at a high level.

Exhibit D.19 IMPORTANCE OF MEASURES TO CUSTOMERS/SUPPLIERS

Respondents were also asked to indicate how these measures were defined—that is, were they jointly defined with the customer or supplier, in the process of being defined, under some discussion, customer-defined, or don't know? Clearly, there is significant work to be completed in making certain that measures are defined—and agreed to—by all participants.

Exhibit D.20 IMPORTANCE OF MEASURES TO CUSTOMERS/SUPPLIERS

Measure	Jointly Defined	Customer-Defined
On-time Delivery	31%	29%
Order Fill	25%	33%
Line Item Fill	29%	29%
Invoice Accuracy	28%	30%
Order Cycle Time	25%	25%

Measurement Issues

The research team also explored the enablers or barriers to logistics measurement within and across companies. The following two exhibits highlight the factors that logistics professionals believe are the most significant enablers and barriers to the development and use of logistics measures within a firm.

Exhibit D.21
MOST SIGNIFICANT ENABLERS FOR THE USE AND DEVELOPMENT OF LOGISTICS MEASURES

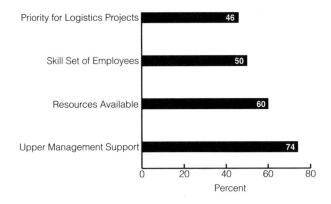

The results indicate that the involvement and support of top management facilitates the development and use of logistics measures. Interestingly, those firms that had achieved a higher level of integration viewed these factors as being more beneficial. Conversely, those firms that were not effectively integrating various activities viewed these factors as significant barriers.

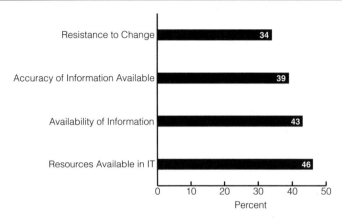

Exhibit D.22
MOST SIGNIFICANT BARRIERS FOR THE USE AND DEVELOPMENT OF LOGISTICS MEASURES

III. PROCESS INTEGRATION

One of the sections of the survey explored how well the seven major processes/capabilities were integrated within and between organizations. In order to assess this integration, a measurement/ integration matrix was developed (please refer to exhibit D.23 below) and provided to respondents. Respondents also could indicate that they were "unaware" of any initiative to measure logistics activities. They were then asked to categorize the state of logistics measurement in each of their processes/capabilities; these results are provided below.

Exhibit D.23 **MEASUREMENT/INTEGRATION MATRIX**

	Intracompany	Intercompany
Integrate	Measuring intracompany cross-functional processes using measures that are both functional and financial in nature. Estimating costs/benefits and implementing initiatives.	Measuring intercompany cross-functional processes using measures that are both functional and financial in nature, estimating costs/benefits to improve, and reaching agreement to implement initiatives that impact both companies.
Coordinate	Identifying underlying factors for performance against measures, estimating costs and benefits to improve performance, and implementing initiatives.	Identifying underlying factors for performance against measures, estimating costs/benefits to improve, and reaching agreement to implement initiatives that impact both companies.
Measure	Measuring functional activities within the company, and comparing to average and/or best in class benchmarks.	Measuring functional activities occurring between two companies, and comparing to average and/or best in class benchmarks.
Aware	Awareness of logistics functions and the potential benefits of logistics management for the company.	Awareness of logistics functions and the potential benefits of supply chain management for the company.

The following exhibits represent the findings of how well integrated (within and between) processes are viewed by the respondents.

The next seven tables define where each of the seven functions responded according to the model.

	Intracompany	Intercompany
Integrate	12%	4%
Coordinate	25	18
Measure	34	37
Unaware/Aware	29	41

One of the major processes in a supply chain is order fulfillment, as it transcends the natural boundaries of the firm. The results of the study show that the level of integration between firms has significant room for improvement.

Exhibit D.25 INTEGRATION MATRIX FOR CUSTOMER SERVICE

	Intracompany	Intercompany
Integrate	11%	5%
Coordinate	27	17
Measure	27	28
Unaware/Aware	35	50

The findings of order fulfillment can also be reiterated for customer service; there is a lot of work yet to be done. It was somewhat surprising to find that only one half of the respondents measured this activity. This also is somewhat inconsistent with those respondents that claim to have had an advantage in customer service.

Exhibit D.26 INTEGRATION MATRIX FOR SOURCING/PROCUREMENT

	Intracompany	Intercompany
Integrate	9%	5%
Coordinate	23	16
Measure	27	21
Unaware/Aware	41	58

The results show that respondents pay less attention to sourcing/procurement activities than to their customer interfaces. Also, this process is the least integrated of the seven processes measured in the study.

Exhibit D.27 INTEGRATION MATRIX FOR TRANSPORTATION/DISTRIBUTION

	Intracompany	Intercompany
Integrate	17%	8%
Coordinate	30	19
Measure	22	25
Unaware/Aware	31	48

As would be expected—given the importance of transportation in logistics—it is not surprising that this process was the most measured and best integrated of the seven. However, it is worth noting that over 30% of the respondents have yet to begin measuring internal activities that are critical to the success of their organization.

Exhibit D.28 INTEGRATION MATRIX FOR WAREHOUSING/STORAGE

	Intracompany	Intercompany
Integrate	**16%**	**6%**
Coordinate	**29**	**16**
Measure	**25**	**18**
Unaware/Aware	**30**	**60**

Warehousing was the second-most integrated process of the seven. However, the focus has been internally oriented; 60% of the respondents have not begun to even measure intercompany activities in this process.

Exhibit D.29 INTEGRATION MATRIX FOR INFORMATION CAPABILITY

	Intracompany	Intercompany
Integrate	**12%**	**4%**
Coordinate	**27**	**17**
Measure	**22**	**25**
Unaware/Aware	**39**	**54**

It is clear from earlier studies and findings that the adoption of information technology is on the upswing. However, the full benefits of these packages have yet to have a significant impact on the integration of information within the firm and between companies.

	Intracompany	Intercompany
Integrate	9%	4%
Coordinate	27	14
Measure	24	24
Unaware/Aware	40	58

Some would argue that planning, forecasting, and scheduling is the most critical process, with the capability of transcending multiple firms. In part, this makes it extremely difficult to efficiently manage. To date, it appears that logistics has been operationally oriented, and has not expended the time and resources necessary to achieve benefits from integration in this area.

IV. DEMOGRAPHICS

To provide context for the findings, respondent demographic information is presented in exhibits D.31-D.33.

Exhibit D.31 PRIMARY BUSINESS OF RESPONDENTS

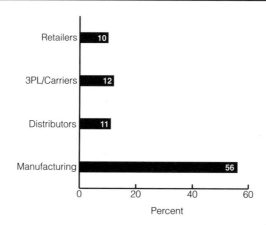

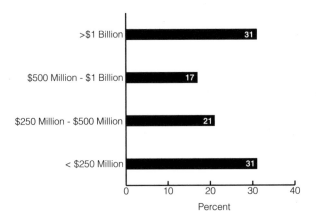

Exhibit D.32 TOTAL SALES OF RESPONDING COMPANIES

>$1 Billion — 31
$500 Million - $1 Billion — 17
$250 Million - $500 Million — 21
< $250 Million — 31

Percent

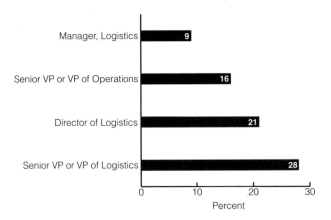

Exhibit D.33 TITLE OF THE SENIOR LOGISTICS POSITION WITHIN THE ORGANIZATION

Manager, Logistics — 9
Senior VP or VP of Operations — 16
Director of Logistics — 21
Senior VP or VP of Logistics — 28

Percent

APPENDIX E
BIBLIOGRAPHY

Adam, Everett E., James C. Hershauer, and William A. Ruch (1981), **Productivity and Quality Measurement as a Basis for Improvement** (Englewood Cliffs, NJ: Prentice Hall, Inc.), pp.126-134.

Aertsen, Freek, "Contracting out the Physical Distribution Function: A Trade-off Between Asset Specificity and Performance Measurement," **International Journal of Physical Distribution and Logistics Management**, Vol. 23, No.1 (1993), pp. 23-29.

Ahire, Sanjay, and Matthew A. Waller, "Incremental and Breakthrough Process Improvement: An Integrative Framework," **International Journal of Logistics Management**, Vol. 5, No.1 (1994), pp. 19-32.

Ailawadi, Jusum L., Norm Borin, and Paul W. Farris, "Market Power and Performance: A Cross-Industry Analysis of Manufacturers and Retailers," **Journal of Retailing**, Vol. 71, No.3 (Fall 1995), pp. 211-248.

Anderson, David L., Frank E. Britt, and Donavon J. Favre, "The Seven Principles of Supply Chain Management," **Supply Chain Management Review**, Vol. 1, No. 1 (Spring 1997).

Anderson, Erin, Leonard M. Lodish, and Barton A. Weitz, "Resource Allocation Behavior in Conventional Channels," **Journal of Marketing Research**, Vol. 24, No.1 (Feb 1987), pp. 85-97.

Anderson, Paul F., and Terry M. Chambers, "A Reward/Measurement Model of Organizational Buying Behavior," **Journal of Marketing**, Vol. 49, No. 2 (Spring 1985), pp. 7-23.

Andre, Rae, "Leading Diverse Management Teams in Logistics," **Journal of Business Logistics**, Vol. 16, No.2 (1995), pp. 65-84.

Andrews, Dorine C., and Susan K. Stalick (1994), **Business Reengineering : The Survival Guide** (Englewood Cliffs, NJ: Yourdon Press Computing).

Anthony, Robert N. (1988), **The Management Control Function** (Cambridge, MA: Harvard Business School Press).

Armitage, Howard M., "The Use of Management Accounting Techniques to Improve Productivity Analysis in Distribution Operations," *International Journal of Physical Distribution and Materials Management*, Vol. 17, No.2 (1987), pp. 40-50.

Armstrong, J. S. (1985), *Long Range Forecasting*, 2nd ed. (New York and Chichester: Wiley).

AT Kearney Inc. (1978), *Measuring Productivity in Physical Distribution: A $40 Million Goldmine* (Oak Brook, IL: National Council of Physical Distribution Management).

AT Kearney Inc. (1984), *Measuring and Improving Productivity in Physical Distribution: The Successful Companies* (Chicago, IL: National Council of Physical Distribution Management).

AT Kearney Inc. (1991), *Improving Quality and Productivity in the Logistics Process: Achieving Customer Satisfaction Breakthroughs* (Chicago, IL: Council of Logistics Management).

AT Kearney Inc. (1995), *Supply Chain Management in the Chemical Industry: A Critical Strategy for Growth*, pp. 2.

Atwong, Catherine T., and Bert Rosenbloom, "A Spatial Approach to Measuring Functional Spin-Offs in Marketing Channels," *Journal of Marketing Theory and Practice*, Vol. 3, No.4 (Fall 1995), pp. 58-72.

Aulakh, Preet S., and Kotabe Masaaki, "Antecedents and Performance Implications of Channel Integration in Foreign Markets," *Journal of International Business Studies*, Vol. 28, No.1 (1997), pp. 145-175.

Austin, Terrence A., and Hau L. Lee, "Unlocking the Supply Chain's Hidden Value: A Lesson From the PC Industry," *Supply Chain Management Review*, Vol. 2, No. 2 (Summer 1998), pp. 24-34.

Baligh, Helmy H., "Components of Culture: Nature, Interconnections, and Relevance to the Decisions on the Organization Structure," *Management Science*, Vol. 40, No.1 (1994), pp. 14-27.

Baligh, Helmy H., "Decision Rules and Transactions, Organizations and Markets," *Management Science*, Vol. 32, No.11 (1986), pp. 1480-1491.

Ballou, Ronald H., and O. K. Helfrich, (1997), *Measuring Physical Distribution Performance*, 1983, National Council of Physical Distribution Management, pp. 836-852.

Ballou, Ronald H., "Reformulating a Logistics Strategy: A Concern for the Past, Present and Future," *International Journal of Physical Distribution and Logistics Management*, Vol. 23, No.5 (1993), pp. 30-38.

Barua, Anitesh, and Byungtae Lee, "An Economic Analysis of the Introduction of an Electronic Data Interchange System," *Information Systems Research*, Vol. 8, No.4 (1997), pp. 398-422.

Bates, Kimberly A., Susan D. Amundson, Roger G. Schroeder, and William T. Morris, "The Crucial Interelationship between Manufacturing Strategy and Organizational Culture," *Management Science*, Vol. 41, No.10 (1995), pp. 1565-1580.

Bechtel, Christian, and Jayanth Jayaram, "Supply Chain Management: A Strategic Perspective," *The International Journal of Logistics Management*, Vol. 8, No.1 (1997), pp. 15-34.

Beier, Frederick J., "The Management of the Supply Chain for Hospital Pharmacies: Inventory Management Practices," *Journal of Business Logistics*, Vol. 16, No.2 (1995), pp. 153-173.

Bensaou, M., and N. Venkatraman, "Configurations of Interorganizational Relationships: A Comparison Between U.S. and Japanese Automakers," *Management Science*, Vol. 41, No.9 (1995), pp. 1471-1492.

Berry, D., and M. M. Naim, "Quantifying the Relative Improvements of Redesign Strategies in a P.C. Supply Chain," *International Journal of Production Economics*, Vol. 46-47 (1996), pp. 181-196.

Bessant, John, Paul Levy, Bob Sang, and Richard Lamming, "Managing Successful Total Quality Relationships in the Supply Chain," *European Journal of Purchasing and Supply Management*, Vol. 1, No.1 (1994), pp. 7-18.

Best, James H. (1990), *The New Competition: Institutions of Industrial Restructuring* (Cambridge, MA: Harvard University Press).

Bhattacharva, Arindam K., Julian L Coleman, Gordon Brace, and Paul J. Kelly, "The Structure Conundrum in Supply Chain Management," *The International Journal of Logistics Management*, Vol. 7, No.1 (1996), pp. 39-48.

Billington, Corey, Hau L. Lee, and Christopher S. Tang, "Successful Strategies for Product Rollovers," *Sloan Management Review*, Vol. 39, No.3 (Spring 1998), pp. 23-30.

Bliemel, Friedhelm, "Inventory Decisions by Trade-Off Analysis: A New Approach in Product-Oriented Marketing Strategies," *Journal of Business Logistics*, Vol. 1, No.2 (1979), pp. 103-119.

Bovet, David, and Yossi Sheffi, "The Brave New World of Supply Chain Management," *Supply Chain Management Review*, Vol. 2, No. 1 (1998).

Bowersox, Donald J., and Phillip L. Carter, "Materials Logistics Management," *The International Journal of Physical Distribution & Logistics Management*, Vol. 15, No.5 (1985), pp. 27-35.

Bowersox, Donald J., and David J. Closs (1996), *Logistical Management*, 4th ed. (Hightstown, NJ: McGraw-Hill Publishing Company).

Bowersox, Donald J., David J. Closs, and Omar K. Helferich (1986), *Logistical Management*, 3rd ed. (New York: Macmillan Publishing Company).

Bowersox, Donald J., M. Bixby Cooper, Douglas M. Lambert, and Donald A. Taylor (1980), *Management in Marketing Channels* (New York: McGraw-Hill).

Bowersox, Donald J., P. L. Daugherty, C. L. Droge, D. S. Rogers, and D. L. Wardlow (1989), *Leading-Edge Logistics: Competitive Positioning for the 1990s* (Oak Brook, IL: Council of Logistics Management).

Bowersox, Donald J., and Cornelia Droge, "Similarities in the Organization and Practice of Logistics Management Among Manufacturers, Wholesalers and Retailers," *Journal of Business Logistics*, Vol. 10, No.2 (1989), pp. 61-72.

Bowersox, Donald J., and Edward A. Morash, "The Integration of Marketing Flows in Channels of Distribution," *European Journal of Marketing*, Vol. 23, No.2 (1989), pp. 58-67.

Bowersox, Donald J., "Introducing the Strategic Visioning Series," *Journal of Business Logistics*, Vol. 19, No.1 (1998), pp. 1-4.

Bowersox, Donald J., "Logistics Paradigms: The Impact of Information Technology," *Journal of Business Logistics*, Vol. 16, No.1 (1995), pp. 65-80.

Bowersox, Donald J., "The Strategic Benefits of Logistics Alliances," *Harvard Business Review*, Vol. 68, No.4 (1990), pp. 36-45.

Bowersox, Donald J., David J. Closs, Thomas J. Goldsby, and Theodore P. Stank, (1998), "World Class Logistics: 1998 North American Research," *Council of Logistics Management Annual Conference Proceedings*, pp.149-166.

Brennan, Charles D., "Integrating the Healthcare Supply Chain," *Healthcare Financial Management*, Vol. 52, No.1 (1998), pp. 31-34.

Brockhoff, Klaus, "R&D Cooperation Between Firms - A Perceived Transaction Cost Perspective," *Management Science*, Vol. 38, No.4 (1992), pp. 514-524.

Bucklin, Christine B., Stephen P. DeFalco, John R. DeVincentis, and John P. Levis, III, "Are you Tough Enough to Manage your Channels?," *McKinsey Quarterly*, No.1 (1996), pp. 104-114.

Busch, Hans F., "Integrated Materials Management," *International Journal of Physical Distribution and Materials Management*, Vol. 18, No.7 (1988), pp. 28-39.

Busher, John R., and Gene R. Tyndall, "Logistics Excellence," *Management Accounting*, Vol. 69, No.2 (1987), pp. 32-39.

Cameron, K.S., "Effectiveness as Paradox: Consensus and Conflict in Conceptions of Organizational Effectiveness," *Management Science*, Vol. 32, No.5 (1986), pp. 539-557.

Camp, Robert C. (1995), "*Business Process Benchmarking*" (Milwaukee, WI: ASQC Quality Press).

Camp, Robert C., and Dan N. Colbert, "The Xerox Quest for Supply Chain Excellence," *Supply Chain Management Review*, Vol. 1, No. 1 (Spring 1997), pp. 82-91.

Caplice, Chris, and Yossi Sheffi, "A Review and Evaluation of Logistics Performance Measurement Systems," *The International Journal of Logistics Management*, Vol. 6, No.1 (1995), pp. 61-74.

Caplice, Chris, and Yossi Sheffi, "A Review and Evaluation of Logistics Metrics," *The International Journal of Logistics Management*, Vol. 5, No.2 (1994), pp. 11-28.

Carlzon, Jan (1987), **Moments of Truth** (Cambridge, MA: Balinger, Inc.).

Carr, Lawrence P., and Christopher D. Ittner, "Measuring the Cost of Ownership," **Cost Management**, (Fall 1992), pp. 42-51.

Carter, Craig R., and Thomas E. Hendrick, "The Development of a Time-Based Construct and Its Impact on Departmental Design and Structure," **International Journal of Purchasing and Materials Management**, Vol. 33, No.4 (Fall 1997), pp. 26-34.

Carter, Joseph R., and Bruce G. Ferrin, "The Impact of Transportation Costs on Supply Chain Management," **Journal of Business Logistics**, Vol. 16, No.1 (1995), pp. 189-212.

Carter, Joseph R., and Jeffrey G. Miller, "The Impact of Alternative Vendor/Buyer Communication Structures on the Quality of Purchased Materials," **Decision Sciences**, Vol. 20, No.4 (Fall 1989), pp. 759-776.

Cavinato, Joseph L., "A Total Cost/Value Model for Supply Chain Competitiveness," **Journal of Business Logistics**, Vol. 13, No.2 (1992), pp. 285-301.

Cavinato, Joseph L., "Evolving Procurement Organizations: Logistics Implications," **Journal of Business Logistics**, Vol. 13, No.1 (1992), pp. 27-45.

Cavinato, Joseph L., "Identifying Interfirm Total Cost Advantages for Supply Chain Competitiveness," **International Journal of Purchasing and Materials Management**, Vol. 27, No. 4 (Fall 1991), pp. 10-15.

Chakravarthy, Balaji S., "Measuring Strategic Performance," **Strategic Management Journal**, Vol. 7, (1986), pp. 437-458.

Champy, James (1996), **Reengineering Management: The Mandate for New Leadership** (New York, NY: Harper Collins).

Charnes, A., W. W. Cooper, and E. Rhodes, "Measuring Efficiency of Decision Making Units," **European Journal of Operational Research**, Vol. 2, No.6 (1978), pp. 429-444.

Checkland, Peter, and Jim Scholes (1990), **Soft Systems Methodology in Action** (New York, NY: John Wiley & Sons).

Chow, Garland, Trevor D. Heaver, and Lennart E. Henriksson, "Logistics Performance: Definition and Measurement," **International Journal of Physical Distribution and Logistics Management**, Vol. 24, No.1 (1994), pp. 17-28.

Chow, Garland, Lennart E. Henriksson, and Trevor D. Heaver, "Strategy, Structure and Performance: A Framework for Logistics Research," **The Logistics and Transportation Review (Canada)**, Vol. 31, No. 4, pp. 285+.

Chow, Garland, "Review of Leading Edge Logistics: Competitive Positioning for the 1990s," **Logistics and Transportation Review**, Vol. 27, No.4 (1991), pp. 384-387.

Christopher, Martin (1992), **Logistics and Supply Chain Management** (London: Pitman Publishing).

Christopher, Martin (1994), **Logistics and Supply Chain Management** (New York, NY: Richard D. Irwin).

Christopher, Martin, "Implementing Logistics Strategy," *International Journal of Physical Distribution and Materials Management*, Vol. 16, No.1 (1986), pp. 52-62.

Churchill, G. A. Jr., "A Paradigm for Developing Better Measures of Marketing Constructs," *Journal of Marketing Research*, Vol. 16 (1979), pp. 64-73.

Clarke, R. L., and K. N. Gourdin, "Measuring the Efficiency of the Logistics Process," *Journal of Business Logistics*, Vol. 12, No.2 (Fall 1991), pp. 17-33.

Clarke, R. L., "The Measurement of Physical Distribution Productivity: South Carolina, A Case in Point," *Transportation Journal*, Vol. 31, No.1 (Fall 1991), pp. 14-21.

Clinton, Steven R., David J. Closs, M. Bixby Cooper, and Stanley E. Fawcett, (1996), "New Dimensions of World Class Logistics Performance," *Council of Logistics Management Annual Conference Proceedings*, p.21.

Closs, David J., and Craig K. Thompson, "Logistics Physical Resource Management," *Journal of Business Logistics*, Vol. 13, No.2 (1992), pp. 269-283.

Cooper, J. C., M. Browne, and M. Peters, "Logistics Performance in Europe: The Challenge of 1992," *International Journal of Logistics Management*, Vol. 1, No.1 (1990), pp. 28-34.

Cooper, Martha C. (1993), "International Supply Chain Management: Implications for the Bottom Line," *Proceedings of the Society of Logistics Engineers*, pp.57-60.

Cooper, Martha C., Douglas M. Lambert, and Janas D. Pagh, "Supply Chain Management: More Than a New Name for Logistics," *The International Journal of Logistics Management*, Vol. 8, No.1 (1997), pp. 1-14.

Cooper, Martha C., and Lisa M. Ellram, "Characteristics of Supply Chain Management and the Implications for Purchasing and Logistics Strategy," *The International Journal of Logistics Management*, Vol. 4, No.2 (1993), pp. 13-22.

Cooper, Martha C., and Lisa M. Ellram, "Meshing Multiple Alliances," *Journal of Business Logistics*, Vol. 18, No.1 (1997), pp. 67-89.

Cooper, Martha C., and Lisa M. Ellram, "Purchasing and Logistics Strategy," *The International Journal of Logistics Management*, Vol. 4, No.2 (1993), pp. 13-24.

Cooper, Martha C., and John T. Gardner, "Good Business Relationships: More than Just Partnerships or Strategic Alliances?," *The International Journal of Physical Distribution & Logistics Management*, Vol. 23, No.6 (1993), pp. 14-26.

Copacino, William C. (1997), *Supply Chain Management: The Basics and Beyond* (The St. Lucie Press/APICS Series on Resource Management).

Copacino, William C., and Donald B. Rosenfeld, "Analytic Tools for Strategic Planning," *International Journal of Physical Distribution and Materials Management*, Vol. 15, No.3 (1985), pp. 47-61.

Cordell, Victor V., "Information Exchange and the Diffusion of Computer Based Information Technologies in U.S. and Japanese Distribution Channels," *Journal of Euromarketing*, Vol. 3, No.3 (1994), pp. 161-175.

Coyle, John J., Edward Bardi, and C. John Langley, Jr. (1988), *The Management of Business Logistics*, 4th ed. (New York: West Publishing Co.).

Cramton, Peter C., "Dynamic Bargaining with Transaction Costs," *Management Science*, Vol. 37, No.10 (1991), pp. 1221-1233.

Croge, C., and R. Germain, "The Impact of the Centralized Structuring of Logistics Activities on Span of Control, Formalization and Performance," *Journal of the Academy of Marketing Science*, Vol. 17, No.1 (1989), pp. 83-89.

Daugherty, Patricia J., Robert E. Sabath, and Dale S. Rogers, "Competitive Advantage through Customer Responsiveness," *Logistics and Transportation Review*, Vol. 28, No.3 (1992), pp. 257-271.

Daugherty, Patricia J., T. P. Stank, and Dale S. Rogers, "The Impact of Formalization on Warehousing Firms," *International Journal of Logistics Management*, Vol. 3, No.2 (1992), pp. 49-61.

Davenport, Thomas H. (1993), *Process Innovation, Reengineering Work through Information Technology* (Boston, MA: Harvard Business School Press).

Davies, Gary, and Eliane Brito, "The Relative Cost of Competing Grocery Supply Chains," *The International Journal of Logistics Management*, Vol. 7, No.1 (1996), pp. 49-60.

Davis, Tom, "Effective Supply Chain Management," *Sloan Management Review*, Vol. 34, No.4 (Summer 1993), pp. 35-46.

Dawe, Richard L., and Dale S. Rogers, (1993), "Using Information Technology to Improve Logistics Competencies," *Council of Logistics Management Annual Conference Proceedings*, pp.79-87.

De Groote, Xavier, Christoph Loch, Ludo Van Der Heyden, Enver Yucesan, and Luk Van Wassenhove, "Measuring Management Quality in the Factory," *European Management Journal*, Vol. 14, No.6 (1996), pp. 540-554.

Delaney, Robert V., "We, The People, Demand Logistics Productivity", *9th Annual State of Logistics Report,* (June 1, 1998), National Press Club, Washington, D.C.

Desai, Preyaas S., and Kannan Srinivansan, "Aggregate Versus Product-Specific Pricing: Implications for Franchise and Traditional Channels," *Journal of Retailing*, Vol. 72, No.4 (Winter 1996), pp. 357-382.

Desiraju, Ramarao, and Sridhar Moorthy, "Managing a Distribution Channel Under Asymmetric Information with Performance Requirements," *Management Science*, Vol. 43, No.12 (1997), pp. 1628-1644.

Dess, G. G., and R. B. Robinson, Jr., "Measuring Organizational Performance in the Absence of Objective Measures: The Case of the Privately Held Firm and Conglomerate Business Unit," *Strategic Management Journal*, Vol. 5, (1984), pp. 267-273.

Dewitt, Fred, "Supply Chain Redesign," *The International Journal of Logistics Management*, Vol. 5, No.2 (1994), pp. 1-9.

Douglas, Susan P., and Samuel C. Craig (1983), *International Marketing Research* (Englewood Cliffs, NJ: Prentice-Hall).

Dowlatshahi, Shad, "Purchasing's Role in a Concurrent Engineering Environment," *International Journal of Purchasing and Materials Management*, Vol. 28, No.1 (Winter 1992), pp. 21-25.

Dresner, Martin, and Kefeng Xu, "Customer Service, Customer Satisfaction, and Corporate Performance in the Service Sector" *Journal of Business Logistics*, Vol. 16, No.1 (1995), pp. 23-40.

Dutta, Shantanu, and Allen M. Weiss, "The Relationship Between a Firm's Level of Technological Innovativeness and its Pattern of Partnership Agreements," *Management Science*, Vol. 43, No.3 (1997), pp. 343-356.

Dwyer, F. Robert, and Sejo On, "A Transaction Cost Perspective on Vertical Contractual Structure and Interchannel Competitive Strategies," *Journal of Marketing*, Vol. 52, No.2 (1988), pp. 23-34.

Eccles, Robert G., and Philip J. Pyburn, "Creating a Comprehensive System to Measure Performance," *Management Accounting*, Vol. 74, No.4 (1992), pp. 41-50.

Eccles, Robert G., "The Performance Measurement Manifesto," *Harvard Business Review*, Vol. 69, No.1 (1991), pp. 131-137.

Eckler, James H., and Paul B. Katz, (1992), "Supply Chain Reengineering for Improved Vendor-Retailer Performance," *Proceedings of Manufacturing International*, pp.113-127.

Edwards, James B. (1986), *The Use of Performance Measures* (Montvale, NJ: National Association of Accountants).

Ellram, Lisa M., and Martha C. Cooper, "Supply Chain Management: Partnerships and the Shipper-Third Party Relationship," *The International Journal of Logistics Management*, Vol. 1, No.2 (1990), pp. 1-10.

Ellram, Lisa M., and Martha C. Cooper, "The Relationship Between Supply Chain Management and Keiretsu," *The International Journal of Logistics Management*, Vol. 4, No.1 (1993), pp. 1-11.

Ellram, Lisa M., "A Managerial Guideline for the Development and Implementation of Purchasing Partnerships," *International Journal of Purchasing and Materials Management*, Vol. 27, No.3 (Summer 1991), pp. 2-8.

Ellram, Lisa M., ""Partnering Pitfalls and Success Factors," *International Journal of Purchasing and Materials Management*, Vol. 31, No.2 (Spring 1995), pp. 36-44.

Ellram, Lisa M., ""Supply Chain Management: The Industrial Organization Perspective," *International Journal of Physical Distribution and Logistics Management*, Vol. 21, No.1 (1991), pp. 13-22.

Emmelhainz, Margaret A., "Strategic Issues of EDI Implementation," *Journal of Business Logistics*, Vol. 9, No.2 (1988), pp. 55-70.

English, Wilke D., "The Impact of Electronic Technology upon the Marketing Channel," *Journal of the Academy of Marketing Science*, Vol. 13, No.3 (Summer 1985), pp. 57-71.

Ernst & Whinney National Distribution/Logistics Group (1987), *Corporate Profitability and Logistics* (Montvale, N.J:, Ernst & Whinney)

Euske, Kenneth J. (1984), *Management Control: Planning, Control, Measurement, and Evaluation* (Menlo Park, CA: Addison-Wesley Publishing Co.).

Farris, M. Theodore II, "Utilizing Inventory Flow Models with Suppliers," *Journal of Business Logistics*, Vol. 1, No.1 (1996), pp. 35-61.

Fawcett, Stanley E., and Steven R Clinton, "Enhancing Logistics Performance to Improve the Competitiveness of Manufacturing Organizations," *Production and Inventory Management Journal*, Vol. 37, No.1 (1996), pp. 40-46.

Fawcett, Stanley E., and D. J. Closs, "Coordinated Global Manufacturing, the Logistics/Manufacturing Interation, and Firm Performance," *Journal of Business Logistics*, Vol. 14, No.1 (1993), pp. 1-25.

Fawcett, Stanley E., and M. Bixby Cooper, "Logistics Performance Measurement and Customer Success," *Industrial Marketing Management*, Vol. 27, No.4 (1998), pp. 341-357.

Fawcett, Stanley E., and D. B. Vellengra, "Transportation Characteristics and Performance in Maquiladora Operations," *Transportation Journal*, Vol. 31, No.4 (Summer 1992), pp. 5-16.

Fawcett, Stanley E., "Logistics and Manufacturing Issues in Maquiladora Operations," *International Journal of Physical Distribution and Logistics Management*, Vol. 20, No.4 (1990), pp. 13-21.

Fawcett, Stanley E., "The Status and Impact of Logistics Issues in the Success of Co-production via Maquiladoras," *International Journal of Logistics Management*, Vol. 2, No.2 (1991), pp. 30-41.

Fernie, John, "International Comparisions of Supply Chain Management in Grocery Retailing," *Service Industries Journal*, Vol. 15, No.4 (1995), pp. 134-147.

Fisher, Joseph, "Use of Nonfinancial Performance Measures," *Journal of Cost Management*, Vol. 6, No.1 (1992), pp. 31-38.

Fisher, Marshall L., "What Is the Right Supply Chain for Your Product?," *Harvard Business Review*, Vol. 75, No.2 (1997), pp. 105-116.

Forrester, Jay W. (1969), *Principles of Systems* (Cambridge, MA: Wright-Allen Press).

Forrester, Jay W., and S. L. Optner (1960), *Systems Analysis* (Englewood Cliffs, NJ: Prentice-Hall, Inc.).

Fortuin, Leonard, "Performance Indicators - Why, Where, and How?," *European Journal of Operational Research*, Vol. 34, (1988), pp. 1-9.

Fradette, Michael, and Steve Michaud (1998), *The Power of Corporate Kinetics* (New York: Simon & Schuster Trade).

Frazier, Gary L., Robert E. Spekman, and Charles R. O'Neal, "Just-In-Time Exchange Relationships in Industrial Markets," *Journal of Marketing*, Vol. 52, No.4 (1988), pp. 52-67.

Fuller, Joseph B., James O'Conor, and Richard Rawlinson, "Tailored Logistics: The Next Advantage," *Harvard Business Review*, Vol. 71, No.3 (1993), pp. 87-98.

Gaski, John F., and John R. Nevin, "The Differential Effects of Exercised and Unexercised Power Sources in a Marketing Channel," *Journal of Marketing Research*, Vol. 22, No.2 (1985), pp. 130-142.

Gassenheimer, J. B., J. U. Sterling, and R. A. Robicheaux, "Long-Term Channel Member Relationships," *International Journal of Physical Distribution and Logistics Management*, Vol. 19, No.12 (1989), pp. 15-28.

Gennotte, Gerard, and Alan Jung, "Investment Strategies under Transaction Costs: The Finite Horizon Case," *Management Science*, Vol. 40, No.3 (1994), pp. 385-404.

Gentry, Julie J., and David B. Vellenga, "Using Logistics Alliances to Gain a Strategic Advantage in the Marketplace," *Journal of Marketing Theory and Practice*, Vol. 4, No.2 (Spring 1996), pp. 37-43.

Germain, R., "Output Standardisation and Logistical Strategy, Structure and Performance," *International Journal of Physical Distribution and Logistics Management*, Vol. 19, No.1 (1989), pp. 21-29.

Germain, Richard, Cornelia Droge, and Patricia J. Daugherty, "A Cost and Impact Typology of Logistics Technology and the Effect of its Adoption on Organizational Practice," *Journal of Business Logistics*, Vol. 15, No.2 (1994), pp. 227-248.

Germain, Richard, Cornelia Droge and Nancy Spears, "The Implications of Just-in-Time for Logistics Organization Management and Performance," *Journal of Business Logistics*, Vol. 17, No.2 (1996), pp. 19-34.

Gilmour, Peter, "Customer Service: Differentiating by Market Segment," *International Journal of Physical Distribution and Materials Management*, Vol. 7, No.3 (1977), pp. 141-148.

Giunipero, Larry C., and Richard C. Brand, "Purchasing's Role in Supply Chain Management," *The International Journal of Logistics Management*, Vol. 7, No.1 (1996), pp. 29-38.

Giunipero, Larry C., and Daniel J. Brewer, "Performance Based Evaluation Systems under Total Quality Management," *International Journal of Purchasing and Materials Management*, Vol. 29, No.1 (Winter 1993), pp. 35-41.

Giunipero, Larry C., "Motivating and Monitoring JIT Supplier Performance," *Journal of Purchasing and Materials Management*, Vol. 26, No.3 (Summer 1990), pp. 19-24.

Glaskowski, Nicholas A., D. R. Hudson, and R. M. Ivie (1992), *Business Logistics*, 3rd ed. (New York: The Dryden Press).

Glassman, David M., and Stern & Stewart Co, "Contracting for Value: EVA and the Economics of Organizations," *The Bank of America Journal of Applied Corporate Finance*, Vol. 10, No.2 (Summer 1997), pp. 110-123.

Gleason, J. M., and D. T. Barnum, "Toward Valid Measures of Public Sector Productivity: Performance Measures in Urban Transit," *Management Science*, Vol. 28, No.4 (1986), pp. 379-386.

Global Logistics Research Team at Michigan State University (1995), *World Class Logistics: The Challenge of Managing Continuous Change* (Oak Brook, IL: Council of Logistics Management).

Global Logistics Research Team at Michigan State University (October 1994), "Global Logistics Best Practice: An Intermediate Research Perspective," *Council of Logistics Management Annual Conference Proceedings*, pp.27-42.

Gomes, R., and John T Mentzer, "The Influence of Just-in-Time Systems on Distribution Channel Performance in the Presence of Environmental Uncertainty," *Transportation Journal*, Vol. 30, No.4 (Summer 1991), pp. 36-48.

Graham, John L., ""The Knowledge Link: How Firms Compete Through Strategic Alliances," *Journal of Marketing*, Vol. 57, No.4 (1993), pp. 149-151.

Graham, T. Scott, Patricia J. Daugherty, and William N. Dudley, "The Long-Term Strategic Impact of Purchasing Partnerships," *International Journal of Purchasing and Materials Management*, Vol. 30, No.4 (Fall 1994), pp. 13-18.

Greis, Noel P., and John D. Kasarda, "Enterprise Logistics in the Information Era," *California Management Review*, Vol. 39, No.4 (Summer 1997), pp. 55-78.

Gustin, Craig M., Patricia J. Dautherty, and Theodore P. Stank, "The Effects of Information Availability on Logistics Integration," *Journal of Business Logistics*, Vol. 16, No.1 (1991), pp. 1-21.

Hakansson, Hakan, and Ivan Snehota (1995), *Developing Relationships in Business Networks* (London: Routledge), pp.18.

Hall, Gene, Jim Rosenthal, and Judy Wade, "How to Make Reengineering Really Work," *Harvard Business Review*, Vol. 71, No.6 (1993), pp. 119-131.

Hall, Richard H. (1999), *Organizations: Structures, Processes and Outcomes,* Seventh Edition, (New York and London: Prentice-Hall).

Hammel, Todd R., and Laura R. Kopczak, "Tightening the Supply Chain," *Production and Inventory Management Journal*, Vol. 34, No.2 (1993), pp. 63-70.

Hammer, Michael, and James Champy (1993), *Reengineering the Corporation : a Manifesto for Business Revolution* (New York: Harper Business).

Hammer, Michael, "Reengineering Work: Don't Automate, Obliterate," *Harvard Business Review*, Vol. 68, No.4 (1990), pp. 104-112.

Handfield, Robert B., and Ernest Z. Nichols (1998), *Introduction to Supply Chain Management* (Englewood Cliffs, NJ: Prentice Hall Press).

Harding, Forrest E., "Logistics Service Provider Quality: Private Measurement, Evaluation, and Improvement," *Journal of Business Logistics*, Vol. 19, No.1 (1998), pp. 103-120.

Harr, David J., and James T. Godfrey, "The Total Unit Cost Approach to Government Financial Management," *Government Accountants Journal*, Vol. 40, No.4 (Winter 1992), pp. 15-24.

Harrington, H. James (1991), *Business Process Improvement: The Breakthrough Strategy for Total Quality, Productivity, and Competitiveness* (New York: McGraw-Hill, Inc.).

Harrington, Thomas C., Douglas M. Lambert, and Martin Christopher, "A Methodology for Measuring Vendor Performance," *Journal of Business Logistics*, Vol. 12, No.1 (1991), pp. 83-104.

Harrington, Thomas C., Douglas M. Lambert, and Jay U. Sterling, "Simulating the Financial Impact of Marketing and Logistics Decisions," *International Journal of Physical Distribution and Logistics Management*, Vol. 22, No.7 (1992), pp. 3-12.

Harrison, Alan, "Co-Makership as an Extension of Quality Care," *International Journal of Quality & Reliability Management*, Vol. 7, No.2 (1990), pp. 15-22.

Haughton, Michael A., and Alan J. Stenger, "Modeling the Customer Service Performance of Fixed-Routes Delivery Systems under Stochastic Demand," *Journal of Business Logistics*, Vol. 19, No.1 (1998), pp. 155-172.

Hauser, John R., and George I. Clausing, "The House of Quality," *Harvard Business Review*, Vol. 66, No.3 (1988), pp. 63-73.

Haves, Robert H., and Gary P. Pisano, "Beyond World-Class: The New Manufacturing Strategy," *Harvard Business Review*, Vol. 72, No.10 (1994), pp. 77-87.

Heide, Jan B., and John George, "Alliances in Industrial Purchasing: The Determinants of Joint Action in Buyer-Supplier Relationships," *Journal of Marketing Research*, Vol. 27, No.1 (1990), pp. 24-36.

Heiko, Lance, "Some Relationships Between Japanese Culture and Just-In-Time," *The Academy of Management Executive*, Vol. 3, No.4 (1989), pp. 319-321.

Hendricks, Kevin B., and Vinod R. Singhal, "Delays in New Product Introductions and the Market Value of the Firm: The Consequences of Being Late to the Market," *Management Science*, Vol. 43, (1997), pp. 422-436.

Hewitt, Frederick (1992), "Supply Chain Integration," *Council of Logistics Management Annual Conference Proceedings*, pp.334-341.

Hewitt, Frederick, "Supply Chain Redesign," *The International Journal of Logistics Management*, Vol. 5, No.2 (1994), pp. 1-9.

Hillman, Willis T., Mike Mathews, and C. Richard Huston, "Assessing Buyer/Planner Performance in the Supply Network," *International Journal of Physical Distribution and Logistics Management*, Vol. 20, No.2 (1990), pp. 16-21.

Hoffman, Gerald M. (1994), *The Technology Payoff: How to Profit with Empowered Workers in the Information Age* (New York, NY: Irwin Professional Publishing).

Hofstede, Geert (1980), *Culture's Consequences* (London: Sage Publications), pp.14 and 373-374.

Holland, Chris, Geoff Lockett, and Ian Blackman, "Planning for Electronnic Data Interchange," *Strategic Management Journal*, Vol. 13, No.7 (1992), pp. 539-550.

Houlihan, John B., "International Supply Chain Management," *International Journal of Physical Distribution and Materials Management*, Vol. 15, No.1 (1885), pp. 22-38.

Huchzermeier, Arnd, and Morris A. Cohen, "Valuing Operational Flexibility Under Exchange Rate Risk," *Operations Research*, Vol. 44, No. 1 (Jan./Feb. 1996), pp. 100-113.

Hunt, Kenneth A., "The Relationship between Channel Conflict and Information Processing," *Journal of Retailing*, Vol. 71, No.4 (Winter 1995), pp. 417-436.

Hunter, J. E., F. L. Schmidt, and G. B. Jackson (1982), *Meta-Analysis: Cumulating Research Findings Across Studies* (New York: Sage).

Jobson, J. D., and R. Schneck, "Constituent Views of Organizational Effectiveness: Evidence from Police Organizations," *Academy of Management Journal*, Vol. 25, No.1 (1982), pp. 25-46.

Johnson, Jean L., Tomoaki Sakano, Joseph A. Cote, and Naoto Onzo, "The Exercise of Interfirm Power and Its Repercussions in the U.S.-Japanese Channel Relationships," *Journal of Marketing*, Vol. 47, No. 2 (1993), pp. 1-10.

Johnson, M. Eric, and Tom Davis, "Improving Supply Chain Performance by Using Order Fulfillment Metrics," *National Productivity Review*, Vol. 17, No.3 (Summer 1998), pp. 3-16.

Jones, Thomas C., and Daniel W Riley, "Using Inventory for Competitive Advantage Through Supply Chain Management," *International Journal of Physical Distribution and Materials Management*, Vol. 15, No.5 (1985), pp. 16-26.

Juran, Joseph M. (1988), *Juran on Planning for Quality* (New York, NY: The Free Press).

Kahn, Kenneth B., and John T. Mentzer, "EDI and EDI Alliances: Implications for the Sales Forecasting Function," *Journal of Marketing Theory and Practice*, Vol. 4, No.2 (Spring 1996), pp. 72-78.

Kaplan, Robert S., and Robin Cooper (1997), *Cost and Effect: Using Integrated Cost Systems to Drive Profitability and Performance* (Boston, MA: Harvard Business School Press), pp.384+.

Kaplan, Robert S., and David P. Norton, "Putting the Balanced Scorecard to Work," *Harvard Business Review*, Vol. 71, No.5 (1993), pp. 134-142.

Kaplan, Robert S., and David P. Norton, "The Balanced Scorecard - Measures That Drive Performance," *Harvard Business Review*, Vol. 70, No.1 (1992), pp. 71-79.

Kaplan, Robert S., "New Systems for Measurement and Control," *The Engineering Economist*, Vol. 36, No.3 (1991), pp. 201-218.

Kaplan, Robert S., "Yesterday's Accounting Undermines Production," *Harvard Business Review*, Vol. 62, No.4 (1984), pp. 95-101.

Keebler, James S., "Logistics Trends in North American Companies", *Proceedings of the 15th Annual German Logistics Conference*, Sponsored by Bundesvereingung Logistik in Berlin, Germany, October 21-23, 1998, published by Huss-Verlag, GmbH, Munich, Germany, 1998, Vol. 1, pp. 47-56.

Keegan, Daniel P., Robert G. Eiler, and Charles R. Jones, "Are Your Performance Measures Obsolete?," *Management Accounting*, Vol. 70, No. 12 (1989), pp. 45-50.

Kendrick, J. W. (1984), *Improving Company Productivity* (Baltimore, MD: The Johns Hopkins Press).

Kerr, Steven, "On the Folly of Rewarding A, While Hoping for B," *Academy of Management Review*, (December 1975), pp. 769-783.

Kestenbaum, Martin I., and Ronald L. Straight, "Acquisition Management Reviews: Typical Findings," *National Contract Management Journal*, Vol. 25, No.2 (1994), pp. 35-41.

Kleinsorge, Ilene K., P. B. Schary, and R. Tanner, "The Shipper-Carrier Partnership: A New Tool for Performance Evaluation," *Journal of Business Logistics*, Vol. 12, No.2 (1991), pp. 35-57.

Kleinsorge, Ilene K., Philip B. Schary, and Ray Tanner, "Evaluating Logistics Decisions," *International Journal of Physical Distribution and Materials Management*, Vol. 19, No.12 (1989), pp. 3-14.

Koota, Pasi, and Josu Takala, "Developing a Performance Measurement System for World-Class Distribution Logistics by Using Activity-Based Costing and Management: Case: Basic Metal Industries," *International Journal of Technology Management*, Vol. 16, No.1 (1998), pp. 267-280.

Korpela, Jukka, Markku Tuominen, and Matti Valoaho, "An Analytic Hierarchy Process-Based Approach to the Strategic Management of Logistic Service: An Empirical Study in the Mechanical Forest Industry," *International Journal of Production Economics*, Vol. 56-57, No.1-3 (1998), pp. 303-318.

La Londe, Bernard J., and M. C. Cooper (1988), *Customer Service: A Management Perspective* (Oak Brook, IL: Council of Logistics Management).

La Londe, Bernard J., and Terrance L. Pohlen, "Issues In Supply Chain Costing," *The International Journal of Logistics Management*, Vol. 7, No.1 (1996), pp. 1-12.

La Londe, Bernard J., and James M. Masters, "Emerging Logistics Strategies: Blueprints for the Next Century," *International Journal of Physical Distribution and Logistics Management*, Vol. 24, No.7 (1994), pp. 35-47.

La Londe, Bernard J., and Terrance L Pohlen, (1998), "1998 Survey of Activity-Based Costing Applications within Business Logistics," *Council of Logistics Management Annual Conference Proceedings*, pp.13-33.

La Londe, Bernard J., and Paul H. Zinszer (1976), *Customer Service: Meaning and Measurement* (Chicago, IL: National Council of Physical Distribution Management).

La Londe, Bernard J., "A Reconfiguration of Logistics Systems in the 80's: Strategies and Challenges," *Journal of Business Logistics*, Vol. 4, No.1 (1984), pp. 1-11.

La Londe, Bernard J., "Supply Chain Management: Myth or Reality?," *Supply Chain Management Review*, Vol. 1, No.1 (Spring 1997).

Lambert, D. M., and T. C. Harrington, "Measuring Nonresponse Bias in Customer Service Mail Surveys," *Journal of Business Logistics*, Vol. 11, No.2 (1990), pp. 5-25.

Lambert, D. M., and R. Zemke, (1982), "The Customer Service Component of the Marketing Mix," *Proceedings, Twientieth Annual Conference of the National Council of Physical Distribution Management*, pp.1-24.

Lambert, Douglas, Margaret A. Emmelhainz, and John T. Gardner, "Developing and Implementing Supply Chain Partnerships," *The International Journal of Logistics Management*, Vol. 7, No.2 (1996), pp. 1-17.

Landy, Frank J. (1989), *Psychology of Work Behavior*, 4th ed. (Brooks/Cole Pub Co).

Langley, C. John Jr., and Mary C. Holcomb, "Creating Logistics Customer Value," *Journal of Business Logistics*, Vol. 13, No.2 (1992), pp. 1-27.

Larson, Paul D., "Buyer-Supplier Co-operation, Product Quality and Total Costs," *International Journal of Physical Distribution and Logistics Management*, Vol. 24, No.6 (1994), pp. 4-10.

Lee, Hau L., and Corey Billington, "Materials Management in Decentralized Supply Chains," *Operations Research*, Vol. 41, No.5 (Sep-Oct 1993), pp. 835-847.

Lee, Hau L., and Corey Billington, "The Evolution of Supply Chain Management Models and Practice at Hewlett-Packard," *Interfaces*, Vol. 25, No.5 (1995), pp. 42-63.

Lee, Hau L., Corey Billington, and Brent Carter, "Hewlett-Packard Gains Control of Inventory and Service Through Design for Localization," *Interfaces*, Vol. 23, No.4 (Jul/Aug 1993), pp. 1-11.

Lee, Hau L., and Corey Billington, "Managing Supply Chain Inventory: Pitfalls and Opportunities," *Sloan Management Review*, Vol. 33, No. 3 (Spring 1992), pp. 65-73.

Lee, Hau L., V. Padmanabhan, and Seungjin Whang, "Information Distortion in a Supply Chain: The Bullwhip Effect," *Management Science*, Vol. 43, No.4 (1997), pp. 546-558.

Lee, Hau L., V. Padmanabhan, and Seungjin Whang, "The Bullwhip Effect in Supply Chains," *Sloan Management Review*, Vol. 38, No. 3 (Spring 1997), pp. 93-102.

Leenders, Michiel R., Jean Nollet, and Lisa M. Ellram, "Adapting Purchasing to Supply Chain Management," *International Journal of Physical Distribution and Logistics Management*, Vol. 24, No.1 (1994), pp. 40-42.

Levy, Michael L. (1979), "Improving Distribution Productivity with Customer Service Activities," *National Council of Physical Distribution Management Proceedings*, pp. 309-320.

Levy, Michael L., "Lean Production in an International Supply Chain," *Sloan Management Review*, (Winter 1997), pp. 94-102.

Levy, Michael L., "Toward An Optimal Customer Service Package," *Journal of Business Logistics*, Vol. 2, No.2 (1981), pp. 87-104.

Lewis, Ira, and Alexander Talalayevsky, "Logistics and Information Technology: A Coordination Perspective," *Journal of Business Logistics*, Vol. 18, No.1 (1997), pp. 141-157.

Livingstone, Geraldine, "Measuring Customer Service in Distribution," *International Journal of Physical Distribution and Logistics Management*, Vol. 22, No.6 (1992), pp. 4-6.

Loar, Tim, ""Patterns of Inventory Management and Policy: A Study of Four Industries," *Journal of Business Logistics*, Vol. 13, No.2 (1992), pp. 69-96.

Loforte, Anthony J. (1993), "The Implications of Multicultural Relationships in a Transnational Supply Chain," *National Association of Purchasing Management Annual Conference Proceedings*, pp.69-77.

Lynagh, Peter M., and Richard F. Poist, "Managing Physical Distribution/Marketing Interface Activities: Cooperation of Conflict?," *Transportation Journal*, Vol. 23, No.3 (Spring 1984), pp. 36-43.

Lynagh, Peter M., "Measuring Distribution Center Effectiveness," *Transportation Journal*, Vol. 11, No.2 (1971), pp. 21-33.

Macbeth, Douglas K., and Neil Ferguson (1993), *Partnership Sourcing - An integrated Supply Chain Management Approach* (London: Pitman Publishing).

Macneil, Ian R. (1980), *The New Social Contract, an Inquiry into Modern Contractual Relations* (New Haven, CT: Yale University Press).

Maisel, Lawrence S., "Performance Measurement: The Balanced Scorecard Approach," *Journal of Cost Management*, Vol. 6, No.22 (Summer 1992), pp. 47-52.

Mallen, Bruce, "Functional Spin-Off: A Key to Anticipating Change in Distribution Structure," *Journal of Marketing*, Vol. 37, No. 3 (1973), pp. 18-25.

Maltz, Elliot, and Ajay K. Kohli, "Market Intelligence Dissemination Across Functional Boundaries," *Journal of Marketing Research*, Vol. 33, No.1 (1996), pp. 46-71.

Manrodt, Karl B., Mary Collins Holcomb, and Richard Thompson, "Supply Chain Management: The Critical Missing Elements," Invited Article, *Supply Chain Management Review*, Vol. 1, No. 3 (Fall 1997), pp. 80-86.

Marr, Norman E., "Do Managers Really Know What Service Their Customers Require?," *International Journal of Physical Distribution and Logistics Management*, Vol. 24, No.4 (1994), pp. 24-31.

Marr, Norman E., "Management Sophistication and Service Performance," *International Journal of Physical Distribution and Logistics Management*, Vol. 21, No.4 (1991), pp. 32-41.

McLaughlin, Edward W., Debra J. Perosio, and John L. Park, "Retail Logistics and Merchandising in the USA: Current Status and Requirements in the Year 2000," *International Journal of Retail & Distribution Management*, Vol. 26, No.2 (1998), pp. 97-105.

Mendez, Eduardo G., and John N. Pearson, "Purchasing's Role in Product Development: The Case for Time-Based Strategies," *International Journal of Purchasing and Materials Management*, Vol. 30, No.1 (Winter 1994), pp. 3-12.

Mentzer, John T., Roger Gomes, and Robert E. Krapfel, Jr., "Physical Distribution Service: A Fundamental Marketing Concept?," *Journal of the Academy of Marketing Science*, Vol. 17, No. 3 (1989), pp. 53-62.

Mentzer, John T., and Brenda P. Konrad, "An Efficiency/Effectiveness Approach to Logistics Performance Analysis," *Journal of Business Logistics*, Vol. 12, No.1 (1991), pp. 33-62.

Mentzer, John T., "Managing Channel Relations in the 21st Century," *Journal of Business Logistics*, Vol. 14, No.1 (1993), pp. 27-42.

Mische, Michael, "DI in the EC: Easier Said than Done," *Journal of European Business*, Vol. 4, No.2 (1992), pp. 19-22.

Mische, Michael, "EDI Strategy: Businesses Shift from Technical to Business Goals," *Chief Information Officer Journal*, Vol. 5, No.1 (Summer 1992), pp. 38-41.

Mock, Theodore J., and Hugh D. Grove (1979), *Measurement, Accounting, and Organizational Information* (New York, NY: John Wiley & Sons, Inc.).

Moore, James F. (1996), *The Death of Competition* (New York, NY: Harper Collins).

Morash, Edward A., and Steven R. Clinton, "The Role of Transportation Capabilities in International Supply Chain Management," *Transportation Journal*, Vol. 36, No. 3, pp. 5-17.

Morash, Edward A., Cornelia L. M. Droge, and Shawnee K. Vickery, "Strategic Logistics Capabilities for Competitive Advantage and Firm Success," *Journal of Business Logistics*, Vol. 17, No.1 (1996), pp. 1-22.

Morash, Edward A., Cornelia Droge, and Shawnee Vickery, "Boundary Spanning Interfaces Between Logistics, Production, Marketing, and New Product Development," *International Journal of Physical Distribution and Logistics Management*, Vol. 26, No.8 (1996), p. 43-62.

Morash, Edward A., and John Ozment, "The Strategic Use of Transportation Time and Reliability for Competitive Advantage," *Transportation Journal*, Vol. 36, No. 2 (Winter 1996), pp. 35-46.

Morash, Edward A., "On the Use of Transportation Strategies to Promote Demand," *The Logistics and Transportation Review*, Vol. 26, No.2 (1990), pp. 53-75.

Morash, Edward A., "Regulatory Policy and Industry Structure: The Case of Interstate Household Goods Carriers," *Land Economics*, Vol. 57, No.4 (1981), pp. 544-557.

Mossman, Frank H., Paul M. Fischer, and W. J. E. Crissy, "New Approaches to Analyzing Marketing Profitability," *Journal of Marketing*, Vol. 38, No. 2 (1974), pp. 3-8.

Naim, Mohamed M., and Towill, ""Establishing a Framework for Effective Materials Logistics Management," *The International Journal of Logistics Management*, Vol. 5, No.1 (1994), pp. 81-88.

Nichols, Ernest L. Jr., and James C. Wetherbe, "Cycle Time Reduction: An Interorganizational Supply Chain Perspective," *Cycle Time Research Journal*, Vol. 1, No.1 (1994), pp. 63-81.

Noordewier, Thomas G., George John, and John R.Nevin, "Performance Outcomes of Purchasing Arrangements in Industrial Buyer-Vendor Relationships," *Journal of Marketing*, Vol. 54, No.4 (1990), pp. 80-93.

Novack, Robert A. (1984), "Transportation Standard Cost Budgeting," *National Council of Physical Distribution Management Proceedings*, pp.309-320.

Novack, Robert A., C. John Langley, Jr., and Lloyd M. Rinehart (1995), *Creating Logistics Value: Themes for the Future* (Oak Brook, IL: Council of Logistics Management), pp.259.

Novack, Robert A., Lloyd M. Rinehart, and Michael Wells, "Rethinking Concept Foundations in Logistics Management," *Journal of Business Logistics*, Vol. 13, No.2 (1992), pp. 233-267.

Novack, Robert A., and Stephen W. Simco, "The Industrial Procurement Process: A Supply Chain Perspective," *Journal of Business Logistics*, Vol. 12, No.1 (1991), pp. 145-167.

Novack, Robert A., "Quality and Control in Logistics: A Process Model," *International Journal of Physical Distribution and Materials Management*, Vol. 19, No.11 (1989), pp. 1-44.

Novich, Neil S., "Leading-Edge Distribution Strategies," *Journal of Business Strategy*, Vol. 11, No.6 (1990), pp. 48-53.

Nunamaker, J.F. Jr., Alan R. Dennis, Joseph S.Valacich, and Douglas R. Vogel, "Information Technology for Negotiating Groups: Generating Options for Mutual Gain," *Management Science*, Vol. 37, No.10 (1991), pp. 13235-1346.

O'Brien, C., and M. Head, "Developing a Full Business Environment to Support Just-in-Time Logistics," *International Journal of Production Economics*, Vol. 42, No.1 (1995), pp. 41-50.

Ohmae, Kenichi, "The Global Logic of Strategic Alliances," *Harvard Business Review*, Vol. 67, No.2 (1989), pp. 143-154.

Oliver, Nick, "JIT: Issues and Items for the Research Adgenda," *International Journal of Physical Distribution and Logistics Management*, Vol. 20, No.7 (1990), pp. 3-11.

Orr, Bill, "EDI: Banker's Ticket to Electronic Commerce?," *ABA Banking Journal*, Vol. 88, No.5 (1996), pp. 64-70.

Pegels, C. Carl, "Alternative Methods of Evaluating Capital Investments in Logistics," *International Journal of Physical Distribution and Logistics Management*, Vol. 21, No.2 (1991), pp. 19-25.

Perry, James H., "Emerging Economic and Technological Futures: Implications for Design and Management of Logistics Systems in the 1990s," *Journal of Business Logistics*, Vol. 12, No.2 (1991), pp. 1-16.

Perry, James H., "Firm Behavior and Operating Performance in Just-in-Time Logistics Channels," *Journal of Business Logistics*, Vol. 9, No.1 (1988), pp. 19-33.

Persson, G., "Organisation Design Strategies for Business Logistics," *International Journal of Physical Distribution and Materials Management*, Vol. 8, No.6 (1978), pp. 287-297.

Pfohl, H. D., and W Zollner, "Organisation for Logistics: The Contingency Approach," *International Journal of Physical Distribution and Materials Management*, Vol. 17, No.1 (1987), pp. 3-16.

Piercy, John E., "Lost, Damaged and Astray Freight Shipments: Some Explanatory Factors," *Transportation Journal*, Vol. 19, No.4 (1980), pp. 33-37.

Pine, Joseph B., Bart Victor, and Andrew C. Goynton, "Making Mass Customization Work," *Harvard Business Review*, Vol. 71, No.5 (1993), pp. 108-119.

Pirttilä, Timo, and Petri Hautaniemi, "Activity-Based Costing and Distribution Logistics Management," *International Journal of Production Economics*, Vol. 41, No.1-3 (1995).

Pirttila, Timo, and Janne Huiskonen, "A Framework for Cost-Service Analysis in Differentiation of Logistics Services," *International Journal of Production Economics*, Vol. 45, No.1-3 (1996), pp. 131-137.

Podsakoff, P., and D. W. Organ, "Self-Reports in Organizational Research: Problems and Prospects," *Journal of Management*, Vol. 12, No.4 (1986), pp. 531-544.

Pohlen, Terrance L., and Bernard J. La Londe, "Implementing Activity-Based Costing (ABC) in Logistics," *Journal of Business Logistics*, Vol. 15, No.2 (1994), pp. 1-23.

Poirier, Charles C., and Stephen E. Reiter (1996), *Supply Chain Optimization: Building the Strongest Total Business Network* (Berrett-Koehler Pub).

Powell, Thomas C., "Total Quality Management as Competitive Advantage: A Review & Empirical Study," *Strategic Management Journal*, Vol. 16, (1995), pp. 15-37.

Powers, Thomas L., and David J. Closs, "An Examination of the Effects of Trade Incentives on Logistical Performance in a Consumer Products Distribution Channel," *Journal of Business Logistics*, Vol. 8, No.2 (1987), pp. 1-28.

Prahalad, C. K., and Gary Hamel, "The Core Competence of the Corporation," *Harvard Business Review*, Vol. 68, No. 3 (1990), pp. 79-91.

Price, Retha A., "An Investigation of Path-Goal Leadership Theory in Marketing Channels," *Journal of Retailing*, Vol. 67, No.3 (Fall 1991), pp. 339-361.

Prokesch, Steven E., "Mastering Chaos at the High Tech Frontier: An Interview with Silicon Graphics' Ed McCracken," *Harvard Business Review*, Vol. 71, No.6 (1993), pp. 134-144.

Rai, Arun, Santanu Borah, and Arkalgud Ramaprasad, "Critical Success Factors for Strategic Alliances in the Information Technology Industry: An Empirical Study," *Decision Sciences*, Vol. 27, No.1 (Winter 1996), pp. 141-155.

Rajagopal, Shan, and Kenneth N. Bernard, "Strategic Procurement and Competitive Advantage," *International Journal of Purchasing and Materials Management*, Vol. 29, No.4 (Fall 1993), pp. 13-20.

Ramsay, John, "The Case Against Purchasing Partnerships," *International Journal of Purchasing and Materials Management*, Vol. 32, No.4 (Fall 1996), pp. 13-39.

Rangan, V. Kasturi, and Andris A. Zoltners, "The Channel Intermediary Selection Decision: A Model and an Application," *Management Science*, Vol. 32, No.9 (1986), pp. 1114-1122.

Rao, Kant, Alan J. Stenger, and Haw Jan Wu, "Training Future Logistics Managers: Logistics Strategies within the Corporate Planning Framework," *Journal of Business Logistics*, Vol. 15, No.2 (1994), pp. 249-272.

Read, William F., and Mark S. Miller, "The State of Quality in Logistics," *International Journal of Physical Distribution and Logistics Management*, Vol. 21, No.6 (1991), pp. 32-47.

Rhea, Marti J., and D. L Shrock, "Physical Distribution Implementation Effectiveness: The Customer Perspective," *Transportation Journal*, Vol. 27, No.1 (Fall 1987), pp. 36-42.

Rhea, Marti J., and David L. Shrock, "Measuring Distribution Effectiveness with Key Informant Reports," *Logistics and Transportation Review*, Vol. 23, No.3 (1987), pp. 295-306.

Rhea, Marti J., and David L. Shrock, "Measuring the Effectiveness of Physical Distribution Customer Service Programs," *Journal of Business Logistics*, Vol. 8, No.1 (1987), pp. 31-45.

Rice, James B., Jr., and Michael Tarr, (1998), "The Global Supply Chain Benchmarking Study for the Consumer Markets Industry," *Council of Logistics Management Annual Conference Proceedings*, pp.121-130.

Richeson, Leslie, Charles W. Lackey, and John W. Starner, Jr., "The Effect of Communication on the Linkage Between Manufacturers and Suppliers in a Just-In-Time Environment," *International Journal of Purchasing and Materials Management*, Vol. 31, No.1 (Winter 1995), pp. 21-28.

Rindfleisch, Aric, and Jan B. Heide, "Transaction Cost Analysis: Past, Present, and Future Applications," *Journal of Marketing*, Vol. 61, No.4 (1997), pp. 30-54.

Rinehart, Lloyd M., and Thomas J. Page, Jr., "The Development and Test of a Model of Transaction Negotiation," *Journal of Marketing*, Vol. 56, No.4 (1992), pp. 18-32.

Rizk, George, and Mike Clough, "Integrated Services Help Drill Horizontal Well Ahead of Schedule," *Oil and Gas Journal*, Vol. 92, No.11 (1994), pp. 65-67.

Ronen, David, "On Measuring the Productivity of Trucks' Dispatches," *Journal of Business Logistics*, Vol. 7, No.2 (1986), pp. 126-131.

Rosenberg, L. Joseph, and David P. Campbell, "Just-in-Time Inventory Control: A Subset of Channel Management," *Journal of the Academy of Marketing Science*, Vol. 13, No.3 (Summer 1985), pp. 124-133.

Rosenbloom, Bert, and Rolph Anderson, "Channel Management and Sales Management: Some Key Interfaces," *Journal of the Academy of Marketing Science*, Vol. 13, No.3 (Summer 1985), pp. 97-106.

Ross, Julie Ritzer, "Logistics Providers take Expanded Role in Supply Chain Management," *Stores*, Vol. 80, No.3 (1998), pp. 57-58.

Rotch, William, "Activity-Based Costing in Service Industries," *Cost Management*, (Summer 1990), pp. 4-14.

Salafatinos, Chris, "Integrating the Theory of Constraints and Activity-Based Costing," *Cost Management*, (Fall 1995), pp. 58-67.

Sandelands, Eric, "Changing Channels," *International Journal of Physical Distribution and Logistics Management*, Vol. 24, No.3 (1994), pp. 23-24.

Sandelands, Eric, "Du Pont's Integrated Vision," *International Journal of Physical Distribution and Logistics Management*, Vol. 24, No.3 (1994), pp. 31-32.

Sandelands, Eric, "Great Expecations for Lean Suppliers," *International Journal of Physical Distribution and Logistics Management*, Vol. 24, No.3 (1994), pp. 40-42.

Sandelands, Eric, "Replenishment Logistics Give Food for Thought," *International Journal of Physical Distribution and Logistics Management*, Vol. 24, No.3 (1994), pp. 17-18.

Schary, Philip B., and Tage Skjott-Larsen, (1995), *Managing the Global Supply Chain* (Copenhagen: Handelshojskolens Forlag, Munksgaard International Publishers Ltd.).

Schmitz, Judith M., Robert Frankel, and David J. Frayer, "Vertical Integration Without Ownership: Strategic Alliances Offer a Managerial Alternative," *Journal of Marketing Theory and Practice*, Vol. 3, No.3 (Summer 1995), pp. 23-30.

Scott, Charles, and Roy Westbrook, "New Strategic Tools for Supply Chain Management," *International Journal of Physical Distribution and Logistics Management*, Vol. 21, No.1 (1991), pp. 23-33.

Scott, Don, "Marketing, Logistics and Inventory," *International Journal of Physical Distribution and Materials Management*, Vol. 19, No.5 (1989), pp. 26-30.

Shapiro, Benson P., V. Kasturi Rangan and John J. Sviokla, "Staple Yourself to an Order," *Harvard Business Review*, Vol. 70, No.4 (1992), pp. 113-122.

Sheombar, Haydee S., "EDI-Induced Redesign of Co-ordination in Logistics," *International Journal of Physical Distribution and Logistics Management*, Vol. 22, No.8 (1992), pp. 4-14.

Sherwood, Dennis, "How Important Is Culture?," *International Journal of Retail & Distribution Management*, Vol. 18, No.4 (Jul-Aug 1990), pp. 3-11.

Shipley, David, and Bill Neale, "The Credit Trap Constraint on Sales Through Industrial Distribution Channels," *Journal of General Management*, Vol. 21, No.2 (Winter 1995), pp. 65-83.

Shycon, Harvey N., and Christopher R. Sprague, "Put a Price Tag on Your Customer Servicing Levels," *Harvard Business Review*, (July-August 1975), pp. 71-78.

Sink, D. S., T. C. Tuttle and S. J. DeVries, "Productivity Measurement and Evaluation: What Is Available?," *National Productivity Review*, Vol. 4, No.3 (1984), pp. 265-387.

Snodgrass, Coral R., "Japanese Distribution Channels," *Journal of Asian Business*, Vol. 12, No.3 (1996), pp. 103-106.

Song, Jing Sheng, and Paul H. Zipkin, "Inventory Control with Information about Supply Conditions," *Management Science*, Vol. 42, No.10 (Oct 1996), pp. 1409-1419.

Speh, Thomas W., and Robert A. Novack, "The Management of Financial Resources in Logistics," *Journal of Business Logistics*, Vol. 16, No.2 (1995), pp. 23-42.

Spekman, Robert E., John W. Kamauff, Jr., and Niklas Myhr, "An Empirical Investigation into Supply Chain Management: A Perspective on Partnerships," *Supply Chain Management*, Vol. 3, No.2 (1998), pp. 53-67.

Sriram, Ven, and Snehamay Ganerjee, "Electronic Data Interchange: Does its Adoption Change Purchasing Policies and Procedures?," *International Journal of Purchasing and Materials Management*, Vol. 30, No.1 (Winter 1994), pp. 31-40.

Stainer, Alan (1997), "Logistics - A Productivity and Performance Perspective", *Supply Chain Management*, pp. 53-62.

Stalk, George, Philip Evans, and Lawrence E. Shulman, "Competing on Capabilities: The New Rules of Corporate Strategy," *Harvard Business Review*, Vol. 70, No.2 (March-April 1992), pp. 57-69.

Stank, Theodore P., and Charles W. Lackey, Jr., "Enhancing Performance through Logistical Capabilities in Mexican Maquiladora Firms," *Journal of Business Logistics*, Vol. 18, No.1 (1997), pp. 91-123.

Stenross, Matthew R., and Graham J. Sweet, (1991), "Implementing an Integrated Supply Chain," *National Association of Purchasing Management Annual Conference Proceedings*, pp.341-351.

Stephenson, Ronald P., and Ronald P. Willett, "Consistency: The Carrier's Ace in the Hole," *Transportation Journal*, (Spring 1969), pp. 28-33.

Sterling, Jay U., and Douglas M. Lambert, "A Methodology for Identifying Potential Cost Reductions in Transportation and Warehousing," *Journal of Business Logistics*, Vol. 5, No.2 (1985), pp. 1-13.

Stern, Louis W., "Reflections on Channels Research," *Journal of Retailing*, Vol. 64, No.1 (Spring 1988), pp. 1-4.

Stevens, Graham C., "Integration of the Supply Chain," *International Journal of Physical Distribution and Materials Management*, Vol. 19, No.8 (1989), pp. 3-8.

Stock, James R., and Douglas M. Lambert (1987), *Strategic Logistics Management*, 2nd ed. (Homewood, IL: Irwin).

Stock, James R., and Douglas M. Lambert, "Becoming a 'World Class' Company with Logistics Service Quality," *International Journal of Logistics Management*, Vol. 3, No.1 (1992), pp. 73-80.

Tagaras, George, and Hau L. Lee, "Economic Models for Vendor Evaluation with Quality Cost Analysis," *Management Science*, Vol. 42, No.11 (Nov 1996), pp. 1531-1543.

Tangeman, Nanci A., "The International Logistics of Freight Forwarding: Performance Measurement at the Harper Group," *National Productivity Review*, Vol. 13, (Winter '93-94), pp. 107-114.

Towers, Stephen (1994), *Business Process Reengineering, A Practical Handbook for Executives* (Stanley Thorns).

Towill, Denis R., Mohamed M. Naim, and Joakin Wikner, "Industrial Dynamics Simulation Models in the Design of Supply Chains," *International Journal of Physical Distribution and Logistics Management*, Vol. 22, No.5 (1992), pp. 3-13.

Tyndall, Gene R., and John R. Busher, "Improving the Management of Distribution with Cost and Financial Information," *Journal of Business Logistics*, Vol. 6, No.2 (1985), pp. 1-18.

van der Meulen, P. R. H., and G. Spijkerman, "The Logistics Input-Output Model and Its Application," *International Journal of Physical Distribution and Materials Management*, Vol. 15, No.3 (1985), pp. 17-25.

Vokurka, Robert J., and Robert A. Davis, "Just-in-Time: The Evolution of a Philosophy," *Production and Inventory Management Journal*, Vol. 37, No.2 (1996), pp. 56-59.

Wagner, William, "Achieving Buyer-Seller Satisfaction Carrier Service," *International Journal of Physical Distribution and Materials Management*, Vol. 17, No.3 (1987), pp. 17-27.

Waller, Matthew A., Dennis Woolsey, and Robert Seaker, "Reengineering Order Fulfillment," *The International Journal of Logistics Management*, Vol. 6, No.2 (1995), pp. 1-10.

Walton, Lisa Williams, and Linda G. Miller, "Moving Toward LIS Theory Development: A Framework of Technology Adoption within Channels," *Journal of Business Logistics*, Vol. 16, No.2 (1995), pp. 117-135.

Walton, Lisa Williams, "Electronic Data Interchange (EDI): A Study of its Usage and Adoption Within Marketing and Logistics Channels," *Transportation Journal*, Vol. 34, No. 2 (1994), pp. 37+.

Walton, Lisa Williams, "Partnership Satisfaction: Using the Underlying Dimensions of Supply Chain Partnership to Measure Current and Expected Levels of Satisfaction," *Journal of Business Logistics*, Vol. 17, No.2 (1996), pp. 57-75.

Walton, Lisa Williams, "The ABC's of EDI: The Role of Activity-Based Costing (ABC) in Determining EDI Feasibility in Logistics Organizations," *Transportation Journal*, Vol. 36, No.1 (Fall 1996), pp. 43-50.

Walton, Steve V., and Ann S. Marucheck, "The Relationship Between EDI and Supplier Reliability," *International Journal of Purchasing and Materials Management*, Vol. 33, No.3 (Summer 1997), pp. 30-35.

Weng, Z. Kevin, "Channel Coordination and Quantity Discounts," *Management Science*, Vol. 41, No.9 (Sep 1995), pp. 1509-1522.

Whipple, Judith Schmitz, Robert Frankel, and David J. Frayer, "Logistical Alliance Formation Motives: Similarities and Differences within the Channel," *Journal of Marketing Theory and Practice*, Vol. 4, No.2 (Spring 1996), pp. 26-36.

Wikner, J., Denis R. Towill, and Mohamed M. Naim, "Smoothing Supply Chain Dynamics," *International Journal of Production Economics*, Vol. 22, No.3 (1992), pp. 231-248.

Williams, Lisa R., "Understanding Distribution Channels: An Interorganizational Study of EDI Adoption," *Journal of Business Logistics*, Vol. 15, No.2 (1994), pp. 173-203.

Williamson, Oliver E. (1975), *Markets and Hierarchies: Analysis and Antitrust Implications* (New York, NY: Free Press).

Withey, John J.,"Realities of Channel Dynamics: A Wholesale Example," *Journal of the Academy of Marketing Science*, Vol. 13, No.3 (Summer 1985), pp. 72-81.

Wouters, Marc J. F., "Economic Evaluation of Leadtime Reduction," *International Journal of Production Economics*, Vol. 22, No.2 (Nov 1991), pp. 111-120.

Yavas, U., M. Luqmani, and Z. A. Quraeshi, "Purchasing Efficacy in an Arabian Gulf Country," *International Journal of Physical Distribution and Logistics Management*, Vol. 19, No.4 (1989), pp. 20-25.